Extraordinary Women in Support of Music

Mona Mender

The Scarecrow Press, Inc.
Lanham, Md., & London
1997

SCARECROW PRESS, INC.

Published in the United States of America
by Scarecrow Press, Inc.
4720 Boston Way
Lanham, Maryland 20706

4 Pleydell Gardens, Folkestone
Kent CT20 2DN, England

Copyright ©1997 by Mona Mender

All rights reserved. No part of this publication may be reproduced, stored in a retrieval system, or transmitted in any form or by any means, electronic, mechanical, photocopying, recording, or otherwise, without the prior permission of the publisher.

British Cataloguing-in-Publication Information Available

Library of Congress Cataloging-in-Publication Data

Mender, Mona, 1926-
Extraordinary women in support of music / Mona Mender.
  p. cm.
Includes bibliographical references (p.   ) and index.
1. Women musicians—Biography. 2. Women in the performing arts. I. Title.
ML385.M37 1997
780'92'2—dc20   96-40068
B   CIP
                                                     MN
ISBN 0-8108-3278-X (cloth : alk. paper)

∞™ The paper used in this publication meets the minimum requirements of American National Standard for Information Sciences—Permanence of Paper for Printed Library Materials, ANSI Z39.48–1984.

Manufactured in the United States of America.

To my husband, Irving,
my children, Judith and Donald,
and my granddaughter, Lynn,

who always give me the encouragement
and support I need.

Contents

Preface   ix

1 A Brief History   1

2 Ladies of the Great Salons   19
    Aspasia *19*
    Isabella d'Este *21*
    Lucrezia Borgia *24*
    Diane de Poitiers *26*
    Marquise de Rambouillet *27*
    Queen Christina of Sweden *29*
    Ninon de Lenclos *35*
    Claudine de Tencin *36*
    Marie du Deffand *37*
    Misia Sert *39*
    Coco Chanel *44*
    Princesse de Polignac *50*

Comtesse de Polignac 52
Gertrude Stein 53

3 Elegant Patronesses of the Old World   55
   Eleanor of Aquitaine 55
   Catherine de Medicis 58
   Queen Elizabeth I 59
   Empress Maria Theresa 62
   Madame de Pompadour 67
   Nadezhda von Meck 72
   Queen Elisabeth of Belgium 80
   Bathsabee de Rothschild 82

4 Wives and Lovers   85
   George Sand 85
   Clara Schumann 96
   Cosima Wagner 100
   Sara Bull 109
   Alma Mahler 110
   Olga Koussevitzky 121
   Aniela Rubinstein 123
   Galina Rostropovich 130
   Felicia Bernstein 140
   Martita Casals 148

5 Inspired Teachers   153
   Isabella Vengerova 153
   Rosina Lhevinne 155
   Estelle Liebling 157
   Olga Samaroff 158
   Nadia Boulanger 158
   Dorothy DeLay 169
   Helen Coates 172
   Phillis Curtin 175

6 Patronesses in the United States   179
   Elizabeth Sprague Coolidge 179
   Mary Louise Curtis Bok Zimbalist 181
   Gertrude Robinson Smith 187

Contents   vii

   Lila Bell Acheson Wallace   *191*
   Alice Tully   *195*
   Elizabeth Nitze Paepcke   *198*
   Ladies of the Hollywood Bowl   *199*
   Ladies of the Metropolitan Opera   *201*
   Others Who Made a Difference   *205*

7 Creative Administrators   211
   Clara Damrosch   *211*
   Helen Mulford Thompson   *219*
   Sarah Caldwell   *222*
   Beverly Sills   *224*
   Loretta Dranoff   *229*
   Others   *231*

8 Remarkable Mothers and Sisters   237
   Maria Anna Mozart   *237*
   Fanny Mendelssohn   *244*
   Rildia Bee Cliburn   *247*
   Jennie Resnick Bernstein   *251*
   Shirley Anne Bernstein   *256*

9 Choreographers and Their Contributions   261
   Isadora Duncan   *261*
   Martha Graham   *265*
   Agnes deMille   *273*

Notes   281
Bibliography   287
Index   295
About the Author   310

Preface

I first became interested in the subject of the involvement of women as supporters of music when I began to serve on the board of trustees of the New Jersey Symphony Orchestra. I then came to understand the problems that music and other arts organizations have with respect to financing—the constant struggle for funds, both public and private. I became involved not only in fundraising directly but in the symphony's programs for the music education of the children of the state, the Young Artists' Auditions, and other programs to serve the public—all of which cost an enormous amount of money. In addition, I participated in the activities of the American Symphony Orchestra League, an organization for all the symphony orchestras in the country. I attended their conventions, which offered courses in fundraising and other areas. These experiences not only revealed the tremendous expenses of the symphonies, but also the high number of women who contribute their time and money individually to support organizations.

The purpose of this book is to celebrate fascinating and diverse women in the Western world who have done us all a great service by furthering music and helping musicians. *Extraordinary Women in Support of Music* starts with a brief history, so that the reader may refer to it in order to place a woman in the proper historic background. In this overview I try to zero in on a woman's historical status with respect to her ability to further the arts, especially music. The main part of the book is devoted to these unusual women, most of whom are well-known. There is no way I could have included everyone I should have, but I found those about whom I have written to be extremely interesting and hope others will too.

Chapter One

A Brief History

Women have been a force in the support of music through the ages. There have been peaks and troughs because of changes of wealth in cultures. When a family is wealthy, it usually follows that the woman has the time and support to become educated and involved in society, with all its pleasures and problems. When the family is poor, the woman must stay at home doing the chores necessary to keep the home running smoothly.

A good point in history at which to start probably would be the 15th century B.C., in order to trace the progress of women's subtle, and sometimes not-so-subtle power.

The Aegean civilization in the 15th and 16th centuries was at its height. It was the golden age of Crete. In that wealthy Cretan society, women were able to enjoy the arts, in spite of the fact that they worked hard physically. Men adored women and made them an important part of the community, both secular and religious. Because women were priests and administered the ceremonies, they had the perfect opportunity to influence the performance of music.

Practically speaking, European history begins in Greece somewhere between 1200 and 800; up to that time, no culture had influenced Europe as much as the Greek civilization. Greek city-states appeared, and by the fifth century Athens and Sparta were the two most powerful.

Historians believe that, by the sixth century there was a great love of music among the people. (In fact, the Greek word "mousike" means "adoration of a muse.") The most respected form of music was choral singing, used extensively in festivals that depended on the cooperation and enthusiasm of women. The presentation of music most enjoyed was a combination of dance, instrumental music and choral singing.

There was a vast difference in the society of the two city-states and the participation of the women in them. Sparta was militarily powerful and socially highly disciplined. Agriculture and military service were the dominant occupations. Women enjoyed a high status and exerted great influence on the men. (At one point, women controlled half the wealth.) In those times they did not have any formal education; therefore, whatever they learned, they learned by themselves or with the help of their families.

In classical Athens, the situation was different. Life was freer and more varied. Adult male citizens were mainly farmers, craftsmen, seamen, and businessmen. They had some input in government. Citizens could attend trials and serve on the city's governing council. This openness of ideas had its effect on the arts and philosophy. (This was the age of philosophers such as Socrates and Plato, and dramatists such as Sophocles, Aeschylus, Aristophanes and Euripides.) Because of the chauvinistic attitudes of men and the change from an aristocratic to a commercial society and the need for labor, women were firmly restricted to the duties of managing the children and the slaves in the household. Even though men dominated, the women were well-respected for their role and very much in charge of the presentation of music and other arts in the home.

Rivalry between the two city-states led to the Peloponnesian War (431-404), in which Athens was conquered.

Under Alexander the Great, who was educated in Greece, Macedonia conquered the Greeks and the now powerful Macedonian army went on to great conquests. These conquests spread the Greek culture through the Mediterranean and the Middle East. This was the beginning of the Hellenistic Age; civilization included both the Greek culture of the Macedonians and the non-Greek Persian culture. (This age lasted until the beginning of the Roman Empire.)

Alexandria, Egypt, in the second century, was a great cosmopolitan city and the center of immense affluence. Courtesans were much in demand and amassed large fortunes. Because of their money and influence on prominent men, they had power, which they used to become active in politics and the arts. Many of their salons attracted the most intelligent and creative men of the time.

Rome began conquering Greece somewhere in the vicinity of 200, B.C. Large fortunes were acquired and noble families lived in great luxury. The middle class, too, was prosperous. Romans began to appreciate the aesthetically beautiful because of their contact with the Greeks. Whereas the people of Greece were creative, imaginative, intellectual, and philosophical, the Romans, in general, had not developed their creativity in the arts at that time.

In "epicurean" Rome in the first century, music was everywhere. Dancing and pantomimes were popular. Each wealthy household had a dancing platform and a dancing master. Performers were plentiful. (Some were famous, went on tours, and were paid handsomely.) Affluent families had their own musicians. Performances took place in theaters, temples, homes, and the church. Women learned to dance, not only because they enjoyed it, but because it taught them grace. The music itself came from Greece. Greek modes and instruments, especially the flute and the lyre, were the rage.

By 30 B.C., music was highly developed in Rome. Many rich women pursued cultural activities and opened impressive salons. Because of the ease with which men could divorce their wives and marry again, women did not put much faith in their marriage vows and lived fairly uninhibited lives. They were concerned about the rights of women, and divorced as freely as men.

Between 70 B.C. and 70 A.D., the Republic of Rome became an empire. This period also saw great creative works. Virgil, Horace, Ovid, Cicero, Livy, Tacitus, and Seneca were some of the most famous of the creative men. At its height, the Roman Empire extended from Britain and northern Europe to the rivers of Mesopotamia. It centered on the Mediterranean. In the "golden age" of Rome (30 B.C. to 18 A.D.) luxurious salons were as popular and intellectually oriented as those in France many centuries later. The power of women grew in society, as well as in government and financial affairs. By 50 A.D., music was part of the lives of all classes of Romans. It primarily was composed for lyric poetry, then sung. Choral music was part of wedding ceremonies and other celebrations, formal concerts, small dinner parties, and musical contests. It was in demand everywhere. Even as the Roman Empire started to decline (at about the beginning of the second century), some important and elegant salons thrived in the homes of royal mistresses, wives, and mothers.

The Middle Ages followed the end of the Roman Empire and lasted until the Renaissance, roughly from the first century until the 14th or 15th century. A slow acceptance of the church in Europe took place. The separation of the Roman Empire into the Greek half (in the East) and the Latin half (in the West) created a division in the church. In 325 Constantine I of Rome, a convert to Christianity, made it the religion of the empire. A second center was created: Constantinople (now Istanbul) was the seat of the Eastern Rites churches (Orthodox Church).

The church, between 96 and 305 became powerful, and dominated Europe after 1000. In 1095, Pope Urban II encouraged the knights of France and Germany to reconquer Jerusalem and Palestine. These crusades lasted two centuries. The structure of Medieval society evolved because no empire was capable of keeping peace. The strongest member of an area's nobility collected taxes or portions of the crops or animals from the local peasants. Ownership of land was the way to power and wealth. A feudal society emerged, and power was decentralized. Among the nobility, the strongest nobleman gave protection or granted land to a lesser nobleman in exchange for loyalty. Peasants were serfs. They did not own the land on which they worked, but were subject to local laws. Manorialism was the system of farming (peasants lived in huts clustered around the manor house).

From the beginning of the Middle Ages, women were forced into submission. (This may have been partly a reaction to the lax morals in Rome.) But they were allowed to work actively for charity and in the administration of the church. Nuns were given great responsibility in the effort to extend the church's influence, but women in secular life remained restricted and under their husbands' rule. By the ninth century, however, their legal position improved. They were able to inherit property and, therefore, exert more power. In addition, because royal and ecclesiastical policy banned divorce, women began to feel more secure.

Between 700 and 1300, the medieval woman was considered a necessary evil. In giving his opinion of the status of women, St. Thomas Aquinas said: "The woman is subject to the man on account of the weakness of her nature, both mind and body . . . Man is the beginning of woman and her end, just as God is the beginning and end of every creature . . . Woman is in subjection according to the law of nature, but a slave is not. Children ought to love their father more than their mother . . ."[1] Civil and canon law permitted wife-beating. Civil law ruled that a woman's word was inadmissible in court, and that the husband had full authority of property.

Aquinas, however, had an unusually unfavorable view of women, and does not necessarily represent general views of the time. In actuality, women shared in a varied life. Home-making, brewing beer, using medicinal herbs, helping with the farming, spinning and weaving for textile guilds were just a few. They received lower wages than the men, but had more and more influence in all aspects of life. They developed charm and grace and were objects of love for the men. The ladies of the aristocracy were idolized. They learned writing and the arts, while the men spent their time working and fighting. They, therefore, controlled the cultural activities, established salons, and ultimately became the leaders of society, with their men following their whims and interests with great admiration. Knights fought for a woman's favors; poets and musicians composed love songs dedicated to her. Men talked of women as if they were servants but treated them as if they were goddesses.

Wealthy households, in 1250 A.D., entertained with minstrels. Some kept their own entertainers on staff. Dancing was not condoned by the church, but was enjoyed by everyone. Pageants and military bands as well as traveling minstrels were popular. Sunday was a day of fun and relaxation, with dancing and feasts. In the 13th century, society was filled with the opportunity for enjoyment.

From 1095 to 1300 A.D. art was kept and treasured in the monastery. Traditions were preserved. There was little if any new art and practically no experimentation. Later society became wealthier and would support the secular artists and musicians.

The church's authority reached its height in the 13th century but began to decline in the 14th century. At that time, the unity of Europe began to disintegrate. The bubonic plague, or "black death," killed a large portion of the population. This caused great economic and social changes, as workers became scarce and more in demand. Because of this demand they were able to leave their old masters and manors and improve their lives. Feudalism weakened.

The troubadour movement in France peaked in the 13th century. Troubadours could be of any class. A few were kings. They trained extensively in music, poetry and gallant speech. They dressed like nobility and fought in armor in tournaments. They usually wrote their own music for their own lyrics for the aristocracy. Minstrels sang them, but often the troubadours would sing and play the lute themselves. The women usually were either married, or, if single, well-chaperoned, and, therefore, the desire of these men was not satiated; it was sublimated in song. The code of chivalry evolved.

Many castles fell in battle and, as a result, some of these singers went to Spain and Italy. England had its share of troubadours as well.

In Germany the minnesinger, like the troubadours of France, helped to raise the status of women. The aristocracy was the center of culture and romantic songs abounded. This movement ended in about 1317.

The Italian troubadour movement extended from 1265 to 1321. The troubadours there preferred to show love for the beauty of women, rather than for the woman herself.

This "courtly love" somewhat compensated for women's lack of independence. They became idealized objects of men's devotion, and were drawn from religious devotion to romance.

Europe changed as a result of the Hundred Years' War (1337-1453), which was fought mainly over English-held lands in France. A feeling of nationalism resulted, not only in France and England but in other countries, as well. Spain, for example, became strong, unified by Isabella I of Castile and Ferdinand of Aragon. Ruling together (they were husband and wife), they were a talented, impressive team—called the "Catholic kings." Isabella used the church to increase her power. 1480 saw the start of the Spanish Inquisition, which helped Isabella and Ferdinand reach their goal of instilling a nationalistic spirit in Spain. In 1492, three important events occurred: all Jews were expelled from Spain, the Muslims from North Africa were ousted from Granada, and Christopher Columbus discovered America. Spanish nationalism was on the rise.

The Renaissance (1378-1534) started in northern Italy, because much old culture remained there, and because the papacy was concerned with matters in other countries. Italian city-states, which were free to develop on their own, became Italy's economic, social, political, and cultural centers. Intellectuality flourished in Florence, Ferrara, Milan, Naples, Venice, Mantua, Genoa, Parma, Perugia, Orvieto, Pisa, and other city areas down to Sicily. Powerful and independent, they each were ruled by "principi," who were given royal titles that became hereditary. Especially important in advancing the cultural life of Italy during the Renaissance were a few wealthy and powerful families. The Medici family in Florence (the most prestigious center for the arts), the Sforza family in Milan, and the Este family in Mantua are well-known examples. Italian culture had enormous influence over all of Europe.

Women were completely subservient to men. Their interests and activities focused on religious service, a socially beneficial marriage, and family service. A girl was raised to marry well, and, for that reason, was given a good education that included music. Even though she was educated, she was required to be feminine, moral, and demure. In reality, she was her husband's equal culturally, socially, and politically (she often served as a substitute for him in governing when he was away). The woman was superior in charm, tact and morality, and was the civilizing force in the family. Music was part of life at home. Ballet, concerts, and pantomimes were presented between Italian comedy acts. It was important to women to appreciate and play music. They formed music clubs, and the number of music academies grew. (Significantly, by that time music notation could be printed.) In the courts, music was the most important art. A ruler usually supported the music of his favorite church, which, in turn, attracted fine musicians and teachers.

High-caliber Flemish music also was enjoyed. Devotion to religion was joyous. The Netherlands School of composition impacted all of Europe, producing beautiful contrapuntal church music.

The Roman Catholic Church had become powerful, corrupt, and extravagant. As agriculture gave way to commerce and business, the people became more secular in their interests and the church lost power. Monarchs became more independent of the church; education in the universities became free of ecclesiastical dictates. The time was ripe for the Reformation, which occurred in the 16th century. The aim of this movement was to restore the purity of life in religion and belief in the Bible's authority. This became known as "Protestantism." Those involved in the

Reformation believed that no one, including the Pope, could grant forgiveness. The only way to obtain salvation was through absolute faith in the will of God. It began in Germany in 1517 with Martin Luther as its leader. When the Reformation took firm hold, there was great emphasis on morality. Religious practices mostly centered in the home in Protestant lands.

Among the common people, the man generally was the patriarch of the family, and the woman was the servant of her husband. The importance of women's participation in their own salvation and marriage was recognized but, nevertheless, there was no equality of the sexes. Among the aristocracy, especially in France, the women were charming and influential. Many were well-educated. The French salon began to emerge. These rich, educated ladies opened their homes to the leaders of society, the arts, politics, education, and philosophy. Morals weakened, probably because of increasing wealth and freedom. Adultery and affairs were rampant. Vanity was at its height.

Although the times seemed somber for the average person, music was much in demand. It was a main subject in education. Every man was expected to read music and play an instrument. Everyone sang and many composed music for dances, ballets, church pageants, court festivals, and plays. Most of the music was vocal, but many instruments were used for accompaniment. The instruments were beautifully made, and became treasures. The favorite was the lute, used to accompany the single voice. The viol also was popular. By the middle of the 16th century, the violin became a favorite. The organ was the most important instrument of the church. Keyboard instruments (clavichord, harpsichord, virginal, and spinet) appeared in homes. Although people came to appreciate instrumental music, which was influenced by the dance form, composing was mostly for the voice and, as a result, opera evolved.

The Reformation affected religious music as well. The middle classes insisted on changes, and two important innovations were the use of language they could understand and participation of the congregation in the service.

A counter-reformation within the Roman Catholic

Church established new religious orders. Especially important in the movement was the Society of Jesus (Jesuits), founded in 1534. This order mainly was concerned with foreign missions and education. In Spain, King Philip II (ruling from 1556-1598) led a crusade to eliminate Protestantism. He ruled Spain, the Netherlands, the Spanish empire in the New World and, from 1580, the Portuguese empire. He tried to conquer Protestant England under Queen Elizabeth I, but failed. Spain was the greatest power of the time because of the wealth from the New World. Its court, between 1556-1665, was magnificent. Religion was *the* force: the Catholic Church was mighty, and those in charge of the Inquisition were extremely powerful. Virginity was prized, and "good" women were kept in seclusion. They did not even dine with men. Suitors, therefore, courted women by playing music in the streets near the windows of the object of their love.

The Holy Roman Empire (1564-1648), which was ruled by the Hapsburgs, included Germany, Luxembourg, Franche-Comte, Lorraine, Switzerland, Austria, Bohemia, Moravia, and part of Hungary. Music was important to everyone. Music education, in fact, was compulsory. Dance and folk songs were the bases for instrumental music. Hymns developed into big chorales, which led up to the great music of Johann Sebastian Bach. The women, who were devoted to their families, ensured good music in their homes. Organists were greatly revered.

In England, the Reformation was in full swing. It started as a result of Henry VIII's desire to divorce his first wife, Catherine of Aragon. The papacy refused his request, and Henry separated the Church of England from the Roman Catholic Church. There was a struggle afterward: Edward VI was in favor of it; Mary I was not. But Queen Elizabeth I resolved the problem by solidifying the Church of England. She sympathized with the aims of the Reformation. At the same time, she encouraged great cultural expression and artistic activity.

One branch of the Reformation, called "Calvinism," included customs somewhat different from those of other countries involved in the Reformation. It was extremely disciplined and serious. (The severity of Calvinism could be seen even in the performance of psalms, which were to be sung only in unison and unaccompanied.)

In the middle of the 16th century, violent religious wars broke out. King Henry IV of France, who became king in 1589, converted to Catholicism, but granted rights and some religious freedom to the Protestants. Religious intolerance continued to plague Europe.

In the 17th, 18th, and 19th centuries, music was dominated by France, Italy and Germany. The Thirty Years' War (1618-1648) slowed Germany's development, but France emerged as a strong nation. England had political and religious problems and, as a result, many English musicians went to Europe, especially to Holland and northern Germany. Austria and southern Germany were particularly influenced by Italy and its music. Venice, in the early 17th century, was a most exciting, cosmopolitan city, filled with the rich and powerful. Geographically, it was exposed to many different cultures. Its music was influenced by a combination of Eastern, French, church, Flemish and southern Italian popular compositions.

In the late 17th century, Rome was a great center of culture. In Cremona, exquisite violins were crafted in the 17th and 18th centuries by the Amati, Guarneri, and Stradivari families. The great Italian violinists became internationally famous. The Italian influence in the 17th century was felt particularly in Vienna, Dresden, London and Paris.

All the great powers were involved in the Thirty Years' War. It was fought mostly on German soil, and the issues were religion, control of the Holy Roman Empire, and boundaries. Religion was one of the main issues in the English Civil War (1642-1648), after which a bill of rights was produced that guaranteed the rights of the individual, a greater degree of religious tolerance, and parliamentary authority. This contributed to the development of parliamentary government and liberalism in Europe.

The baroque period (1600-1750) was a time of growth of the middle class culture. Church patronage of the arts regained favor as Rome became the center of the arts;

royalty and wealthy merchants also joined in the support. A demand arose in Europe for public entertainment. Music academies sprang up, and coffee houses held concerts (Johann Sebastian Bach ran weekly concerts for years in Zimmermans's Coffee House in Leipzig). In the 18th century, opera houses were supported by royal patronage. Attending the opera became the fashionable thing to do. Women who wanted to advance their social status actively supported music and musicians.

By the middle of the 19th century, the middle class grew large and powerful. Independent commercial establishments for music were established. In the 19th century, women comprised the highest proportion of servants, but earned half the salary of men. A woman might rise from maid to housekeeper or cook, but that was the highest position to which she could aspire. Women of all classes still exerted only behind-the-scenes power.

German music was at its height from 1685 to 1897 (from Bach and Handel to the death of Brahms). Music was in every home. In school it was taught to girls as well as boys. Independent thought and morality were emphasized. University students were encouraged to develop as individuals as well as citizens of the state. Music criticism developed. In the 18th century, the popularity of concerts grew. Because there were many courts in Germany, centers of music were sprinkled throughout the country, helping to spread musical culture to the middle class, since it was not concentrated in one large court. In Mozart's time (1756-1791), composers no longer were content to be servants of nobility; they wanted to be part of the bourgeoisie. No longer was there only the patronage system. One could obtain a commission for compositions to be performed at public concerts, the fee being paid by businessmen and others. Teaching continued to be a means of livelihood.

In the middle of the 17th century, the Western use of polyphony began to seep into Russian music. Peter the Great in the early 18th century took an interest in European, especially Italian, music. By the 19th century, foreign musicians dominated Russia's musical life. Russian violinists (particularly dedicated Russian-Jewish violinists, who often were gifted and well-educated) became the interpreters of centuries of violin music, especially Romantic music. At the same time, native talents started to be recognized. There was renewed interest in Russian culture and folk music. By the first half of the 19th century, national art music emerged.

In Europe in the 18th century, each state ruler had some sort of musical establishment. The courts at Berlin, Mannheim, Dresden, Paris, Esterhaza, and Vienna are known to have had an unusual quantity and quality of music. But, because it was so costly, more and more wealthy private citizens were called upon and volunteered to become patrons. Benefit concerts were soon seen as a way to support charities.

With the rise of capitalism and industrialization there developed a labor force in which women participated. The goal for women became equal wages and opportunity. In the 18th century, women still did not have citizenship, but the French and American Revolutions did bring about some benefits for them. The "Age of Reason" brought about individualism and enlightened thought based on reason, not faith. Individual rights were glorified, launching today's feminism. Nevertheless, all classes of women were subservient to men. Divorce was difficult and adultery was rampant among the higher classes. The middle class followed the Puritan tradition, however.

In France, the period between 1648 and 1715 was called the "French Zenith." It was the era of King Louis XIV, the "Sun King" (1648-1715), who was an absolute monarch. Versailles, one of the largest palaces in Europe, was the glittering center for musicians and other artists, as well as intellectuals. (The middle class was taxed heavily to finance the king's projects and way of life.) Versailles set standards in taste. The aristocracy was considered very "civilized," and aristocratic ladies were influential. Men had mistresses. Married women had affairs. Prostitutes were acceptable if they were educated and were well-mannered. The salons of Paris in the 18th century were at their most brilliant. Paris was the cultural capital of the world. Hedonism reigned. Women were sought after and spoiled and, with this power, they set the tone. They felt free of the restrictions of religion and were completely immersed in society. Great effort and time were spent on educating themselves so they could be involved in the intellectual and artistic life of society, and men followed their lead. These ladies were informed, well-dressed, elegant, and desirable. They were skilled in the art of manipulating men. Intrigue was part of the game. Knowledgeable in the art of makeup, dress, jewels, and culture, they were dazzling. Yet, with all that, they still did not have actual legal power.

At the same time it was the Age of Enlightenment, with emphasis placed on the intellectual. France was at its center, but other countries were involved as well. These intellectuals believed in reason and freedom of thought, and that individuals have natural rights. These beliefs and the opposition to absolutism led to the American and other revolutions. The philosophers Voltaire (born Francois Marie Arouet), Denis Diderot, Baron de Montesquieu, John Locke, Jean Jacques Rousseau, and Thomas Jefferson were part of this Age of Enlightenment.

The modern era of Europe began with the French Revolution (1789-1815) and the Industrial Revolution (which began in the mid-18th century and actually was an evolution). The first great industry in England was textiles. Germany and Belgium led in coal, steel, and other metals. By the end of the 19th century, Germany was the most powerful state in Europe.

The Napoleonic wars, which lasted about 15 years, ended at Waterloo in 1815. The congress of Vienna (1814-1815) took on the job of structuring Europe, striving to create a balance of power among France, Britain, Prussia, Austria, and Russia. The problem was that, except for Britain, all the victors were monarchies, and revolutionary changes transpired. In 1848, after a bitter winter, revolutions erupted all over Europe. They subsided by 1850, and Italy was unified under King Emmanuel II in a constitutional monarchy in 1861. By 1870, the seat of the Italian government was Rome. In 1867, there was a dual monar-

A Brief History

chy of Austria-Hungary. Otto von Bismarck, a Prussian autocrat, succeeded in his efforts to build a united German federation under the rule of Prussia. King William I of Prussia was proclaimed German emperor in 1871.

In spite of the chaos caused by the French Revolution and the Napoleonic wars, the famous Paris Conservatory and the national opera were established. Patronage moved from the courts to the wealthy financiers who sponsored concerts and operas. Some fees were charged for public performances. Casual outdoor concerts were performed in the Tuileries Gardens.

After the defeat of Napoleon in 1814, corruption increased. The revolution of 1848 established the second republic, which eventually became the second empire under Napoleon III. After the Franco-Prussian War, when Napoleon III was defeated, the third republic was established. All these changes in regimes resulted from political restriction on the people; aristocrats and the clergy were favored. Tensions developed, too, because of the growth of industrialization, unions and social movements.

In the 19th century, Paris became the center for foreign musicians, such as Frederic Chopin from Poland and Franz Liszt from Hungary. It was an exciting city in the 1830s and 1840s. People had enormous desire to live to the fullest, and greatly appreciated artists and intellectuals. France was in a period of prosperity which freed its citizens to concentrate on culture rather than merely on economic survival. France has always focused on cultural activities, but since 1870 they have been a constant priority.

In England, in the 17th century, the Puritan revolution assigned the women an even more domestic role. However, the growth of individualism and liberal institutions encouraged them to begin thinking in terms of equal opportunity and rights.

In 1702, singers began to appear in England, and opera became popular. The royal court encouraged music, especially that of George Frideric Handel. The first half of the 18th century saw a big increase in the number of concerts. London was a great cultural center—an affluent society in which the women were influential. Men joined exclusively male clubs, however, where they spent much of their time. These clubs were second homes to which men could and did escape, spending much of their time there. At that time, a women's group cropped up, called the "Blue Stockings." They met to discuss art, literature, and other matters of the intellect. By the 19th century, the term was one of ridicule, and used to show contempt for intellectual women, but progress had been made toward women's independent thought. This group was important as one of the only intellectual salons in England in the 19th century. Among the wealthy, dances and musical entertainment were held at court or at home. In that respect, women had the opportunity to support music and musicians.

In the last part of the 19th century, democracy seemed to advance and the frustrations of the subject peoples led to tension and, ultimately, to World War I in 1914. The Austrian empire under the Hapsburg Dynasty was the center of Europe and important between the 13th and the 20th centuries. It was at its largest in the first half of the 18th century. Vienna was one of the most important cities for music. Franz Joseph Haydn, Beethoven, Mozart, the Strauss family, Schubert, Brahms, Bruckner, Mahler, and Schoenberg all worked and lived there. The empire broke up in 1918 after World War I.

In the 20th century, greatly improved communication and means of travel brought the people of different countries closer. In the early years of this century, Paris was the center of study for music for Americans as well as Europeans. At the same time, American blues, ragtime and jazz evolved and European composers and other musicians came to America to experience this new music. Each culture influenced the other.

Women aggressively pursued equal rights. Despite progress they still do not have full political, legal, economic, social, educational, or sexual equality even today.

German music dominated the United States in the 19th century. Singing families became popular, including the Hutchinsons, who linked their musical activities to social causes. New York City became the center of the arts in

America; Boston and Philadelphia also became hubs. The love of concerts spread to cities with large European populations, such as St. Louis, Milwaukee, Cincinnati, New Orleans, and Chicago. Opera companies, orchestras, and choral and chamber groups appeared. Women organized support organizations. The growth in the number and quality of American musicians brought about the founding of music schools and conservatories. Today, almost all educational institutions of higher learning have music departments.

At the end of the 19th century, the movement for birth control strengthened under the women's rights movement. Smaller families and shared responsibilities allowed more free time outside the family. Teaching was one of the main fields in which women earned a living. Music teachers were in demand, and by 1900, music teaching ranked fifth as a vocation for women. Other, more affluent, women became patronesses, either individually or as part of organizations supporting music institutions and individuals.

Aside from concert and opera series, music festivals and competitions interest patronesses. Music festivals date as far back as the 17th century. Originally they were choral concerts sponsored by the church. In the last part of the 20th century, festivals have sprung up all over. Many European and American cities and some smaller towns have festivals. In the United States, festivals began in the 19th century. The Handel and Haydn Society of Boston presents this country's oldest music festival. Today, some of the most famous outdoor concert festivals are the Berkshire Music Festival at Tanglewood in Lenox, Mass., with the Boston Symphony Orchestra in residence; the Saratoga Springs Festival with the Philadelphia Orchestra; Ravinia, Ill., with the Chicago Symphony; and Wolf Trap, near Washington, D.C., maintained by the National Park Service. They all have visiting conductors, artists, and music groups, as well as those in residence. In Europe, some of the most prestigious festivals are the Bayreuth Wagner Festival in Germany, the Glyndebourne Opera Festival in England, the Salzburg Festival in Austria, and the Maggio Musicale in Florence, Italy. Jazz, popular, and folk music festivals are held in Vienne, France; Montreux, Switzerland; New York City; New Orleans; and Austin, Texas, to name a few.

Music competitions, which were held as long ago as the sixth century B.C. in Greece, have now developed into major tests in the careers of musicians. Some of the most well-known are the Tchaikovsky International Competition in Moscow, the Chopin Competition in Warsaw, the Queen Elisabeth Competition in Belgium, the Rubinstein Piano Competition in Israel, the Van Cliburn International Piano Competition in Fort Worth, Texas, and the international Naumburg Competition for piano, violin, voice, and chamber music.

In the United States, support for music institutions, performance and training depend on federal, state, local, and private sources, as well as on income from ticket sales. (The income from box-office receipts makes up only a small portion of the money needed for productions.) In 1965, the National Endowment for the Arts was established. It provides grants to music groups, but is now in jeopardy. Those who argue for the NEA maintain that a federal grant is a stamp of approval and will, therefore, encourage private institutions, foundations, corporations and individuals to match the grant of the NEA. Above all, music is a necessity that civilizes and enriches society and the individual.

Chapter Two

Ladies of the Great Salons

Aspasia (fifth century B.C.) a famous courtesan, was born in Miletus, Greece (near Turkey), and moved to Athens in 450 B.C. She belonged to the highest class of Greek courtesans, who, collectively, had lost their respectability or had escaped the seclusion required of women. These women usually bleached their hair yellow to attract men, and they wore flowery robes (perhaps because of some legal requirement). They had no civil rights and were forbidden to enter a temple other than that of their own goddess, Aphrodite Pandemos. However, they were admired by many, and it was not considered shameful for men to be seen with them. At that time Pericles was the political leader of Athens (from about 460 to 429). Athenian culture and military power dominated, and Pericles' leadership led to impressive democratic reforms and cultural accomplishments in the Greek empire. (The Parthenon, one of the great contributions to the culture of the world, was built during this era.) Aside from his commitment to fair laws, merit rewarded, efficiency in the military, and the development of trade, he encouraged the advancement of the arts. It was important to him that the people were educated enough so that they could participate in government, fine drama, all the arts, and philosophy.

Pericles and his wife had been married for many years when he met Aspasia. From all accounts, he was a man of great dignity, but susceptible to the charms of beautiful women. He was a handsome and politically powerful man and, of course, women were attracted to him. But meeting Aspasia was an electric event for him. He was intrigued by the fact that she was different, a new type of woman in the society of Athens. He fell deeply in love with her and she with him. Traditional married life did not attract her; instead, she wanted the freedom and the opportunity to participate in cultural life. She was ahead of her time in her active advocacy of education for women. In fact, she opened a school of rhetoric and philosophy in which her lectures were so popular that men attended as well. Fortunately, Pericles' wife wanted to marry another man, and they divorced. He was then free to live with Aspasia. From that time on, his social life revolved around his home. As much as he wanted to marry her, legally he could not, because, according to a law for which he was responsible, an Athenian could not marry a foreigner. Aspasia created a fascinating salon in their home, attracting artists and scientists, statesmen, and philosophers. (Among them was the great Socrates, who said he learned the art of eloquence from her.) At that time, it was unusual for a woman in Athens to have access to the cultural life of men. Athenian women were poorly educated, except in domestic affairs, and were kept in seclusion. (In Sparta, however, the women were much more involved in society.) Aspasia set the fashions for women and, by her example, opened their minds to moral and intellectual freedom. She began a trend in which this class of courtesans played an active part in Athenian life.

Ladies of the Great Salons

Eventually Pericles' political enemies brought a "writ of impiety" against Aspasia. It was a celebrated scandal. Pericles defended her when she was brought to trial, and the case was dismissed; but, for both of them, this was the beginning of the decline of their influence. They remained devoted to each other. After the death of his two legitimate sons, he arranged to have his and Aspasia's son legitimized. He died three years after the trial and left his fortune to her.

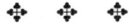

Isabella d'Este (1474-1539) was one of the most admired women of the Renaissance. She was famous for her beauty, accomplishments, exquisite taste, and devotion to the arts, as well as her intelligence and skill in diplomacy. A woman of enthusiasm and charm, she was generous, warm, and gracious and, at the same time, elegant and aristocratic. Statesmen, royalty, and other eminent people of her time sought her out. Artists and musicians were inspired by her. Her salon was the center of culture in Italy.

The Este family was one of the most powerful and impressive dynasties in Italy for about two centuries. Members of the Este family were important in the church, as well as in affairs of state. Isabella was born in Ferrara, daughter of Ercole I of Ferrara and Eleanora of Aragon, granddaughter of King Ferrante I of Naples. Her younger sister, Beatrice, with whom she was very close, was sent to Naples to her grandfather's court to learn the ways of court life. But Isabella stayed at home and was surrounded by fine musicians, artists, scholars and others who contributed to the brilliance of that court. Even at the age of 6, she was said to have held intelligent conversations with astonished diplomats. At that time, one of the men who had heard about this prodigy was the Marquis Federigo of Mantua in 1480. He suggested to her father that she and his son, Gian Francesco, become engaged. Ercole, who needed Mantua's support against Venice, agreed. Isabella remained at home for 10 more years, sopping up knowledge and becoming beautifully accomplished. She learned to play the clavichord and the lute, to dance, and to write. Her childhood was a rich and happy one.

When Isabella was 16 years old, she became the marchioness, or marquesa, of Mantua. The marriage started out well enough, but, during Isabella's first pregnancy, her husband was unfaithful and became increasingly so. This may have been partly her fault, since she was often away, visiting Milan in order to spend time with Beatrice, her sister, who was duchess of Milan. (Beatrice, too, was beautiful and accomplished. She and her husband had one of the most splendid courts in Italy. Among those at her court were Leonardo da Vinci, Niccolo da Correggio, and Donato d'Angelo Bramante. She served as ambassador to Venice for her husband, and helped him in his successful effort to become duke of Milan. She and her husband were part of the negotiations of the peace congress of Vecelli between Charles VIII and the princes of Italy.) There were many visits to Urbino as well, because she also was very close to her sister-in-law, Elisabetta Gonzaga, duchess of Urbino. (When the duke and duchess of Urbino were deposed, she warmly received them to her court.) She also visited her parents in Ferrara. Still, Francesco did not behave very well, not only in her absence but when she was at home. He embarrassed her by parading his mistress publicly and by having one adventure after another. Isabella acted as if she was not hurt, giving him support and advice in politics and diplomacy. Nevertheless, this situation probably contributed to her deep immersion into the arts and literature, and into friendships. Her relationship with her sister may have helped her cope with her feeling of rejection by her husband.

Her first priority was maintaining Mantua's independence and economic health. Her husband became ill with syphilis, at which time he depended on Isabella to help govern Mantua. Because of her great skill in diplomacy, she prevented takeovers by Cesare Borgia, Louis XII, Francis I, and, finally, Charles V. In 1519, her son Federigo succeeded his father. He was a good ruler, but foolishly allowed his mistress to take his mother's place in court.

Isabella, who was made to feel increasingly uncomfortable in Mantua, traveled to Rome with the desire to have her son Ercole made a cardinal. Pope Clement VII was undecided, and, in order to convince him, she decided to remain for a while and settled in a suite in the Colonna Palace at the invitation of the cardinals. There she established a fascinating salon. She found herself imprisoned during a battle in Rome in 1527. She managed to escape, and, eventually, she was able to win the cardinalate for Ercole.

In 1529, she helped the rulers of Urbino and Ferrara avoid having their principalities absorbed by the papal states. She also convinced Charles V to make her son Federigo a duke.

Isabella remained vibrant, attractive, and famous throughout her life, and was known as La Prima Donna (The First Lady). She was particularly devoted to music, which was the theme of decoration in her inner rooms. The leading lutist of the time, Marchetto Cara, lived at her court. Bartolommeo Tromboncino, a well-known composer of madrigals (whom Isabella encouraged to create music for poetry), also lived at the court, as did other gifted people. The "frottola," an Italian song form that was popular from 1490-1530, originated and was developed in her court, and became fashionable in other city-states in Italy. Many of the texts for the frottola were written by the poets of Isabella's circle. This song form eventually gave way to the madrigal and the French chanson.

Isabella was a generous patroness, commissioning works by Raphael and other great artists. She not only encouraged musicians but commissioned many beautiful instruments to be built. She had a valuable antique collection, and was knowledgeable about these and other instruments. As a performer, she was no dilettante; her singing was excellent, as was her command of the clavichord. Her contribution to the arts, in particular, and culture, in general, was outstanding.

Isabella d'Este died at age 64, revered by all.

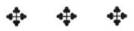

Chapter 2

Lucrezia Borgia (1480-1519) was a fascinating and tragic figure in history. There has been a great deal of conjecture that she possibly has been unjustly maligned. Pope Alexander VI (Rodrigo Borgia) was her father. He had several illegitimate children by his mistress Vannozza Cattani. His two favorites were Cesare and Lucrezia.

The Borgias were a noble family from Spain. Alexander's uncle Alphonso de Borgia was the first of the influential Borgias, becoming Pope Callistus III in 1455. By the time Alexander became pope, the family's power was in the ascendancy. He made his oldest son, Cesare, cardinal as a means of exerting power on the church. After a time, Cesare renounced his cardinalate and became deeply involved in politics and war, becoming a ruthless and wily general and administrator of the army of the church. He relentlessly pursued his father's goal of recapturing the papal states, in the process becoming the most powerful man in Italy.

Alexander loved his daughter Lucrezia with a passion. In fact, there was much gossip about their possibly incestuous relationship. (Cesare, her brother, too, loved her more than he was able to love anyone else.) She was attractive, but not an outstanding beauty, with a sweet face and long, heavy blond hair. He taught her about political intrigue and the skills of his office. (Much to the consternation of others, he once left her in charge of the Vatican.) She loved and was completely devoted to her family all her life.

Lucrezia was educated in a convent and then lived with a cousin of Alexander's. Hers was a privileged and happy childhood. Her father chose Giovanni Sforza, nephew to the regent of Milan, as her husband. This was done for political reasons, as was customary in those days. At age 13, she was married. Apparently, it was not a successful union. She was lonely, missed her father, and went back to Rome. Alexander had the marriage annulled on the grounds of impotency, which Giovanni denied. He retaliated by hinting that the father and daughter had an incestuous relationship. (Giovanni did finally have a son with his third wife.)

At this point, it was advisable to arrange another marriage for Lucrezia. This time the husband was Don Alphonso, Duke of Bisceglie, the illegitimate son of King Alphonso II of Naples. Lucrezia fell in love with him. Unfortunately, politics interfered in their otherwise happy relationship. Her brother Cesare married a French woman, and Alexander allied himself with Louis XII of France, an enemy of Naples. French agents were all over Rome. Her husband became frightened and fled back to Naples, leaving Lucrezia. When Alexander realized that his daughter was heartbroken, he made her regent of Spoleto, where her husband joined her. After being reassured that it was safe, they returned to Rome. The fly in the ointment was that Lucrezia's brother and her husband did not like each other. Mysteriously, one night Don Alphonso was stabbed as he was leaving St. Peter's. However, under his wife's care, he recovered. One day, as he was walking in a garden, he saw Cesare and, convinced that his brother-in-law had hired the would-be assassins, shot Cesare with an arrow from his bow. The arrow missed, whereupon Cesare sent his guards to his brother-in-law's rooms, where they suffocated Don Alphonso, very likely in front of his wife. Lucrezia was devastated. Strangely, she did not hold this act against her brother, feeling that it was a natural reaction. It is interesting to note that scholars of this era came to believe that she was a gentle person and that the malicious stories about her, including those about incest, were not true.

Again, her father arranged a marriage for her. With great ceremony and magnificent extravagance, Lucrezia was escorted from Rome to Ferrara to marry Alphonso, the future Duke of Ferrara and brother of Isabella d'Este of Mantua. She was completely accepted and loved by the people of Ferrara, and her husband was delighted with his charming and lovely wife. This was a turning point in her life. There was no more scandal about her. She was accepted unconditionally. At this point in her life she became involved in the arts, and wrote poetry in several languages. She established a brilliant court in Ferrara, which included the great artist Titian, as well as the poet Pietro Bembo. She encouraged musicians to compose for the many festive events at the court. The emphasis with respect to her commissions was on music for dance, from which dance forms for instrumental music evolved. Lucrezia contributed enormously to Italian music.

Alphonso and Lucrezia had four sons and a daughter. She died at the age of 39 after having given birth to her seventh child, who was stillborn.

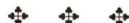

Diane de Poitiers (1499-1566) was the daughter of Jean de Poitiers, Comte de Saint-Vallier, and grew up in a court in which the arts were respected and loved. When she was 16 years old, she married Louis de Brèze, who was 56 years old. After he died, having been married about 15 years, she never married again. However, she became the influential mistress of King Henry II of France.

She met Henry when he was 7 years old. His mother had died and Diane, at age 27, had the opportunity to comfort him. Eleven years passed before he met her again. He was married, not by choice, to Catherine de Medicis. They had married four years previously and, although old enough for marriage, he was quite immature. He really wanted a mother, not a wife. Diane was quiet and maternal. He listened to her advice, and she helped him gain the knowledge and wisdom that would be needed when he was king. He became more secure, but, at the same time, depended on her. Eventually, she became his mistress, bringing up her two daughters by Brèze with their own child and with his illegitimate child (or children). Although he strayed a few times, he became more and more devoted to her. He spent his evenings with his wife (probably at Diane's insistence) but his life was really with Diane.

As king, he was even more devoted to her, and showered her with riches. With all this wealth, Diane rebuilt the mansion of the Brèze family at Anet. It was designed by Philibert Delormé. This famous chateau became Henry's second home. It housed a fine museum of art and had a splendid salon, attracting the cream of society, the most noted diplomats, intellectuals, cardinals, and the finest artists and musicians. This was actually the seat of the government, with Diane as chief advisor. The symbol of their love was seen on dishes, coats of arms, and works of art. The symbol was an H made up of two D's back-to-back, with a dash between the D's. It appeared everywhere for all to see.

When King Henry died at age 40, after having been injured in a tournament, Diane de Poitiers retired to her chateau in Anet and lived only 7 more years.

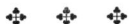

One of the most celebrated salons in France was that of **Catherine de Vivonne, Marquise of Rambouillet** (1588-1665). She was born in Rome, and was the daughter of Jean de Vivonne, the marquis of Pisani, who was the French ambassador to the Vatican. Her mother was Giulia Savelli, an heiress in the Orsini family, one of Rome's leading and most powerful families. Her education was exceptional for a girl in the 16th century. When, at age of 12, she married Charles d'Angennes, marquis of Rambouillet, she brought to France an excellent knowledge of language and fine manners. She had definite ideas, particularly disapproving the separation of the intellectuals and the nobility. She was kind and decent, and elegantly beautiful. Her special ability to attract and mix all the most interesting people at her salon created an irresistible atmosphere.

The marquise was not happy with the intrigue, superficiality, and lack of refinement in the French court (her husband had a very prestigious position under Henry IV and Louis XIII), and, after the birth of her eldest daughter, began to gather interesting people around her. In 1618, she designed the Hôtel de Rambouillet on the Rue St. Thomas-du-Louvre in Paris. One room was decorated with blue velvet, gold, and silver and was called the "salon bleu." This spacious room became her distinguished and famous salon. Among those who frequented the salon were great men of the church, ladies as well as gentlemen of the nobility, generals, musicians, poets, scholars, ladies and gentlemen of letters, scientists, visual artists, and humorists. The combination was electrifying and stimulating—aristocrats became more educated and cultured, men learned gracious manners from the women, and the art of conversation became highly developed. Among the guests were French classical moralist François de La Rochefoucauld, Cardinal Richelieu, the princess of Conti, the duchess de Rohan, novelist Madame de La Fayette, writer Madame de Sevigné, poet Guez de Balzac, and the playwright Corneille. Good taste and good manners were required. The marquise's tact and guidance led to healthy discussion, not destructive argument. Many imitations of her salon sprang up that contributed to the development of French culture, particularly in the area of literature. These lesser salons were often pretentious and were the object of satire and ridicule in Moliere's "The Affected Ladies."

Catherine had 7 children, but this did not impair her beauty or her activity. She was the inspiration for much of the poetry written by poets of her salon, in spite of the fact that her fidelity to her husband (a man who was considered dull) and her decency were never in doubt. When she retired, she drew up a code of correctness in speech and deed that helped to clarify language and was the seed from which the French Academy grew. (L'Academie Française was established in 1635 by Cardinal Richelieu for the purpose of developing and purifying the French language. It is the oldest of the five societies that make up the Institut de France.) Future salons continued the practice of including both women and men, thus raising the status of women and their influence on literature, language, intellectual affairs, and the arts. A great sense of beauty developed and respect for knowledge increased. The Marquise of Rambouillet, deservedly, is known for her positive impact on French culture.

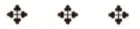

Ladies of the Great Salons

Queen Christina of Sweden (1626-1689) was born in Stockholm, Sweden, to King Gustavus II and Marie-Eleanore of Brandenburg. Gustavus loved her very much and accepted the fact that his heir was a girl. Her mother, on the other hand, never forgave her for not being a boy. (Perhaps this was the reason for her masculine attire and activities.) When she was 6 years old, her father was killed in his war to save Protestantism. She inherited the throne. Her education was well-guided by a learned man named Johannes Matthiae. The regent, who governed wisely during the 12 years of her minority, was the chancellor, Count Axel Oxenstjerna. Christina became of age to govern in 1644, when she turned 18. She made a point of neglecting her appearance, wore mannish attire and no jewelry, and participated in sports, such as hunting. She had a pretty face and blond hair, her eyes sparkling and lively. Although she supported the institutions of family and marriage, she did not want to marry, believing it would ruin her freedom. Sex to her was an act of subservience.

She was aware of her faults: too much pride, egotism, ambition, and impatience with others. Her strength was that she had definite ideas based on her great intellect and study. Her interests and knowledge included philosophy, languages (German, French, Italian, Spanish, Latin, Greek, Hebrew, and Arabic), literature, science, and music. In her court, she not only collected great art, but great thinkers. Many came to consult with her in her library. Her passion was philosophy. In 1649, she invited René Descartes to come to Stockholm to teach her philosophy. After much correspondence with her, he accepted. When he arrived, she insisted that the classes take place at 5 o'clock in the morning, three times a week. He walked through the snow to the queen's library. This was definitely not his cup of tea. He was used to sleeping late and to warmer weather. In February 1650, he caught a severe cold, which developed into pneumonia, and he died.

Christina was an individualist and generous to the point of extravagance, at the expense of Sweden. She was brilliant with commanding presence, but she was unruly and arrogant, completely unconcerned about public opinion, for which she showed contempt. Her court was luxurious and extraordinary, but she was not particularly interested in the food she ate nor the clothes she wore. She was jealous of the admiration and acclaim given to the chancellor, and made it difficult for him to pursue his diplomacy. Yet she was instrumental in bringing about great advances for her country. During her reign, the school system of Sweden vastly improved. She issued the first school ordinance for the country, built a college at Dorpat, founded six other colleges, and turned a college at Abo in Finland into a university. Students were sent abroad to learn. Scientists were urged to write in such a way that their papers could be understood by laymen. A publishing house was established in Stockholm. Trade and manufacturing were encouraged. Towns were given more privileges. In international matters, peace was important to her, and she worked hard for it.

Eventually, it became evident that she was getting tired of ruling. She began to show her contempt for the Protestant religion (the religion of her countrymen), ignored the feelings of her people, and spent more and more time with her favorite foreign guests, rather than attending to affairs of state. An ongoing source of irritation for her: Members of the government were anxious for her to marry to establish a successor to the crown. Christina would not marry. She was tired of work and tired of lectures by her counselors. The public's annoyance was obvious to her; the warmth and stimulation of France and Italy beckoned.

In 1654, at age 28, she left the throne to her cousin, friend, and lover, Charles X. The people of Sweden probably were delighted. Still, the ceremony was traumatic for Sweden, and it caught the attention of all Europe.

Charles gave Christina 50,000 crowns for her journey, and the Swedish Diet gave her a salary and the rights of a queen with regard to the people escorting her. She left Sweden (dressed as a man and calling herself Count Dohna). Her travel took her to Denmark, then to Hamburg, where she shocked all by staying at the home of her financial agent, who was Jewish. From there she went in disguise through Protestant Holland, then, in traditional dress, to Antwerp, which was Catholic. Going through

Brussels, she received a warm reception, but it was at Innsbruck, Austria, that she converted to Catholicism and was rechristened "Alexandra." Christina had long since concluded that, because one cannot know the truth, one should join a religion that appeals to one's emotions and sense of the aesthetic. It was a difficult decision for her, because of her attachment to her father, who had fought so ardently in defense of Protestant Europe.

Her triumphal entry into Italy was glorious. Town after town turned out to celebrate her arrival with festivals and entertainment. When she arrived in Rome, she was given a formal welcome by Pope Alexander VII. After all, in the eyes of the Catholic Church this conversion was a great victory.

At that time, the visual arts were only a small part of Rome's culture. It had many musicians, writers and scholars, great museums, libraries, and colleges. Italian lyric poetry was exciting and beautiful. Christina was welcomed by the most prominent people, not only as the former queen of Sweden but as a great patroness. Europe was fascinated with her—by her abdication, her conversion, her travel through Europe to the pope, and her independence.

In France, which she visited twice, she was greatly admired. In 1656, she was honored as a queen, with great ceremony. She stayed in the king's apartments in the Louvre. Men admired her, especially her splendid mind. Generally, however, women of the salons were offended by her neglect of dress, her free speech, especially in matters of sex and religion. In no way would she conform. She visited France again in 1657. This time she was given only an apartment at Fountainbleau. While there, she had her majordomo assassinated, because she discovered that he had been part of a conspiracy against her. The French court was stunned. This was not the act of a gracious guest. She spent the winter there, but the offended court was glad to see her leave for Italy.

Having established her salon in Rome, she received the most powerful and wealthy families and was overwhelmed with gifts and invitations. She was pious, but that did not interfere with her enjoyment of secular life. Her religion did not translate into prejudice. In the last 20 years of her life, her salon became the most celebrated in the city. She had one of the finest collections of art works and manuscripts. She influenced Italian poets to move from an artificial style to a direct, pure one. In her establishment, she had her own private theater, where she had excellent performances produced.

In her salon were performers and composers, as well as other artists. When Alessandro Scarlatti, who wrote music mostly for the voice, composed his first opera, Christina was so taken with it that she produced his next operas in her theater. He was her music director from 1679 to 1683. Scarlatti's operas were the models used for the next 50 years.

Arcangelo Corelli, considered by many to be the foremost violinist of his time, as well as the leading composer of violin music, dedicated his first printed sonatas to Christina. These sonatas for violin paved the way for wonderful 18th century chamber music. He set the form of the "concerto grosso," in which there are two violins and one violoncello playing with a string orchestra. This was the forerunner of the concertos of Vivaldi and Handel, and the suites of Bach. He was known for his trio sonatas and violins sonatas, as well. This age focused on the violin. In the 16th century, Andrea Amati, a gifted violin maker, brought his craft to Cremona. His grandson, Nicòlo, was considered by many to be the greatest craftsman of the family. Nicòlo's pupils, Andrea Guarneri and Antonio Stradivari, improved violins even further. (The oldest violin signed by Antonio Stradivari was dated 1666. He was 22 years old. He lived 93 years and made more than a thousand violins, violas, and violoncellos.) The dynasties of the Amati, Guarneri, and Stradivari families represent the peak of fine violin-making. Orchestral music and the composition and performance of instrumentals advanced.

Christina died in 1689 at age 63, and was buried in the Vatican. After her death, the Arcadian Academy was founded in her memory. Its first members were those who benefited from her friendship, patronage, and knowledge.

❖ ❖ ❖

Ladies of the Great Salons

The years 1660 to 1760 mark a period in which civility in French society was at its height. Women combined beauty, elegance, and sexuality with intelligence and the acquisition of knowledge. They taught men the fine art of conversation, so that it became courteous, eloquent, clear, and substantial. The exchange of ideas between men and women was free and beneficial to both. By this time, the hostesses of the great salons in Paris had fine-tuned their roles, and Paris was the center of world culture. These *salonières* were awe-inspiring. The stimulating gatherings blended brilliant, important conversation with gossip. The salons were *the* places to be. These elegant and bewitching women ruled this rarefied society cleverly and intelligently. To be invited to one of these salons was to have arrived. At this point, feminine influence was probably at its zenith, perhaps greater at that time than later when women obtained more legal power. The way to influence a man was to win the confidence of the woman he loved.

Those who assembled for these fascinating exchanges of ideas were some of the most creative minds of the time. Denis Diderot, the philosopher, and Jean Le Rond d'Alembert, the mathematician, were participants. Both men were responsible for the editing and publishing of the celebrated French *Encyclopedie,* which had profound effects on society, politics, and general knowledge. The articles were written by the most accomplished of the French Enlightenment, such as the Swiss-born French author, musician, and philosopher Jean-Jacques Rousseau; the great philosophical historian Charles Louis de Secondat, Baron de La Brede et de Montesquieu; and the writer and philosopher Voltaire (François Marie Arouet). Applied sciences and arts were included. Opinions stated in the articles were not dogmatic, although influenced by the aims of the Enlightenment. Reason, tolerance, and respect for the individual made up the underlying philosophy. These men joined other extraordinary people at the salons. The marquise de Sevigné and the comtesse de La Fayette (exceedingly talented and successful writers) were great additions. The mixture of philosophers, writers, visual artists, and musicians with those in power in government and with interesting members of the old aristocracy created an exciting intellectual environment.

Jean Baptiste Lully (1632-1687) was the most known name in French music of the 17th century. He made a name for himself in the court of Louis XIV, who also was a proficient musician. In addition to Lully's talent for politics at court and his close friendship with the king, he was a truly gifted musician: a violinist, singer, dancer, and a composer. An Italian, he adapted his music to the French taste. He was a brilliant theatrical composer. (In the field of religious music, however, he was surpassed by composer Marc Antoine Charpentier.)

The "sun king" appointed Lully as superintendent of music, founded the Royal Academy of Dancing, established the Royal Academy of Music, and appointed composers such as Lully and François Couperin (1668-1733) to his court. An unusual monarch, he was responsible for establishing the tradition known as "the music of Versailles." This tradition lasted through his reign and into that of Louis XV, who, although he considered music to be merely ornamental and not an art in itself, encouraged the performance of fine music at court in order to please his mistress, Madame de Pompadour, a lady of superior taste in music (see Chapter 3).

Music in France during the reign of Louis XV was dominated by Jean-Philippe Rameau (1683-1764), known for his theoretical writings and his operas, and Jean-Jacques Rousseau (1712-1778), known for his philosophical ideas and musical works. The ideal in music in the 18th century was accessibility, no strain in understanding, entertaining yet noble, and "naturalness" (in terms of feelings and speech). It was not an experimental age with respect to music. There was, however, strong feeling about the music that one wanted to hear. When an Italian opera troupe presented Pergolesi's *La Serva Padrona*, a classic of comic opera, a war of taste in music erupted. This was the War of Buffoons, between those who loved Italian music and those who preferred French music. The members of the salons and the royal courts joined in the argument.

Ladies of the Great Salons

Rameau fought for French music, Rousseau for Italian. Rameau was victorious.

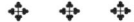

Ninon de Lenclos (1620-1705) was the daughter of a nobleman who believed one must have a questioning mind and use it freely without preconceived ideas, but her mother was a rigid woman with strict morals. Ninon was not provided with a formal education, but she accumulated knowledge on her own. She learned to speak Italian and Spanish, read books, and, like her father, developed a fine and inquiring mind. As a freethinker, she believed there was no moral obligation connected with love, and, at age 15, she became a prostitute and courtesan. Because of her flamboyant behavior, she was confined to a nunnery by the queen mother. This experience was fortuitous, in that it provided her with positive guidance in social etiquette and furthered her education in many areas. Because of her wonderful personality and sharp wit, the nuns thoroughly enjoyed having her stay with them, and she happily regarded it as a fine vacation. She was released by order of the king in 1657.

She had developed into an interesting and charming woman with elegant manners (a necessity, especially in the Parisian society of the day). Her admirers included some of the most distinguished men in France: members of the court, such as composer Lully, who enjoyed hearing her excellent harpsichord playing and her singing, and the great condé (Louis II, Duc de Bourbon), as well as members of great families and talented figures in the field of literature. Men came from near and far to court her. In 1657, she opened one of the first of the famous salons of that age. She invited those with the greatest minds and talent. Paris was astounded by her mind, beauty, and exquisite taste in the management of her salon. She became quite respectable in the minds of others and extremely well-liked for her honesty and kind nature. Having heard about her, King Louis XIV arranged to meet her, and he, too, was charmed.

As she grew older, she took great comfort in writing to her surviving friends. In one of her letters, she discussed her feelings about old age. She was philosophical and gracious, but, nonetheless, resented aging. She died at age 85.

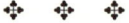

Claudine Alexandrine Guerin de Tencin (1681-1749) was born in Grenoble. Her salon became one of the most brilliant in the reign of King Louis XV. She was one of the most powerful and interesting women in France, second only to Madame de Pompadour, mistress to the king. Her parents placed her in a nunnery, but after 16 years, at age 32, she escaped, and hid in the rooms of an artillery officer, who fathered her son (the influential philosopher, scientist, encyclopedist, and academician and mathematician, Jean Le Rond d'Alembert). The infant was left on the steps of a church when he was a few hours old. His father claimed him and paid Madame Rousseau, a glazier's wife, to raise him with love and care. At age 7, the father presented him to his mother, who refused to have anything to do with him because she felt that a child would interfere with her career as a *salonière*. Claudine proceeded to have one liaison after another. Her lovers included some of France's most prominent men. (This promiscuity seemed to dominate the lives of her parents and siblings as well. Her father, who was president of the Parlement of Grenoble, was a known "ladies' man," her mother was considered a flirt, her sister admitted to affairs, and the fact that her brother had taken holy orders did not prevent him from philandering.) Included on her list of paramours was regent Philippe, Duc d'Orléans. She was extremely attached to her brother, and used her power to help his career.

In Paris, she lived on the Rue St. Honoré. Her first step was to gather money, which she did by investing well and by stealing from a friend who had asked her to be the guardian of his fortune. She refused to return it to him, so he killed himself, and she was sent to the bastille. Her friends managed her release, she kept most of the money, and, eventually, the scandal faded.

Her next step was to establish her own salon. Her guests were mostly male, because she wanted no competition. They included all ranks, but each participant had to be extraordinarily interesting and distinguished. It has been said that the conversation at her salon was the most brilliant in the reign of King Louis XV. Through her associations, she developed enormous power, so much that she was able to have her brother made an archbishop, then a cardinal, and, finally, a minister in the Council of State. She used her influence to have Madame de Châteauroux become the king's mistress, then persuaded her to convince the king to lead his army in war. She considered herself wise and was not shy about exerting her influence. Louis and his government were sources of constant discussion in her salon.

When La Tencin grew old, she became an ardent Jesuit. She was in constant communication with Pope Benedict XIV. In spite of her faults, she was kindness itself when it came to helping her gifted friends. In this way, she performed a great service to the culture of France. In her declining years, she became a successful author whose work was very well-received. She died at age 68.

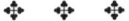

Marie de Vichy-Champrond du Deffand (1697-1780), a marquise, was orphaned at age 6. She was educated extremely well in a convent in Paris. From an early age she was curious and anxious to learn. At 21, she married the marquis du Deffand, a man she hardly knew; that relationship did not last and they were soon separated. She then became addicted to gambling, and lost a great deal of money, but with enormous self-control, was able to cure herself. She became the mistress of the regent Philippe II, the duke of Orléans. When he died, she relied on her wits.

As a frequent guest at the court of the political and ambitious duchesse du Maine, she began to collect many aristocratic and politically powerful friends—among them Charles Hénault, president of the Court of Inquiry. (He was her lover for a while, and they remained devoted friends.) She was beautiful, witty and brilliant, but unprincipled, cynical, and manipulative. She had great imagination and a clear mind, but her suspicious nature interfered with her judgment. One of her great gifts was her ability to see through to the character of a person and judge it accurately; one of her problems was her intense need for people. She could not bear to be alone. She had deep periods of depression, and some of the most interesting letters by Voltaire dealt with his attempt to help her cope.

Madame du Deffand established a salon in Paris to which celebrities flocked. Her salon was the center of French society and intellectual life for almost 40 years, and nearly as brilliant as Tencin's salon. Others rivaled hers, but had different emphases. Marie Thérèse Rodet Geoffrin's salon was known for her literary guests and her support of those involved with "The Encyclopedie". That of the Marquise de Lambert concentrated on intellectual discussions and discouraged such distractions as music. Meanwhile, Madame du Deffand drew from the aristocracy more than the literary world, although she had an ongoing friendship and correspondence with Voltaire. (Their letters are considered classics in French literature.) Montesquieu, Fontanelle, Diderot, and Madame de Staal-Delaunay were some of the regular participants. Hénault introduced her to D'Alembert, with whom she was impressed. Because of him, she tolerated the other encyclopedists, although she did not sympathize with them.

In 1754, she went blind, and by 1764 her salon closed. From then on her closest friend was Horace Walpole (20 years younger than she), who visited her often, and with whom she carried on a fascinating correspondence for 15 years. Because of Walpole's influence, her writings grew in eloquence and style. These later writings are highly regarded. Although she no longer had her salon, she was surrounded by friends and constantly visited by people of distinction, including foreign visitors such as Benjamin Franklin. Her fame as a *salonière* was worldwide.

The Marquise du Deffand died, leaving her papers and her dog, Tonton, to Walpole.

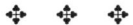

Madame de Pompadour (1721-1764), discussed in Chapter 3, was one of the great *salonières* before she became the mistress of King Louis XV. Her later career as a patroness at the royal court is of greater historical significance, although her dazzling reputation as a *salonière* had a lot to do with the king's interest in meeting her.

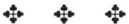

According to the fascinating book *The Life of Misia Sert* by Arthur Gold and Robert Fizdale (see Bibliography), in the early 20th century, there appeared in Paris one of the most influential *salonières* of all time. Her salon was the center of one of the most talented group of artists, writers, musicians, and dancers Paris has ever known. It epitomized the "belle époque." She was **Misia Sert** (1872-1950)—fascinating and beautiful, witty and highly intelligent, and with a talent for attracting and manipulating people. Men of genius immediately fell in love with her. She, in turn, did all she could to help them.

Misia was born in St. Petersburg, Russia. Her background was rich and interesting: her father was from an old and well-known Polish family, the Godebskis; her great-grandfather was a well-known poet; her grandfather had been deeply involved in the struggle for Polish independence, then moved to France, where he wrote for the stage. Her father, Cyprien Godebski, was a sculptor, talented but not inspired. He became famous and successful—a man of infinite charm, good looks, and irrepressible *joie de vivre*. Much of his life was spent traveling because of his important commissions. One woman after another fell in love with him, and, if they were rich, he often fell in love with them. His friends included artists and socialites.

Misia's maternal grandfather was a famous cellist, Adrien-François Servais. He was a native of Halle, Belgium, near Brussels, where he lived for most of his life. His wife loved music and, in order to entertain in an appropriate manner, they built a huge villa in Halle. They had one of the most active and prestigious salons where everything was unimaginably extravagant. Franz Liszt, Hector Berlioz, Anton Rubinstein, Henri Vieuxtemps, Hans Richter, and Hans von Bülow were among their friends who often visited this villa. Cyprien Godebski, a guest, met and married their daughter, Eugènie. They had two boys and Misia. Cyprien left for Russia before his last child was born, and there had an affair with his wife's aunt. Eugènie, even though pregnant, went after him, but soon after arriving, died in childbirth. Misia was left with her father, who had his mistress take care of her. Her father's behavior seemed to have created a pattern in her life, for she was always attracted to men who were virile, artistic, and unfaithful. In Warsaw, Cyprien met Matylda Natanson, the widow of a wealthy banker. She was a musician and sculptor. They established an elegant salon in Warsaw. Misia was sent to live in Belgium with her grandmother and her brothers. She loved everything about it. The house was filled with love and music, pianos and musicians. As it turned out, Misia was extremely musical and became a gifted pianist. (When she was 5 years old, she sat on Liszt's lap and played the piano for him while he worked the pedals.) She was, in fact, a child prodigy, and a student of Gabriel Fauré for years. Although Fauré cultivated Misia, it was her grandmother who loved and encouraged her, and introduced her to the world of famous musicians, beautiful music, and extravagant elegance.

But this happy time at her grandmother's did not last. She was brought to live in the new home of her father and step-mother in Paris. The relationship with her step-mother was not warm, but Matylda did recognize Misia's great talent and arranged for her to take lessons. She was sent to live at a school, then back to her grandmother's, then to her aunt's, then back to a school in Paris. The instability of her environment had a lasting effect. Nevertheless,

Ladies of the Great Salons

during that time she studied with Fauré, and his influence served her well throughout her life. Matylda died, and her father married yet again, but he and his new wife soon moved away. It seems that all those years of loneliness taught her to be independent and strong.

At 18, she left home to live on her own. She had known the Natansons because Matylda's first husband was a member of that family. Misia met Thadée Natanson again and he fell in love with her. They were married. Thadée, an intellectual, was a good influence on Misia. They were involved in the intellectual and social life of Paris. Fauré was disappointed that Misia had married, for he had planned a brilliant career for her. But Misia loved her new world, with its exciting young artists, writers, and musicians. They had plenty of money, were surrounded by stimulating people, and were both interested and knowledgeable about new art. Unknown painters such as Edouard Vuillard, Auguste Renoir, Pierre Bonnard, and Henri de Toulouse-Lautrec, became their friends and often spent days at a time in their summer home. Misia was the subject of paintings by these extraordinary artists. Thadée became involved in his "Revue Blanche," a literary revue that grew to be very successful. Because of her influence on her husband with respect to the periodical, Misia was able to dispense favors to those who wanted to be included. This gave her power of her own. Because the revue developed into an international periodical that dealt with social, artistic, and literary issues, contributors included people such as Count Leo Tolstoy, Anton Chekhov, Jane Austen, Oscar Wilde, André Gide, Emile Zola, and Marcel Proust. Misia had "open house" every day and in this way her salon was created. Musicians were invited as well. Fauré and his student, Maurice Ravel, and Claude Debussy were frequently at their house.

Eventually, Thadée became obsessed with liberal politics and less and less concerned with his "Revue Blanche," although he was still interested in increasing his fortune. But Misia was bored with politics. (She was never able to tolerate boredom.) In 1900, she met Alfred Edwards, a man of extreme wealth who was capable of great crudeness and, sometimes, violent behavior. Although he was married, he pursued Misia relentlessly. Thadée's fortune had slipped and, because Alfred had offered him the directorship of his coal mines in order to lure him away from Misia, Thadée persuaded his wife to satisfy Alfred's desires, to become his mistress, and, eventually, his wife. She agreed, in part because she would be the wife of the richest man in Paris, in part because of her growing disrespect for her weak husband. She lived with Alfred as a pampered mistress until they were both divorced from their respective spouses. They were married in 1905.

Alfred continued to overwhelm her with luxury, which she thoroughly enjoyed. Misia enjoyed everything: concerts, opening nights, bicycle racing, art shows, operas, ballets, cafe-concerts. But she was easily bored. Her one enduring interest and love was art and artists of all kinds. On her yacht, she entertained prominent artists, including the great singer Enrico Caruso and the brilliant composer Maurice Ravel. She grew more and more interested in such creative people. At one point, through her husband's newspaper empire, Misia was instrumental in publicizing the dustiness of the *Conservatoire* and was influential in reforming it. Fauré was appointed the new director.

Eventually, Alfred became obsessed with another woman—a beautiful actress named Geneviève Lantelmle. He divorced Misia in 1909 and married his new love. Misia was young and humiliated, but wealthy.

The next stage in her life found her devoted to two men, each in a different way. She met José Maria Sert, a Spanish painter and member of a wealthy family. He was extremely well-known, a favorite of the Spanish royals. She and Sert became lovers, and finally married in 1920, after years of living together. Misia had fallen deeply in love for the first time. Their life together was filled with art; they both were dedicated to beauty and its creators.

The other important man in her life was Serge Diaghilev, the famous impresario who was a genius in combining many different talents in his productions. As soon as he and Misia met, they became inseparable friends. She was his closest woman friend, supporter, confidante, and advisor. It was because of her help that he was able to bring the Russian Ballet to Paris. The well-connected Comtesse Greffulhe and Misia formed a committee of influential people to help him. Misia was the center of this society. She was the link to Diaghilev. Her salon became the home of Russians and their friends. Some of the regular guests were Nijinsky, Cocteau, Proust, and Stravinsky, all of whom became involved in Diaghilev's ballets. Misia introduced Ravel, Satie, and Debussy to him, and they too became important to his ballets. It was an astonishingly brilliant group.

Her value to Diaghilev cannot be overstated. Aside from their deep friendship, her knowledge and her connections to artists and members of the highest society in Paris paved the way for him. As an example, in 1917, Diaghilev produced the ballet "Parade." He used Jean Cocteau's stunning scenario, Erik Satie's orchestral score, Pablo Picasso's stage design, Leonide Massine's choreography and the work of other now famous artists, most of whom were brought together by Misia. With her powerful influence on Diaghilev, she manipulated situations so that egos were soothed and paths were smoothed.

After World War I, more and more talented people arrived in Paris, and many met regularly at a nightclub called "Le Boeuf Sur Le Toit." One could have seen Artur Rubinstein, Erik Satie, the prince of Wales, the Diaghilev crowd, as well as Francis Poulenc, Germaine Tailleferre, members of the French nobility, other patrons of the arts, and Misia and her husband. The '20s had arrived, and Misia was the bridge between the past Belle Époque and the new flamboyant and "roaring twenties." Thanks to Misia, Diaghilev came to know and commission the music of Les Six (Georges Auric, Louis Durey, Arthur Honegger, Francis Poulenc, Germaine Tailleferre, and Darius Milhaud). Rubinstein included in his autobiography many interesting anecdotes about Misia and her support of and involvement with illustrious musicians and other artists. "Misia Sert invited me to have tea with Diaghilev, Massine, and Eric Satie, whom I met for the first time. . . . With the great help of Misia, who was of Polish origin, we tried to interest

Diaghilev in Szymanowski and his music and we succeeded."[1]

When Igor Stravinsky confided in him about his desperate financial situation, Rubinstein replied, "Misia Sert is a woman of great resources. I have no doubt that when I talk to her, she will find a way to give you solid financial help. Diaghilev and his ballet couldn't have survived the war without her help."[2] He went on to say that Misia did manage to provide him with money so that he could spend the summer in Biarritz and work on a project for Diaghilev.

Unfortunately, Sert fell in love with a young Russian girl, Roussadana Mdivani, left his wife, had the marriage annulled, and married "Roussy." It was another humiliation and a damaging loss for Misia. Another great loss, the death of Diaghilev in 1929, left her grief-stricken. But she and Coco Chanel, her dearest friend (and one with whom she was in constant competition), remained close, sharing their lives and secrets, depending on each other, although always rivals. Regrettably, as they grew older, they depended on drugs more and more. Misia's health deteriorated badly, and in 1950, she died. When Coco was told about her friend's death, she went to Misia's deathbed immediately to wash and dress her in white and apply makeup so that even though she was 78 when she died, Misia was still amazingly beautiful.

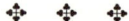

Gabrielle (Coco) Chanel (1883-1971) probably was this century's most famous couturière. She is known for her high-fashion classic clothes and accessories, most of which have been copied over and over, and for her extraordinarily successful perfume business. For her time, Coco's clothes were revolutionary. Her hats were severe, her dresses were made of unusual materials such as jersey, her suits were cut simply but distinctively. Trench coats and pea jackets were introduced, and the Chanel hemline became popular. Modesty and taste were important.

The story of Coco Chanel has been difficult to reconstruct, in part because she relayed a version that she evidently wanted people to believe. She was the daughter of peddlers. Her father was great fun, but unreliable, and her mother was sickly and gloomy. They had five children, two boys and three girls. When her mother died of tuberculosis, Coco was 6 years old. Her brothers were given to public officials, and the girls were deposited by the father at the home of his parents. He left, never to return. Coco was devastated, and began to develop her philosophy at this point. She defined it by saying, "I have never been interested in money, but I was concerned with independence. If I analyze myself a little, I see immediately that my need for independence began to develop when I was still a very young girl."[3] She had learned from the young domestics in her grandmother's home that, if one worked hard, one could earn money and, more to the point, not be dependent on anyone.

Her grandmother placed her in a convent at Moulins. As a charity student (therefore, having poor food and accommodations), she was required to do many chores to earn her keep. This situation humiliated her, and affected her entire life. It was always important to Coco to have people believe she had a father who sent money, and she insisted over and over again that she was not an orphan. She would tell anyone who would listen that her father was in America and that, since she was his favorite child, he would take good care of her.

At age 20, Coco was a beauty. In Moulins, there was a cavalry garrison, where she met Étienne Balsan, a handsome and dashing second lieutenant from a wealthy family of industrialists. Étienne, however, did not work in the family business. He was a horseman, madly in love with riding. At that time, Coco was living with her father's young sister Adrienne, who was only two years older than she. They were both dressmakers. (Even as a child, Coco enjoyed designing clothes, basing her styles on those described in the romantic novels she read.) Adrienne and Coco's younger sister Antoinette were also raised by the grandmother, and the three young ladies were known as

"The Three Graces." They were beautiful, and all three were eagerly looking for security. The regiment attracted the most eligible young men of Paris, and the three girls enjoyed entertaining them. When Étienne left the army, he entered his career as a gentleman jockey. He was exciting, knew the most important people, and was very much in demand socially. Yet he was no snob. He simply did what he wanted. He was interested only in the world of horsemanship, polo, hunts, and racing; beautiful and exciting women; and his independence. He became the first of Coco's lovers who was important to her.

Étienne invited Coco to leave Moulins, go with him to Paris, and move into his home at Royallieu, where he had racing stables. He had a mistress established there, Emilienne d'Alençon, a famous and beautiful "cocotte" (professional paramour). Therefore, Coco was forced to take a back seat. This did not seem to bother her, because she felt that this was a step in the right direction. She had left Moulins without a backward glance, convinced that her future lay in Paris. She was an adorable playmate for Étienne—amusing, bright, and completely devoted to his interests, spending her time at Étienne's training grounds at La Croix-St. Ouen with the trainers and jockeys. He began to take her into Paris, where she stayed at the Ritz and met the cream of society. She knew nothing about high society, or how to eat exotic foods such as oysters. But in a very short time she learned everything she needed to know and more. Everyone was charmed by her manner, wit, and individualism. An important lesson she learned was that it paid to be aggressive. Another was that most people who seemed secure were not truly self-confident, so it was not difficult to destroy their defenses. It goes without saying that, because of her experience with her father, she did not trust men. She used them.

She began to dress as she wanted. She once said, "All those ladies were badly dressed, in their body armor, with their bosoms out, their behinds jutting out, too, bound in at the waist until they were almost cut in two. They were dressed to the teeth. Actresses and cocottes set the fashions, and the poor society ladies followed, with birds in

Ladies of the Great Salons 47

their hair, false hair everywhere, and dresses that dragged on the ground and gathered mud."[4] She could not understand how the cocottes could use their brains when they wore these enormous hats smothered with flowers, and she began to design a simpler and more masculine hat. Women began to talk about her style and want it for themselves. Coco started thinking about establishing herself in business and becoming independent. She opened a little hat shop, but this first venture was short-lived.

At this time, the second important lover entered her life. Boy Capel was a handsome English playboy she met at Étienne's winter training quarters, and with whom she fell in love. She left a note for Étienne and went to Paris with Boy. She had been with her former lover at his home outside of Paris for four years and still had no promise of security. He had kept her in his home with not a thought for her future. In Paris with Boy (whose life and escapades were followed avidly in all the newspapers), she became well-known and admired, even envied. Now that he was without her, Étienne became jealous and pursued her again. The three were together so much that they were the talk of Paris. She was about 26 at that time, living at the Ritz with all her bills paid, but still no security.

Coco decided that she could not live like a kept woman. Étienne left the country for a while (perhaps to forget her), but, before he left, he set her up in an apartment on avenue Gabriel, where she could live and make hats. Boy Capel did his part by opening a bank account for her to provide the means to proceed with her business. By this time she was almost 30 years old. The hat business became successful. She was no longer intimidated by anyone and was not afraid to charge enormous prices for her hats. Happily, she was able to bring her sister Antoinette and her aunt Adrienne to work for her at her shop. The *Three Graces* were together again. The little workshop was moved to rue Cambon, at the corner of rue St. Honoré. And that was the beginning of the great House of Chanel.

Coco described her entry into dress designing: "One day I put on a man's sweater just like that, because I was cold. It was in Deauville. I tied it with a handkerchief at the waist."⁵ This was her first jersey dress. She had a genius for cutting and draping, getting the effect she wanted quickly. She adapted the English masculine style to feminine styles, in that way allowing women more freedom of movement, but with incredible *chic*! Women loved it and flocked to her.

By 1919, Coco Chanel was famous. During the war, the Germans allowed her to sell her clothes, and she lived a luxurious life with her wealthy and titled friends. At the same time, she met Misia Sert and José Maria Sert, who gave her an extensive education in the arts and exposed her to beauty of a kind she had never experienced. She became interested in the *Ballets Russes* and in the career of Serge Diaghilev, the impresario. When Coco was visiting Misia at the Hôtel Meurice, she met Diaghilev, who was much in need of money. She invited him to visit her at the Ritz, where she lived, and gave him a check for the full amount immediately. This was the beginning of her support of the arts and, more important, her intellectual independence. She no longer needed the guidance of Misia or anyone else. Her salon attracted everyone that mattered in the culture of Paris. She was in her 40s (although she looked at least 10 years younger), dynamic, and beautiful.

Boy Capel was killed in a car accident in 1919. Although he had married someone else, Coco had remained friendly with him and his wife. Yet when he died, she was truly desolate, and if it had not been for the Serts, who took her with them to Italy to distract her, it would have been most difficult for her to cope with her feeling of loss.

Grand Duke Dmitri, the grandson of Czar Alexander II, was the third important man in Coco's life. She had met him before the war, and after he was forced to flee Russia because of his collaboration with Prince Felix Yusupoff in the murder of Rasputin, he went to Coco for help. From 1919 on she was seen everywhere with him. But in 1929, when she was about 45 years old, she met the Duke of Westminster at the Hôtel de Paris in Monte Carlo. He was the richest man in Great Britain. She said, "My real life began with Westminster. I'd finally found a shoulder I could

Ladies of the Great Salons

lean on, a tree against which I could prop myself"[6] He took Coco back to England with him, where she lived in the lap of luxury. On his estate, she went hunting, riding, and fishing, and relaxed. Theirs was a relationship between equals: a free, successful, and independent woman and a man of great wealth and position. They lived at all his homes and on his yacht, the *Flying Cloud*. At his home in La Pausa, in the south of France, their romance finally came to an end when Winston Churchill made it clear that, because the duke was divorced and free to marry, it was his duty to wed the daughter of the chief of Protocol at Buckingham Palace.

In 1939, when war was declared, Coco closed her House of Chanel. No one seems to know why. She claimed it was because of the war. A German was known to visit her frequently. During the occupation, her handsome and charming "gentleman" friend was Baron von D. (called "Spatz" by her friends), who had been sent to Paris in 1940 by Joachim von Ribbentrop, the foreign minister of Germany. His job had been to supervise the textile industry. He and Coco were never seen in public because of his desire for anonymity but it was known that they were together often. Although some people suspected her of favoring Germans, there were many who thought that she worked for the British, and that she was on a special list of people to be protected by the British. Artur Rubinstein, with whom she had been especially close before the advent of the Nazis, said upon returning to Paris after the occupation, ". . . Here [in Paris], some of my best friends, especially Misia Sert, were full of praise for the Nazis' 'good manners' during the occupation, but were incensed about the American 'invasion,' as they called it, and their 'vulgar' familiarity. . . . Of course, this put me out terribly, but soon enough I discovered that Misia and her like were made up of the most concentrated kind of egoism, incapable of realizing the real tragedy of the war . . ."[7]

In 1954, Coco Chanel reopened the House of Chanel. She was 71 years old. It was a huge success, due largely to the American market and the dress industry on

Seventh Avenue. Copies of the Chanel style were comparatively inexpensive and became available to the average woman. She was again the talk of the fashion world.

Coco died on January 10, 1971, at her apartment at the Ritz Hotel, alone except for her maid. Her House of Chanel was as successful as ever.

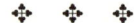

Misia Sert drew many powerful friends into her world. They, like Coco Chanel, established salons and became great patrons and patronesses. Perhaps the most well-known, elegant salon of that time was that of the **Princesse Edmond de Polignac,** born Winaretta Singer (1865-1943), who was the heiress to the Singer Sewing Machine fortune. She was talented in many areas, especially in painting and music. In fact, she was so talented that Artur Rubinstein said about her, "We once performed the *Valse romantique* for two pianos by Chabrier brilliantly for her friends."[8] The prince was a gifted amateur composer, and thoroughly sympathetic with his wife's artistic interests. The couple had a good relationship, in spite of the fact that Winnie was a practicing lesbian. She was perfectly honest about her sexual preference, but conducted herself with discretion in public. Whether artists were homosexual or not had no bearing on whether they were invited to her salon. In the world of artists, homosexuality seemed to be prevalent, or perhaps just freely acknowledged. Talent and gentility to Winnie were the all-important qualifications. Members of the aristocracy, socially prominent friends, and exceptionally gifted artists were invited to her soirées, concerts, recitals, and balls. She was a bold, free-thinking woman and yet very proper in appearance. Virginia Woolf said of Winnie, "Looking at her, you would never guess that she had ravaged half the virgins in Paris."[9] Be that as it may, she was the most well-known patroness in the artistic world in Paris at that time.

Through Misia, she became deeply involved in the Diaghilev group. At one point, she arranged to have the

Ballets Russe produced in Monte Carlo. (Her husband was uncle to Prince Pierre de Monaco.) The ballet troupe was in residence there for six months each year. It finally had a permanent home.

Winnie was indefatigable in her efforts to help great artists. Among the many that benefited from her support were Igor Stravinsky, Francis Poulenc, and Erik Satie, whose compositions she commissioned. She arranged a private hearing at her salon of Stravinsky's *Les Noces*, in which the composer conducted his own work. This production included voices, winds, percussion, and four pianos (played by Poulenc, Auric, Marcelle Meyer, and Hélène Ralli) on Pleyel double-pianos. Stravinsky was anxious for the dancers to become familiar with the score, so Winnie arranged this elaborate presentation.

Many connections were made among the creative people meeting at her salon. Cole Porter met Rolf Mave, who wanted American music for his ballet. Fauré, de Falla, Nijinsky, and Diaghilev had the opportunity to mingle with the fine poet, the Duchesse Anna de Noailles.

Other musicians whose talent she promoted were Gabriel Fauré, Ernest Chausson, Vincent d'Indy, Emmanuel Chabrier, Maurice Ravel, Ethel Smyth, Claude Debussy, Artur Rubinstein, and Manuel de Falla. She arranged to have great artists such as Wanda Landowska perform on the harpsichord. She was very supportive of Nadia Boulanger (see Chapter 6), arranging, for example, a concert in which Boulanger conducted a complete concert of baroque music in her private auditorium. (This was one of the occasions on which the princess played the organ.) She had hired a full orchestra and chorus, and invited some of the most important people of Paris. Although they were not close friends, when the princess died, she left Nadia Boulanger 500,000 francs and established a charitable organization named The Singer-Polignac Foundation, making Boulanger its musical director.

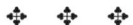

Winnie's niece by marriage, the beautiful **Comtesse Jean de Polignac** (Marie-Blanche), also was a friend of Misia Sert. She was the daughter of Jeanne Lanvin, the couturière. Her interest lay in music, and she was a gifted amateur singer. She assumed Misia's role as hostess of a salon devoted to music. Gifted musicians were invited to work at length in her music room, and were introduced to colleagues and lovers of music who could further their careers. Nadia Boulanger, the well-known teacher, composer, conductor, and organist, performed privately with her. When Nadia gave a series of lecture-recitals on French choral music, she arranged to bring her own soloists with her, among them Comtesse de Polignac. It was unusual for a woman of Marie-Blanche's social position to be "working." It also was unusual for the rehearsals to be held in her luxurious suite in the Claridge Hotel. Nevertheless, it was a good working relationship. The countess arranged to have the House of Lanvin create Nadia's performing clothes (always black and severe). In 1938, she was one of the singers who accompanied Nadia Boulanger on her tour in the United States.

Misia's half-brother Cipa, and his wife, **Ida Godebski**, had a salon of the highest quality in Paris, frequented by people such as Gide, Vuillard, Bonnard, Satie, Milhaud, Poulenc, and Stravinsky. Ravel, a special friend, was made to feel as if he were part of the family. He composed the wonderful *Ma Mere L'oye* especially for their two children. The finest music was performed.

Others in Misia's circle were committed to supporting these talented people. **The Comtesse Adhéaume de Chevigné, the Comtesse Henri Greffulhe, and the Princesse Lucien Murat** were impressive patronesses, particularly of Diaghilev.

❖ ❖ ❖

This was a splendid age for the arts in Paris. The great salons, although they attracted musicians, seemed to be more concerned with visual and literary artists. American artists who found themselves in Paris were delighted to meet one another and others at the exciting salons. One such salon was **Gertrude Stein's** (1874-1946), located on the left bank. Its philosophy was one of equality, as opposed to that of the Princesse de Polignac, who insisted that her guests be "well-bred." The Gertrude Stein salon was composed mostly of talented Americans. (There were some in Paris who preferred a salon that was more "discriminating.")

Her great contribution to music, aside from the stimulating atmosphere of her salon, concerned Virgil Thomson, a composer of remarkable originality, and, later, a brilliant music critic. He was a member of her circle, and she was particularly helpful in the development of his ideas. The librettos for his operas, *Four Saints in Three Acts* (1934) and *Mother of Us All* (1947), were written by Gertrude Stein. Through her he met Jean Cocteau, Erik Satie, and the composers of *Les Six*, all of whom influenced his work.

Gertrude Stein was born in Allegheny, Pa., but was raised in California. She graduated from Radcliffe College in 1897, and, because she was a woman of independent means, she was able to settle in Paris. For a while, she shared an apartment with her brother Leo, but she soon developed a deep relationship with Alice B. Toklas, with whom she lived for the rest of her life.

Gertrude became known for her avant-garde writings and fascinating friendships, as well as for her magnificent collection of modern paintings. She was a prolific writer, having produced more than 40 books. Her style became abstract, paralleling the paintings of Picasso, Matisse, and others. For a long time she had difficulty finding a publisher for her work, but, with the help of her friends Sherwood Anderson and Ernest Hemingway, she succeeded. Her writings were difficult for most people to read and understand, but in 1933, her book, *The Autobiography of Alice*

B. Toklas, became a best-seller and her fame increased. She returned to the United States for a lecture tour 30 years after she left. But her home was Paris, where she continued to live until her death.

Chapter Three

Elegant Patronesses of the Old World

Eleanor of Aquitaine (1122-1204) was one of the most important of the great medieval women, with great beauty, intelligence, power, and wealth. She was the daughter and heiress of Duke William X of Aquitaine in France, who was a leader and supporter of the troubadours. From him she inherited her love of amorous poetry and songs. Eleanor grew up and was educated at his court at Bordeaux, where she was exposed to some of the best minds of southwestern France. She absorbed it all and developed beautifully, becoming a young woman of culture, intellect, love of life, powerful passions, and physical grace and ability. She was raised to be a queen, in the best sense of the word.

When she was 15 years old, she married Prince Louis, the heir to the French crown. A month later, he became King Louis VII. They had two daughters but no sons. They were complete opposites in personality and interests. Whereas she was delightful, lovely, and full of fun, he was serious, plodding, and interested almost exclusively in affairs of state.

Determined to be a good queen, Eleanor and her attendants accompanied her husband to Palestine on the Second Crusade. She was badly neglected by him, but nevertheless managed to enjoy herself. Included in her good times were affairs with other men. The king tolerated her behavior, but St. Bernard of Clairvaux of the church exposed her activities to the world. In 1152, Eleanor finally sued for divorce. Both she and King Louis wanted an annulment, which the church granted under the pretext that the king and she were too closely related.

Eleanor returned to Bordeaux, where she was courted by many suitable men. She chose Henry of Anjou, who succeeded to the crown of England, becoming King Henry II, and she became a queen again. King Louis was concerned about the fact that Aquitaine would be lost to his daughters. This was the beginning of the stress between England and France that continued throughout medieval history.

The troubadours adored Eleanor. She, in turn, was their great patroness. She gathered singers and poets around her and was the inspiration for many of their love songs. Amorous poetry became popular in southern France, and when she moved to England, the troubadours followed her, bringing their style of love songs, including ballads, with them. A favorite was the "pastourelle," which told the story of a knight who tries to make love to a reluctant shepherdess who, inevitably, is rescued by her brother or lover. This and other ballads were sophisticated versions of folk songs and stories. However, it was their Provençal love songs that were mostly associated with the troubadours. This type of song glorified love that was chivalrous and spiritual, rather than physical. The object of that adoration was a woman (usually someone else's wife). She was unattainable and the object of worship and respect. The plots' interest lay in the intellectual intricacies of the situations. The gentle and chivalrous ideals of these songs traveled to Germany, where they were sung by "minnesingers" (very much like the troubadours of southern France and the trouvères of northern France). This kind of music and its influence on society traveled on to the Iberian peninsula and the growing city-states of northern Italy. Because of her great support and encouragement, Eleanor was largely responsible for its dissemination throughout Europe and England. Some of the songs inspired dancing, which was becoming more and more popular, and instrumental music with dance forms evolved.

Eleanor and Henry had five sons and three daughters. Now that she was older and the fires were banked, she remained faithful to him. However, Henry, who was 11 years younger than she, was very much taken with the ladies of the court. Eleanor was consumed with jealousy. Their relationship deteriorated into indifference, then into hatred. Henry arranged to have her dethroned and, although she fled to Aquitaine, he had her captured and imprisoned. She remained confined for 16 years, but never lost her spirit. In fact, she encouraged her sons' rebellion of 1173. It failed, and Henry stayed in power until his death in 1189.

Because of her close involvement with and support of the troubadours, and their own influence and popularity, they successfully persuaded the people of Europe that the king was at fault. When her son Richard the Lion-Hearted succeeded his father, he freed his mother. He spent little time in England because of his involvement in the crusades, so he made Eleanor regent of England while he was away. She became important politically, not only because of her position and astuteness, but because of her popularity in Aquitaine, which she had inherited. As a result of her marriage to Henry II of England, part of Aquitaine became united with England and remained so for approximately 400 years. During that time the relationship between England and France was one of hostility and stress.

When Richard died, his brother John succeeded him as king, at which time Eleanor withdrew to a convent in France, where she died at age 82.

❖ ❖ ❖

Catherine de Medicis (1519-1589) was born in Florence, Italy, into the great Medici family. She had a difficult childhood. Both her parents died within 22 days of her birth, her mother in childbirth and her father as a result of syphilis. She was moved from place to place in the care of Medici relatives at a time of violence and intense scheming. At one point, she was held hostage by those in Florence who had expelled the Medicis and who wanted to keep them under control. Her family did return to retake the city, in spite of the fact that Catherine was threatened with death.

Pope Clement VII, her uncle, sent Catherine to France to marry Henry, duke of Orléans, son of Francis I and heir to the French throne. They were both only 14 years old. Francis I had taken over a large part of Italy and was threatening to take even more. This marriage was the pope's attempt to create peace between Italy and France. Catherine was desperately unhappy: Henry hardly spoke to his young bride and, because she had brought so many Italians with her, she seemed to have alienated the Parisians. She remained childless for 10 years but then had 10 children. Seven of the children survived. Three of her sons became kings of France: Francis II, Charles IX, and Henry III. Her daughter Elizabeth married Philip II. Her daughter Marguerite of Valois married Henry of Navarre. Other than bearing her husband's children and spending a few hours with him in the evening, she had no relationship with him. He was completely involved with Diane de Poitiers (see Chapter 2), who was his mistress and who dominated him. Although he did not love Catherine, after his death she mourned him for the rest of her life.

Her son Francis II (1559-60) succeeded to the throne, but was too young to govern. He died soon after. His brother Charles IX became king of France. He, too, was too young to govern, and was under Catherine's guardianship. Even after he came of age, he left the governing to her. She was highly intelligent, extremely cultured, and had the Medici talent for skillful and crafty diplomacy. For 30 years, she was a power in the governing of France. She was officially regent on two occasions. She had one goal—to keep her sons in authority (first Charles IX, then her favorite, Henry III). Although ruthless and not averse to treachery to achieve her aims, she knew the art of compromise and tried to use it to bring about peace between the Catholics and the Huguenots (Calvinists). She tried to give the Protestants some measure of freedom of worship, but the Catholics vehemently opposed this. As a result of this intolerance, the Wars of Religion began, consisting of lootings and massacres, and lasted 40 years.

Her adored son Henry III became king in 1574. She continued to be active in negotiations with the Catholic League, which wanted to control the throne. But in December 1588, her son murdered the league's leaders, and Catherine, horrified to the point of physical illness, died two weeks later. Henry was assassinated in 1589, just after Catherine died.

When Catherine arrived in France with her Italian entourage and her Italian culture, she introduced Italian dances. Ballet became the most popular entertainment in her court. (These new forms of dancing encouraged instrumental accompaniment. The dance forms led to the suites of movements, each movement a different dance form. This, in turn, led to the symphony and the chamber music quartet.) Balthazar de Beaujoyeux, the first well-known violinist, appeared at her court, and she was instrumental in bringing many other violinists there. Violin music became popular. France had been resistant to the music of other countries, but Catherine de Medicis helped to break down that barrier.

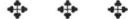

Queen Elizabeth I of England (1533-1603) greatly impacted the development and enjoyment of music. She was highly intelligent and well-educated. In music, especially in performing on the virginal and the lute, she was quite proficient. She also composed poetry and music. Her interest in the virginal was a large factor in her encouraging keyboard music.

Elizabeth was the daughter of Henry VIII and his second wife, Anne Boleyn, who was executed when she was not able to produce a male heir and suspected of infidelity. Anne had never really played the role of mother to her daughter; therefore, Elizabeth was not emotionally affected by this loss. She was brought up in the care of Henry's subsequent wife, Catherine Parr, who treated her with affection. She had a fairly happy childhood which she shared with her younger half-brother Edward and her half-sister Mary who was 17 years older. She read omnivorously, and became fluent in French, Italian and, later, Spanish. Classical Greek, Latin, philosophy and history also fascinated her.

When Edward died, Mary became queen. When Mary died, Elizabeth became the reigning monarch. Henry VIII had practiced Protestanism after breaking with Rome. His son Edward continued that policy. But Mary was an ardent Roman Catholic, and restored that religion to England. Elizabeth re-established Protestanism as the religion of England, but she was moderate in her beliefs, and tolerant of Catholic composers who wrote for the Catholic church. (William Byrd, one of the greatest composers in England, benefited from her policy and encouragement, as did England, in general.)

Although Elizabeth had never married and was said to be a virgin, she had many suitors. Robert Dudley, the earl of Leicester, was an important object of her affections. (It has been said that she would have married him if she had not been suspicious that he was involved in his wife's murder.) Philip II of Spain proposed marriage, but she rejected the offer. She was courted for long periods by the duc d'Anjou (the future King Henry III of France) and his brother duc d'Alençon. These relationships may have been politically inspired. She was a master of diplomacy and, doubtless, her shrewd mind and understanding of human character served England well.

The period extending from the defeat of the Spanish Armada in 1588 to 1603, when James I became king, was a golden age in England. The queen's love of music and drama created an atmosphere of excitement in those arts.

In Shakespeare's plays, music was important. Composers collaborated with dramatists. Music-making in England was extremely popular, but there were no large public concerts. Nevertheless, there were many amateurs among the general public who demanded musical publications. Most sang madrigals and played lutes. Viols and the virginal were found in many households. It was expected that young men could sing or play an instrument. All this activity inspired composers, and the result was a wonderful combination of folk and art music. There were various kinds of music, and the keyboard and chamber music were exceptional. In spite of the nationalistic spirit of England in political matters, musicians were happy to borrow from the music of other countries, particularly Italy. In the last 20 years of Elizabeth's reign and beyond, the madrigal became the rage. They were derived from the Italian madrigal, but English madrigals were lighter. Most of the composers wrote for amateurs.

The queen constantly entertained at her court. Musicians were hired to perform and compose, keyboard music being her particular love. Dancing was a joy to her, as were plays. It was a lively court. Masques were imported from Italy. The combination of poetry, music, pageantry, fun, and ballet was thoroughly enjoyed.

Elizabeth I, through her encouragement and example, brought the arts to the people of her country. In addition to her support of secular music, she helped the development of church music by taking on the role of patroness of chapel masters, their large choirs and their music. She encouraged the development of polyphonic music in religious services, even though she favored secular music. Because she enjoyed being courted, she promoted the development of the love song in the form of the madrigal. The best-known Elizabethan musicians probably were William Byrd, Orlando Gibbons, and John Bull. (Gibbons and Bull were her royal chapel organists.) These three composers wrote the first book of keyboard music in England.

❖ ❖ ❖

Chapter 3

Empress Maria Theresa (1717-1780) was one of the most interesting and impressive rulers of the Hapsburg dynasty, which dated back to the 10th century, and it was the longest-ruling European group. The Hapsburg lands and peoples were incohesive and widespread. At the beginning of her reign, the empire included Austria, parts of Italy, Yugoslavia, Bohemia, Moravia, Silesia, Hungary, Croatia, some areas of southern Germany, the Austrian Netherlands, which became Belgium, the duchies of Milan, Mantua, Piacenza, and Parma, and Tuscany in Italy, and Lorraine (as a result of her marriage). The focal points of Austria were Vienna, the Danube valley, and the Hungarian Plain.

Maria Theresa, the elder daughter of Emperor Charles VI, was born in Vienna. Although Charles's court was grandly ceremonial, his life at home with his family was relaxed and comfortable. He thoroughly enjoyed his children. (His daughters Maria Theresa and Marianne survived into adulthood. Two other children died.) Elizabeth Christine, Maria Theresa's mother, was a beautiful, tender, and lovely woman, but seems not to have made much of an impression on anyone, including her elder daughter, who was extremely close to her father. Charles' love of music was almost as strong as that of his family and the crown. He was a talented composer, producing musicals at his court. His two daughters were encouraged to study music and to sing some of the roles in his operas. Maria Theresa had an excellent music teacher who taught her not only voice but musicianship, and her voice became strong, beautiful, and of professional quality. (Some who were qualified to judge thought she could have had a career in opera.) The rest of her education, unfortunately, was not adequate for someone destined to be an empress. She was taught mostly by Jesuits, whose main accomplishment was the strengthening of her already extreme faith in the Catholic religion. Perhaps it was just as well that she was not encumbered with preconceived ideas, because, as it turned out, she did not approve of many of her father's policies and was free to depend on her own commonsensible theories and humane impulses. The most important knowledge she retained from her early education was in the areas of music, manners, religion, and Italian poetry.

The archduchess, Maria Theresa, was good-looking, at times even beautiful. She had clear blue, direct eyes, although her outstanding physical feature was an abundance of corn-colored hair. Her charm was evident from an early age, as were her fine character and intelligence. When she was young, she fell in love with Francis Steven, heir to Lorraine, when he was brought to her father's court in Vienna to be educated. He was nine years older than she. A determined and spirited girl even then, she made it clear to her father that she wanted to marry Francis. Charles finally agreed, and she married him when she was 19. There was never anyone else for her, not only because she truly believed in the sanctity of marriage but because she always truly loved him. At the same time, she was clear-headed about his faults, and knew that he probably would be of little or no help in affairs of state when she became empress. She also was quite aware of his good qualities. She knew, for example, that he was very able in the managing of money. It is interesting to note that her self-control and common sense were evident even where her husband was concerned. Although she discovered after a few years that he was unfaithful, and even though she disapproved heartily and was terribly jealous, she kept him happy in their family life. It was apparent that, though she had extreme religious convictions and absolutely disapproved of illicit sex, this did not interfere with her immense sexual appetite for her husband. They had 16 children, 10 of whom survived. Among those who survived were the future emperors, Joseph II and Leopold II, as well as Marie Antoinette, queen of France. Francis and Maria Theresa both enjoyed their children, who were raised in a strict but loving environment. (Unfortunately, these children were inadequately prepared for adult life—strange, considering Maria Theresa's knowledge of her own educational shortcomings.) Francis had many affairs, but the most important and lasting infatuation was with Countess Wilhelmina Auersperg, a grasping, cold woman. Maria Theresa knew about their affair, and, when Francis died, she went out of her way to be kind to the countess, giving her a great deal of money, which she knew Francis had promised the countess.

Because he had no male heir, Maria Theresa's father, Charles, had proclaimed the "Pragmatic Sanction," which declared that the Hapsburg holdings and realm were to be inherited by his eldest daughter. A few years after she was married, when she was 23, Charles died and Maria Theresa became empress. She was very young and inexperienced, but extremely self-confident. Unfortunately, no one else had the same confidence in her and she had to show her strength. She was a complicated woman. On the one hand, she was good-hearted, on the other, she was coldly intolerant of non-Catholics. Nevertheless, she could overcome her intolerance for the sake of her goal. She did not agree with the ideas of the Enlightenment, which was an intellectual movement in the 18th century that followed a long period of religious conflict. (The views of this movement were based on reason and the focus was on human understanding of the individual.) Yet, one of her great achievements was the improvement of the lives of the peasants. She was a peaceful woman, but fiercely protective of her realm to the point of going to war. She was a puritan when it came to sex without marriage, yet for the sake of the relationship between Austria and France, she insisted that her daughter Marie Antoinette, who was the French dauphine, be pleasant to the influential Madame Dubarry, the mistress of King Louis XV of France.

She made her husband co-ruler, but she was the real power. She proceeded to discard her father's old and ineffective advisers, and began surrounding herself with unusually effective ministers. Her ability to keep on top of everything, her shrewd judgment of people, her ability to use charm or anger to manipulate people, and the goals on which she focused made her a great administrator. Two of her most admirable traits were honesty and a distaste for personal greed and selfishness.

Maria Theresa was mostly interested in domestic problems, especially because she could see that they directly affected the success of her dynasty. However, during her reign, in order to protect the Hapsburg domain, she involved her people in two great European wars, the War of the Austrian Succession and the Seven Years' War. Her domestic reforms were impressive. The administration of the state became centralized, and the powers and privileges of the nobility were reduced; in spite of her devotion to the Catholic religion, she subordinated the church to the state; she abolished tax exemptions for the nobility and the church; teaching methods, medical education, and the study of science were modernized and vastly improved; music and architecture were high priorities (Vienna became the center of the arts and the court was the center of opportunity for musicians); there were judicial system and land reforms. Her greatest achievement was to make her scattered lands and people part of a well-knit society that lasted into the 20th century.

Music was glorious during this period. Even though her court is remembered for its music, Maria Theresa, in spite of her musical background, was more a patroness of entertainers, rather than the arts. The emphasis on music in her court is legendary; yet, despite her fine musical education and talent, her taste was superficial. All she expected of the musicians was a lovely performance in the accepted traditions. She appreciated Italian composers, but of all the Germans she preferred Christoph Willibald Gluck (who had been influenced by Italian music when he lived and studied in Milan) and Antonio Salieri (who was born in Italy).

She never did understand the genius of Bach, Handel, Haydn, and Mozart. (She did not even understand the importance of her dear kapellmeister, Gluck, whose ideas reformed opera. He stressed drama, character, and realism, pulling the music, dancing, story, and staging into an expression of the whole). In fact, these great composers were not appreciated in her court. When Mozart and his sister were youngsters, they performed for the empress at her court. Maria Theresa was entranced by them because they were so very young, but when Mozart became a mature musician, she lost interest. She could have secured a place for herself in the history of music if she had helped him, but she missed her opportunity. Her son, Archduke Ferdinand, governor of Milan, was overwhelmed by Mozart's genius as a composer when he fulfilled a commission for the archduke's wedding. He wrote to his mother that he wanted to take Mozart into his service. His mother advised him not to because she felt that it would be a burden to have inconsequential people in his service. Mozart was 15 at the time, and employment might have given him the security he needed. Perhaps he would have lived a longer, less frustrating life and the world would have been blessed with more of his mature music.

Mozart absorbed the aims of the Enlightenment, which he incorporated into his operas *The Magic Flute* and *The Marriage of Figaro*. Some claim that these ideals colored his view of court life, and that *The Magic Flute* was about Maria Theresa and other ruling court members. One of Mozart's most ardent admirers was Haydn, who thought that the young composer was one of the greatest, if not *the* greatest, composers of all time. He was particularly distressed that Mozart did not have a prestigious and supportive court appointment.

Vienna was the place to be in order to further one's musical career. Haydn was one well-known example. He came from humble beginnings, went to live and study music in Vienna as a youngster, and, eventually, met and impressed Pietro Mestastasio, who was Maria Theresa's chief court poet and the greatest opera librettist of the time. Through him, Haydn met many influential people and his career was launched.

The engagement which proved to be the turning point in his life was the one offered him by Prince Anton Esterhazy. He signed a contract to be second kapellmeister at his estate. Haydn, like all musicians at that time, was considered to be and was treated as a servant, and it seems that he accepted this without complaint, although much was demanded of him. When Prince Anton died, his brother, Prince Nikolaus, a great patron of the arts, took Haydn to his new palace at Esterhaza where the composer remained as first kapellmeister for about 30 years until 1790, when he moved to Vienna. He went on to London, where he was widely acclaimed and respected, as he was in Paris, Petersburg, other capitals. Eventually, he returned to Esterhaza and his position as kapellmeister. By that time, attitudes toward talented musicians had changed. He knew he was a great artist, and was treated as one. He received many honors and medals in his lifetime, acknowledged by all as one of the greatest talents in the history of music. But he was never formally acknowledged by Maria Theresa or her son Joseph. Finally, after Haydn's death in 1809, Emperor Francis II bestowed the Leopold Medal on him. He had composed a national hymn for Austria during the Napoleonic Wars. In 1848, this became the music for *Deutschland uber Alles*.

Music was one of the greatest glories of Maria Theresa's reign. Even though the love of music existed everywhere in Europe and in England, and musicians regularly traveled to Paris, London, Rome, Naples, Hamburg, Potsdam, Leipzig, St. Petersburg, Prague, and Dresden, Maria Theresa, particularly, is remembered for her encouragement of music and musicians in her court and in Vienna. As a result of her educational reforms, every child received an education in music and its appreciation. The years of her life encompassed a period of great artistic, intellectual, and political change and she was responsible for much of it.

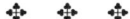

Madame de Pompadour, born Jeanne Antoinette Poisson (1721-1764), was one of the most exceptional women in history. Her strong influence on King Louis XV affected the way the country was governed. Her exquisite taste in all the arts became the model for Europe to emulate. Her intellect, charm, and great beauty, as well as her clever management style, were the magnets that drew exceptional and creative minds to the court at Versailles, where she was Louis's official mistress and the person to whom he was closest for two decades, until her death. Versailles was the main home of the royal family and the focal point of France. The courtiers lived, played, and prayed there, always at the pleasure, and according to the rules, of the king.

The future marquise de Pompadour was born in Paris, which at the time was like an overgrown village. Her mother was a great beauty and, although married to François Poisson, thought nothing of having liaisons with other men. Her father was a jolly middle-class man who became involved in a black market scandal when Jeanne was 4 years old. He fled to Germany, leaving his wife to cope. This she did admirably by cultivating M. Le Normant de Tournehem, a powerful and wealthy man who was a former ambassador to Sweden. This big-hearted fellow loved Madame Poisson and took care of her whole family. He provided a fine education for Jeanne and her brother Abel. Jeanne absorbed all that she was taught, and became one of the most accomplished women in France. She was a fine singer, actress, and clavichord player. Her knowledge and taste developed rapidly in the areas of botany, painting, music, literature, philosophy, and minor arts, such as the design of fine china and furniture. After eight years, her protector was able to bring Poisson back to France, where he was exonerated and given a good job. Tournehem and the Poissons proceeded to live happily together.

Jeanne (called *Reinette,* as a child) was a charmer from birth. She had every desirable trait a woman could want. Her one problem was delicate health. When she was of marrying age, there was a difficult obstacle to overcome in securing an advantageous match: the questionable reputations of her parents. M. de Tournehem bribed his nephew, M. Charles Guillaume Le Normant d'Etioles, with a large dowry, an invitation to share his beautiful homes, and the promise of being named heir to his fortune. They were married, and the young man fell in love with his wife at once. They were happy together and had two children. The son died in infancy. Her beloved daughter, Alexandrine, lived until she was 9 years old.

Madame d'Etioles was now in society. She made up her mind that she would have a salon of intellectuals of the time. The writers of the day, known as the *philosophes,* were in the process of preparing a huge encyclopedia, parts of which were opposed by the church and the court. Voltaire belonged to this group, which was centered in Paris. There already were other great salons in Paris, but with the help of Voltaire and others, she succeeded in creating one of the finest. When her mother became ill and retired from society, Jeanne was invited on her own by the most desirable people. Her charm and elegance, love of life and people, wit, and astonishing sophistication in the field of philosophy and art made her an extremely attractive guest. She was invited to every important event, and her name soon was known at Versailles.

King Louis XV was handsome, charming, and an intelligent ruler. He tried to reform a worn-out government, but died before he could implement his proposed reforms. (His grandson, King Louis XVI, reversed his plans, with well-known, negative repercussions.) At a young age, he was married to the daughter of the exiled king of Poland (Stanislas Leczinski). Marie Leczinska, dressed plainly, wore no cosmetics, and spent her time embroidering altar cloths. Her father was penniless, and youth was not on Marie's side (she was seven years older than Louis), but she was healthy, sweet, and queenly in demeanor. The king fell in love with her. They had 10 children. He may have preferred to be faithful (he loved his family), but he found his wife to be a bore. Louis began to have not just little affairs, but important liaisons. His mistresses were the Marquise de Vintimille until 1741, her sister, the Duchesse de Châteauroux until 1744, the Marquise de Pompadour until her death in 1764, and the Comtesse du Barry from 1769. Because of his lack of self-confidence, their influence was great.

Madame Poisson, who was a shrewd schemer, decided that her daughter was to be the king's next mistress. Jeanne had always said that the only man for whom she would leave her husband would be the king. (When she was 9, an old woman predicted that she would be the king's mistress. As a girl of 15 she was described as *a morceau de roi*, a morsel for a king.) Madame Poisson saw to it that her daughter met the king in the woods where he hunted, that he saw her face at the balls, and that he was made continually aware of her. He finally invited her to supper. Her mother taught her how to amuse him. He was captivated and offered her an apartment at Versailles. Without a minute's hesitation or thought for her husband, she accepted. The husband was advised by M. de Tournehem to take this philosophically, which he did. The king made him a farmer general. Jeanne was made the marquise de Pompadour, and received the appropriate property. She was presented in court, where the queen accepted her as a necessary evil. The dauphin, on the other hand, remained her opponent.

Madame de Pompadour realized that Louis was bored, and made it her mission to provide him with superb entertainment. Because of her the Théâtre des Petits Appartements was established at Versailles. Operas, dances, comedies, parties, hunts, and side excursions were some of the fruits of her efforts. He was delighted, not only with these diversions, but with her. She was witty, intelligent, lively, and completely devoted to him. They were inseparable, night and day, and he was utterly dependent on her for his happiness. The marquise's power was great. Louis listened to her advice about state affairs. He gave her unlimited funds with which she collected the most beautiful and expensive works of art, furniture, and jewelry. She built and furnished palaces which she claimed were for the purpose of entertaining the king. She owned her own houses, cottages, and apartments.

Madame de Pompadour became a power in France, because those who wanted favors were forced to go through her to the king. It was important to her to care well for those to whom she was close. Those artists, musicians, artisans, writers, and others whom she admired were the recipients of her largesse. Her influence extended from governmental and societal affairs to French culture. It is probable that she was the most cultured and well-read woman of the time. It is certain that, because of her reputation as a connoisseur, European art was influenced to a great degree by the art of France.

Although at this time patronage of music was moving from royalty to financiers and to the public, the French court, under the guidance of the musical and forceful mistress of the king, contributed to it extravagantly. When Jean Philippe Rameau, a French composer (still known for his theories of composition with respect to chords and for some of his works), was having a problem with his career, Madame hired him to write the music for Voltaire's *La Princesse de Navarre*, which was extremely successful, and his career was restored. In 1752, there was a war, called *Guerre des Bouffons* (War of Buffoons), between advocates of Italian and French music. The court was divided: Madame de Pompadour supported French music and Rameau; the queen supported Italian music, led by Jean-Jacques Rousseau. French music triumphed (although Rameau conceded that there was much to learn from Italian music). It is interesting to note that French music was played at all German courts, because some of the great German composers, such as Handel and J. S. Bach, who were pupils of Francois Couperin, understood and enjoyed French music. Mozart, Haydn, and Gluck were influenced by the composition principles of Rameau.

Eventually, Jeanne grew physically exhausted (her health was always delicate). The sexual relations between the king and his mistress were discontinued, and she resigned herself to the king's dalliances in the *Parc aux Cerfs* (Stag Park) at one end of Versailles, where a few young girls were housed in a cottage for Louis's pleasure. Madame preferred this arrangement to being displaced by another woman as royal mistress. The king remained devoted to and delighted by her to the end of her days.

Her influence was still felt with respect to appointments and policies. Unfortunately, one of her policies did not turn out well: she (and Louis) favored France's alliance with Austria under Empress Maria Theresa, rather than with Prussia under Frederick the Great. (It is possible that her decision was determined by her personal feelings; Maria Theresa treated her with respect and Frederick treated her as a kept woman.) She and two others, appointed by the king with her advice, negotiated an alliance with Austria after she learned that Prussia had signed an alliance with England. This was a reversal of alliances, and may have contributed heavily to the conditions that brought about the Seven Years' War. It has been said that, if France had stood alone and remained outside the quarrel between Austria and Prussia, the conflagration would have been contained. Although she was blamed for it, ultimately the responsibility belonged to the king and the Council of State.

After the beginning of the war, she stayed in her apartment, working with the king and his ministers. She was devastated by the events of the war and weighed down with guilt because of her perceived part in it. By this time she had lost her looks, and her health had started to deteriorate. But her fascinating personality and intellect remained. She and the king were deeply content with each other.

Despite the rule that only royals may die at Versailles, Louis refused to move her when it was apparent that the end was near. He hardly left her room. Madame de Pompadour was buried near her daughter, Alexandrine, in the Place Vendome.

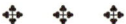

Nadezhda Philaretovna von Meck (1831-1894), beloved patroness and friend of Piotr (Peter) Ilyich Tchaikovsky, was the daughter of Philaret Vasilievitch Frolowsky, who was of the landed gentry. A quiet man, Frolowsky played the violin and loved music. Nadezhda's mother, Anastasia Potemkin, in contrast, was a forceful and autocratic woman. She inherited traits from both. Her father was the parent Nadezhda deeply loved. She would listen to his playing for hours, and became an accomplished performer on the pianoforte, often playing duets with her sister.

At age 17, she married Karl George Otto von Meck, a commanding man from a proud family. Nadezhda was not a woman of independent means (her father had used up the family money) and she was dependent on her husband. This was unfortunate because she did not enjoy marriage. However, they had 12 children, six sons and six daughters. Money was a problem at first, because her husband was an engineer in the service of the government and earned little. At this point in her life, she worked hard. She nursed her children, made their clothes, and was a good housekeeper. She disliked her husband's working for the government, where he had to take orders, and she convinced him to resign. Karl was a talented engineer but not a businessman, so his practical wife took over the business part of his work, and eventually he became highly successful. He was widely known for the railroad he built and for his famous map of Russia with railroads of the future on it. He made a fortune, then died in his 60s, leaving his wife a very wealthy woman.

Vladimir was her favorite son. He was charming and forceful, as talented as his father, but stronger socially and administratively. He managed the private railroad. His charm and expertise were so impressive that he became one of those special men who were able to deal successfully with the House of Rothschild. He lived lavishly, married, and had a son whom his mother adored. Nadezhda depended on him, and began to withdraw socially after her husband died, seeing only her children. She had many houses and estates and went from one to the other, always surrounding herself with people who would do things her way. Her children were ruled by Nadezhda, who even arranged their marriages. A domineering woman, Madame von Meck was tall, poised, with a low voice, dark expressive eyes, and long dark hair. She was never idle, writing letter after letter, inspecting her houses, playing the piano. Her third and favorite daughter, Julia, was devoted to her, but Nadezhda was still lonely. She was an agnostic, so religious worship did not occupy her time. The more reclusive she became, the more she needed music. A musician always was living in the house to teach her children or to play duets with her. (In 1881, she hired Claude Debussy to teach music to her children and to be the pianist in residence. Unfortunately, he paid too much personal attention to her daughter and, when Madame von Meck discovered this, he was sent away.) Music affected her so deeply, that at times she was physically upset. It was her consuming passion. In her drawing room, there was a Steinway at one end and a small "pianino" at the other. Although she was in a position to thoroughly enjoy herself, her great emotional swings and frequent colds and headaches prevented it. The stage was set for her friendship with Peter (Piotr) Ilyich Tchaikovsky.

Nicholai Rubinstein had a friendly relationhip with Nadezhda and visited her frequently. Nicholai was the director of the Moscow Conservatory and an educator of great stature, as well as a pianist, conductor, and composer. Madame von Meck was a patroness of the conservatory. (Nicholai's brother was Anton Rubinstein, who was considered to be the finest pianist in Europe, even though Liszt, who was aging, was still idolized. Anton founded the St. Petersburg Conservatory in which a musician at long last was able to earn a bachelor's degree in music. The Grand Duchess Helena Pavlovna, a great patroness of the arts, gave Anton the money to found the conservatory. Piotr Ilyich Tchaikovsky was one of its first pupils.)

There was a great difference between Moscow and St. Petersburg with respect to an artist's lifestyle: Moscow had a decidedly Bohemian flavor, whereas Petersburg was stiff and snobbish. Anton sent Tchaikovsky to Nicholai's conservatory, where he was much more comfortable. Nicholai, who was always welcome in Nadezhda's house, brought a piano transcription of Tchaikovsky's *Tempest Fantasia* to her house to play for her in 1876. She was overwhelmed when she heard it and agreed to commission a work by him. Tchaikovsky and she were both shy, which was a bond between them. (They discussed this problem in their letters to each other. Their correspondence is one of the most celebrated, extensive, and enlightening in history. Although they shared some of their innermost feelings, they did not want to meet face-to-face and never did, although they lived near each other for long periods. They did catch glimpses of each other and exchange photographs.) After listening to his composition, she wrote, "For several days after hearing your *Tempest* I was in a delirium from which I could not emerge."[1] At this point, their relationship developed rapidly. Nadezhda was exactly what Tchaikovsky needed, for she was extremely musical and knowledgeable, and she understood and felt at once the emotional content of his work. She wrote, ". . . I think that, more than contact, similarity of opinion and feeling brings people together; two persons can thus be close though very far. I am interested in everything about you; I should like at all times to know where you are and approximately what you are doing."[2] At the time they started their relationship, Nadezhda was 45 years old and Tchaikovsky was 37.

At first, Madame von Meck offered the composer commissions, and she paid handsomely. But Tchaikovsky was financially insecure. He needed an income on which he could depend, so she arranged to give him a yearly allowance of 6,000 rubles so that he would be able to compose without worrying about financial matters.

Two years later, Tchaikovsky wrote that he was going to be married. (Madame was unhappy about it, to say the least. At first she wrote a restrained, proper letter, simply urging him to continue their correspondence.) Without acknowledging it, he may have felt this marriage was bound to be a disaster. He was an extremely sensitive man. His homosexuality was a deep, festering secret that made him so unhappy, fearful, and psychologically unstable that he thought, at times, that he was on the edge of insanity. (Nadezhda never knew about his homosexuality.) His marriage, he hoped, would bring him respectability. Unfortunately, his wife, Antonina Ivanova Miliukova, was an attractive, oversexed woman of subnormal intelligence. She was passionately in love with Tchaikovsky and concentrated only on its physical expression. He was on the verge of a severe nervous collapse. After nine weeks, his brother Modeste rescued him and took him to St. Petersburg where he was in such terrible condition that he seemed to be unconscious for hours. He and his brother decided that the only way out was for their brother Anatol to tell Antonina that the marriage was over and to bring her back to her mother. The distraught husband then escaped to Berlin, and then to Lake Geneva, Switzerland. She would not give him a divorce and he continued to support her. She was a problem to him for the rest of her life. Antonina often blackmailed him for money. She continued to have lover after lover and had children who were put in an orphanage. She finally was committed in 1917 to a mental institution where she resided until her death.

He had never wanted a wife; he wanted a mother. He turned again to Nadezhda. When he left his wife, he wrote to his benefactress, explaining his misery. Her letter to him was one of comfort and reassurance. She even offered to pay for a divorce. She had been terribly upset, not only because of his unhappiness with Antonina, but because he had married at all. When she realized from his letters that he hated his wife, she was extremely relieved. She now felt free to say what she wanted to him. This was a terrible period for Tchaikovsky: he was a terrified man, whose psyche was fragile; as a result, he had constant physical problems (colitis and pains). He was completely dedicated to and immersed in his music. Socializing was difficult for him. He needed solitude and to be surrounded by natural beauty. At the same time, he wanted to be famous. He needed the comfort and support of Nadezhda, especially during this time. It is probable that, without her, he would not have been able to compose at all between 1877 and 1878. Tchaikovsky was becoming more and more dependent on Madame and her letters. When he wanted desperately to leave his teaching position at the Moscow Conservatory where he worked under Nicholai Rubinstein, he asked Nadezhda's opinion. She told him to leave, explaining that she felt that teaching took up too much of his time, that he needed his freedom and rest. With her support, he was able to. This was the second time she saved him from a nervous collapse; the first time, she had made it possible for him to go abroad, where Antonina would not be able to follow him. He was rescued from his misery, not only by Madame von Meck, but again and again by his sister Alexandra, who always offered him refuge and the warmth of her own family life. But the real support, in terms of finances, career, close emotional friendship, and uninterrupted concern came from Nadezhda. Her money and moral support gave him freedom from fear and from Antonina. In addition, he was able to regain his strength after he retired from his particularly difficult teaching schedule. He expressed his feelings in a letter to Madame von Meck on October 25, 1877: "Nadezhda Filaretovna, every note which comes from my pen in future is dedicated to you! To you I owe this reawakening love of work, and I shall never forget for a moment that you have made it possible to carry on my career . . ."[3]

His dear friend and patroness idolized Tchaikovsky. Here was a powerful and wealthy woman who bowed to no one and was extremely demanding. But with her beloved friend, she was completely giving. Her letters are full of love, deep commitment to him and his music, and gratitude for the opportunity to help. She asked for nothing in return.

Madame von Meck traveled often with her children and servants to her different homes and abroad. But she always was eager for Tchaikovsky's letters. She had a deeply passionate and sensuous nature that she did not acknowledge, except in her feelings for Tchaikovsky and his music. She loved him in spirit, and her letters to him were her means of expression. She was very Victorian and had little idea of sexual perversion. Tchaikovsky wanted his "weakness" to be a secret, especially from Madame. The only women who knew about his sexual orientation were his sister, Alexandra, with whom he was very close, and Antonina who was using this knowledge to blackmail him. He was miserable about his secret and felt that his redemption for manhood was in his music.

Nadezhda and Tchaikovsky became closer and closer through their correspondence. She wrote, ". . . And you know, my wonderful friend, how precious your talent is to me, how I long to take care of it . . . We are far apart only in distance; but for that we should be nearly one person, we feel the same about everything, usually even at the same time."[4] One of the subjects on which they disagreed was Mozart's music. Mozart was one of Tchaikovsky's idols, and he felt that Mozart had all the qualities that he himself lacked. Nadezhda preferred the romantic school, and she was shocked by Mozart's classicism.

Although they did not arrange to meet, she invited him to stay at her estates (but not her houses). When she was in Europe, she sometimes would arrange for him to stay very near her, and would make sure that he was comfortable. As time went on, they did catch glimpses of each other at concerts, theater, or when passing each other on a walk or ride. Despite the thrill of being near each other, each respected the other's privacy and need for solitude. There seems to have been a great deal of uneasiness on the part of Tchaikovsky. He writes to his brother Anatol from Florence, Italy in 1878, "I am happily living in peace and luxury, but I cannot deny the proximity of Nadezhda Philaretovna slightly disturbs me. She often drives and walks past my windows. What if we meet? What ought I to do? She does not seem to be afraid of it . . ."[5] The beautiful apartment she provided for him was only a quarter of a mile away from her.

Madame von Meck owned a house in Moscow, a very large country estate in Brailov in the Ukraine, and a villa on the French Riviera, where it pleased her to spend the winter. She would usually tell Tchaikovsky her schedule so that he would know how *not* to meet her. She would pass by his house just to see the lights on and know that he was there. They were happy at this time, and became accustomed to seeing each other from afar. When they did meet accidentally, he apologized for miscalculating the time and she replied, "I cannot tell you how comforting it was to meet you like that. It convinced me of the reality of your presence . . ."[6]

In their letters, they discussed his music at length, as well as his career. She once asked him about his method of composition, and he answered in deep, soul-searching detail. In these answers he gave the world fascinating insight into his composing. Evidently, she was highly knowledgeable, and he was delighted to discuss these things with her. In his letter on July 7, 1878, he writes, ". . . you display a technical knowledge rarely found even among educated amateurs . . ."[7]

It would be difficult to say whether or not Nadezhda von Meck influenced Peter Ilyich Tchaikovsky's music, but it appears that he was under her influence when he was composing the Fourth Symphony (which she called "our symphony") and *Eugene Onegin*. When she received the piano arrangement of his Fourth Symphony, she played it over and over. She became so emotional that she wrote an extraordinary confession to Tchaikovsky in which she talked about her suffering at the time of his marriage two years before, ". . . Do you know that when you married it was terribly hard for me, as though something had broken in my heart? The thought that you were near that woman was bitter and unbearable . . . I love you more than anyone and value you above everything in the world. If this knowledge bothers you, forgive my involuntary confession. I have spoken out. The reason is, the symphony . . ."[8] But she went on to assure him that she did not want any change in their relationship. Tchaikovsky answered quickly, responding only to her statement about her love of his symphony. That was the last time she overstepped where he was concerned. Their relationship was to be based on their mutual interest in his music and career. She then proceeded to arrange to have his symphony performed in Paris to spread his reputation. That performance was the beginning of Tchaikovsky's fame in Europe.

Nadezhda later began to write him letters about large financial losses, suggesting that she was on the verge of bankruptcy. Of course, he became alarmed, and offered to go back to teaching, but she said she could afford the pension. She started to complain more and more about wickedness and ingratitude. Then, in September 1890, he received a letter from her that destroyed their relationship and his happiness. She wrote that she had very little money and could not send him any more. The letter was short and cold. Actually, the von Meck fortune was intact. He realized that the von Mecks were public figures, and that news of a financial loss probably would have been publicized. He did not need the money at that point, although, as usual, he was giving money to friends and family. But he was not as upset about his financial situation as he was devastated by her sudden coldness. He became hurt, then bitter and humiliated, thinking of himself as a kept man. In 1891, when writing to her son-in-law, who acted as a go-between in their relationship, he said what offended him most was that she had stopped writing to him: ". . . Perhaps it is because I have never met Nadezhda Philaretovna that I always idealized her. In such a person, half-divine, I could not imagine such treason; it seemed to me the earth would fall to pieces under my feet sooner than that Nadezhda Philaretovna's feelings toward me would change. . . . My peace is gone and whatever happiness fate intended for me is poisoned . . ."[9] He was 51 years old and tired.

The explanation for her behavior may have been not only her physical and mental illnesses but the slow mortal disease of her eldest son, brilliant and charming Vladimir. Her spirit broke as she watched him slowly die. Possibly she blamed herself for neglecting her favorite son and devoting so much to Tchaikovsky, and by cutting herself from her friend felt she was atoning. It also is possible that her mind was affected. Her daughter said that her mother suffered from a "terrible nervous affliction."[10.]

The two friends of the spirit had met when Tchaikovsky was at his lowest and Nadezhda at her highest. He began to climb and she to slip, physically and emotionally. Tchaikovsky became more and more active and social and, as he became more successful, gained strength emotionally. She, on the other hand, grew less and less active socially, having become ill with tuberculosis and frequent migraine headaches. They were both emotional and intense, but he knew himself and fought his weaknesses. She did not. Because of his honesty with himself, he was able to grow. She wasted away.

Madame von Meck died four years later in Wiesbaden. (Peter Ilyich Tchaikovsky died three months before her in St. Petersburg.) She was buried in her beloved Moscow, next to her husband.

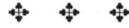

Queen Elisabeth of Belgium (1877-1966) was unique, a truly noble woman of great character, intelligence, and sensitivity. She was a German princess and daughter of Duke Theodor of Bavaria. He, too, was unusual in that he was extremely cultured, and surrounded himself with fine writers and artists. In addition, he was a physician with an excellent reputation. His daughter became interested in medicine, too, and received her medical degree at the University of Leipzig. That interest and a deep love of the arts, particularly music, shaped her life. Violin was her instrument of choice, and she studied it seriously with Eugène Ysaÿe, the celebrated Belgian violinist, conductor, and composer.

At the turn of the century, she married Prince Albert of Belgium. Her subjects adored her. They knew that the problems of the working people and various social causes were always of great concern to her. She founded a medical clinic in her new country, and proceeded to teach nursing. During World War I, she refused to leave Belgium, and it was only when the Germans approached Brussels that she retreated with the Belgian army, continuing her job of nursing. When there was only a very small piece of her country left, Prince Albert and she stayed in a little house in a little town on the coast, even though it was continually being bombed. In that small piece of remaining territory, she set up a hospital where she continued to nurse those in need. There, too, she started a school for refugee children. It was not until the Germans began to retreat that she returned to her home.

After the war, Queen Elisabeth continued to work for liberal causes. After World War II, she became one of the advocates of the Stockholm Peace Appeal, which called for a ban on atomic weapons. Causes outside of Belgium interested her as well, and she traveled all over the world working toward her goals. Throughout her life, music remained her great love. She invited musicians to the palace, and often performed in trios or quartets. She was especially close to Pablo Casals, who would visit her whenever he was in Belgium. During these visits they would play chamber music together. Casals and the queen were the same age. They had met when she was in her mid-20s and remained devoted to each other for more than 60 years. Elisabeth would frequently attend his music festivals in Prades, France, and later San Juan, Puerto Rico, and Marlboro, Vt. Casals described her as a "small fragile-looking woman, but she had a will of iron. When she did something, it was because she believed it was the right thing to do . . . In may ways she was the most unconventional member of royalty I have ever met. But in every way she was queenlike—she had an inner nobility." He also described an incident that illustrates her fine character and independent spirit: "There was a conference sponsored by the Royal Institute . . . Again, I was invited to the royal box. When I came there, Queen Elisabeth indicated an empty chair beside her and invited me to be seated. I realized the chair was the king's and I hesitated . . . But she smiled and said again, '. . . Please be seated, Pau.' So I sat down . . . I later learned that the episode had created something of a scandal . . ."[11]

In 1937 Queen Elisabeth founded the annual competition *Prix International Eugène Ysaÿe* for violinists and pianists in Brussels. The first winner was the Russian violinist David Oistrakh. Later the name of the competition was changed to the *Concours International Reine Elisabeth* (Queen Elisabeth International Competition). It became one of the world's most prestigious music competitions. The rules require that those who enter the contest be between 17 and 30 years old, of any nationality. There is a four year cycle for violin, piano, composition, and a year of rest. The competition takes place on Elisabeth's birthday. The winners are awarded prize money and medals.

In 1966, Queen Elisabeth died at age 89. Her granddaughter, Queen Fabiola of Belgium, succeeded her as the sponsor for the Queen Elisabeth competition.

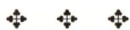

Bathsabee (Batsheva) de Rothschild was born in England and raised in France. Her family was the very well-known European banking family, which was pivotal in the rise and fall of royal dynasties and governments. They were very philanthropic and ardently Jewish. It is a fascinating family. In 1880, Bathsabee's great-uncle Baron Edmond de Rothschild began financing the Jewish settlement of Palestine and helped to establish the agriculture and industry of the country, even though he was not a Zionist. Her brother, Guy, who ran the French branch of the bank, was president of the United Jewish Appeal in France. Her sister Jacqueline married the celebrated cellist Piatigorsky. The English branch of the family has raised great amounts of money for Israel. It has been a family tradition to support and spend money in Israel, but never to take any out of the country.

Bathsabee attended the Sorbonne in Paris, studying biology. When France fell to the Germans in World War II, she went to America and attended Columbia University in New York City. While the war was still in progress, she went back to England and enlisted in the Free French Army under Charles de Gaulle. The war had a terrible effect on the Rothschilds; some members died as a result, a few quite horribly.

After the war, she married Donald Bloomingdale of the department store family. They had a child who died, and she and Donald divorced. Tragically, he then died of a drug overdose. Because of her baby's death, Bathsabee became interested in scientific research and philanthropy and eventually established foundations in Israel for science and for the arts. It was science, after all, in which she had been educated and which engaged most of her attention. Yet, when she was living in New York City, she studied at the Martha Graham dance studio (see Chapter 9). This created a powerful love of the dance, particularly modern dance as performed by the Martha Graham group, and she began to follow them unobtrusively on tour. Enormously wealthy, spirited, and bright, Bathsabee was shy and unassuming, and it was quite a while before the members of the troupe noticed her. But when they did, they adored her. For many years, she provided them with great financial support and remained Martha Graham's dear friend. The one country in which Bathsabee would not help Martha and her troupe was Germany. She had promised her father never to spend any money in that country.

In 1958, Bathsabee settled in Tel Aviv, Israel, and spent much time and a large part of her vast fortune on the Bat

Dor Dance Company, which was influenced and, in some cases, trained by Martha Graham or her disciples. Classical music concerts were appreciated in Israel, but music and dance together was a different experience. In 1963, Bathsabee and Martha Graham founded a new Israeli dance company, called the Batsheva Dance Company, featuring native Israeli dancers and Martha as the top artist.

Bathsabee de Rothschild is beloved in Israel. The Bathsabee de Rothschild Foundation for the Advancement of Science in Israel, Inc. and the Batsheva de Rothschild Fund for the Advancement of Science and Technology enhance the country and, in fact, everyone. Agnes deMille reported: ". . . the Israeli government has enlarged and developed de Rothschild's plans, in many instances following along the trails she blazed. But she was the pioneer, and Israel calls her blessed."[12]

Chapter Four

Wives and Lovers

Ainö Sibelius, wife of the great Finnish composer Jean Sibelius, once said, "I am glad that I have lived near him. It seems that I have not lived in vain. I will not claim that it has always been easy. Merciless self-discipline has been always necessary. Yet, I consider myself a fortunate person. My husband's music is like the word of God. It springs from a holy source and near that source it is good to live."[1] There are others who have felt the same commitment to the special genius of their husbands or lovers.

George Sand, born Amantine Aurore Lucile Dupin, but called "Aurore" (1804-1876), was the most celebrated woman in the literary world of the 19th century. Although she is known to most people as Frederic Chopin's lover, she was extremely famous in her own right and in her own time, known as a writer of enormous talent and popularity, as well as a woman who lived so fully and freely that gossip followed her everywhere.

Not only was she influential in literature and drama, but she was actively involved in the chaotic politics of France from the 1820s to the 1830s. She lived as she saw fit, according to her own opinions and sense of morality. She was against the monarchy and staunchly for the rights of the people. Aurore and her close friends (including people such as Franz Liszt, Heinrich Heine, Victor Hugo, Alexandre Dumas *fils*, Honoré de Balzac, Alfred de Vigny, Prosper Merimée, and Alfred de Musset) all were devoted to freeing the arts from the old static and academic values. It was important to them that artists be acknowledged as valuable contributing members of society, and that their social status be comparable to that of other great achievers (scientists and philosophers, for example). Their belief was that the artist's goal was to create beauty and to work for the benefit of all members of society, not just for the privileged few. Paris became the center for the romantic artists and musicians.

Aurore was born in the year of Napoleon's coronation. Her father, Maurice Dupin, who was the grandson of the famous Maréchal de Saxe and descended from royalty, was an army officer and aide-de-camp to Joachim Murat, who later sat on the throne of Naples. Her mother, Sophie-Victoire Delaborde, on the other hand, was of humble origin. Her father was a tavern keeper. It was a difficult life for little Aurore, because money was scarce and her parents did not have a permanent home. In 1808, when the child was 4, Maurice Dupin was killed in a riding accident. His widow and his daughter went to live at his mother's Nohant estate in the country.

Madame Dupin de Francueil, Aurore's grandmother, was an elegant woman who was of the old school, surrounded by luxury and servants and people with beautiful manners. She had lost her husband when Maurice was only 9 years old, and, from then on, passionately concentrated on her beloved son. Not surprisingly, she was appalled when he married Sophie, whom she considered completely unworthy of him. Of course, this made for an unhappy relationship between the two women. Sophie was persuaded to sign a paper naming Madame Dupin de Francueil as Aurore's teacher and guardian, in exchange for which Sophie would be given a pension. The child pleaded with her mother not to "sell" her and not to leave her, but Sophie left for Paris. Aurore loved her grandmother, but was in awe of her and resentful of the constraints put on her for the purpose of teaching her the ways of a lady. She was attached to her mother even though Sophie, whose temperament was far from controlled, would create scenes and often would spank her. When she and her grandmother spent the season in Paris, she would often see her mother and her half-sister Caroline, but her grandmother did her best to keep them from having too much contact with Aurore. Because she missed them so terribly, there were periods when her mother was allowed to stay at Nohant. Sophie did not enjoy these visits and, eventually, they stopped. After begging Sophie to take her home with her, Aurore finally adjusted and settled down with her grandmother.

Her music education was provided by Madame Dupin de Francueil, who played the harpsichord and was knowledgeable about 18th-century music. Aurore always had a great love of music, becoming quite a connoisseur as she grew older. She was tutored, along with her half-brother Hippolyte, in French, Latin, arithmetic, hand-writing, history, geography, dancing, and music. She advanced quickly in the area of music, particularly with respect to the piano. Her other loves were drawing and writing. By the time she was 11 she already wrote compositions. When she was 12 or 13, her grandmother decided that she needed better teachers and placed her in a convent in Paris. At first she disliked it, but soon grew to love life there, to such a degree that she decided to take her vows and become a nun. This was a development her grandmother had not expected and did not like. She removed her from the convent and took her back to Nohant, even though Aurore had spent three of her happiest years at that convent.

During this next period, she was very lonely. Her main focus was caring for her grandmother, who was old and ill. She did not have a father to guide her or a dependable mother (even Sophie's letters to her daughter were rare). And she now had the sole responsibility of administering the estate. The advantage, however, was that she was free to live as she liked. Although it was frowned upon, she and her first "beau," Stephane Ajasson de Grandsagne, spent a great deal of time alone. Stephane introduced her to exciting new activities such as target practice with a pistol, and encouraged her to wear masculine riding clothes in order to be comfortable. He understood her desire for freedom and the satisfaction she felt in resisting the constraints imposed on women. Together, they read and discussed books and her love of knowledge grew. Unfortunately, because of her disregard for appearance, she was the subject of gossip that became more intense and widespread as she grew older and more well-known.

In 1921, her grandmother died. It was the end of her youth. When the will was read, Aurore was named heiress of Nohant. Her mother wanted to take her back to Paris with her. Her daughter did go to live with her, but by this time their relationship had deteriorated. To add to Aurore's misery, she was considered a social outcast because of her mother. Sophie constantly created scenes, and the 17-year-old girl finally escaped by accepting an invitation to visit the du Plessis family in the country. It was so satisfying an experience for all that she was soon adopted as a member of their family, although her home was officially with her mother. By this time she was a lovely, exciting young woman with dark hair and beautiful eyes. While on these lengthy visits to the du Plessis home, she was besieged by suitors. She wanted to be married to limit her mother's control, and promptly fell in love with one of the young men. Unfortunately, Aurore soon realized that he wanted her only as his mistress, not his wife. She then accepted a proposal of marriage with a man with whom she was not in love. At age 18, she married Baron Casimir Dudevant, a country squire, with whom she was very unhappy. They had two children: Maurice and Solange, and, although she truly believed in marriage, the young wife was not able to adjust to his ignorance and his drinking.

In 1825, when on a trip with some friends, she met Aurelien de Seze, with whom she had a passionate love affair. This soon came to an end, but not before her husband was aware of it. She came to an understanding with him that she would do as she wished. She never advocated "free love." All her life she believed fervently in the equality of a husband and wife in marriage, and fought against the social and legal system that made the man the dominant partner. In no way was she a feminist, as defined today. She said, "I hope that the fathers of Saint-Simonism [Count Henri Saint-Simon, a social theorist, taught that division of labor should replace aggression in society] will not undermine the great belief that the love of *one* man for *one* woman is the holiest element of human greatness . . . Let women . . . wait for marriage to cease being a degrading tyranny, albeit remaining a sacred link. What will women achieve by revolt? When the male world has been converted, woman will also be converted without one's having had to bother oneself about her."[2] It was her conviction that the only way marriage would be reformed was by reforming society. She said she did not advocate infidelity, an act to which a woman should only resort in order to cope with her status of marital "slave." In addition, one should not condone the bad behavior of men while condemning any deviation from absolute purity in women. When discussing the equality of women with respect to men, she made it quite clear that she thought women were suited to be artists of various kinds but not politicians, simply because of their education and innate character. Different roles were suited to men. Nevertheless, this did not mean that women were inferior.

In 1831, after coming upon some of her husband's papers that were addressed to her, she finally called a halt to their relationship. One of the papers was his will, in which he expressed his anger against his wife and condemned her character. After confronting him with it, she left him. At the time, Aurore was having an affair with Jules Sandeau, a writer. When she left her husband in 1931, she and Jules went to Paris, where she established herself in an apartment and got a job as a journalist so that she could arrange to take care of her children.

Aurore and her husband were legally separated in 1836.

Casimir had been living off the income from his wife's property. The settlement stated that he would receive the income from the town house in Paris as long as he paid for his son's education and gave him an adequate allowance when he was 20 years old. Aurore was given custody of Solange, her daughter, and the possession of her estate, Nohant. In those days, there was no alimony for a wife, and Nohant barely supported itself, so she had to earn a living. She began to write, and thanks to her grandmother's training, she was accustomed to long, hard work. She wrote at a furious pace, as she did everything. Her literary output was astounding. At first she collaborated with Jules in writing articles and a novel, signing them *J. Sand* (a shortened form of Sandeau) in order to disguise the fact that a woman was one of the authors. When she started writing alone (Jules was spending little time writing, and Aurore was disgusted with his laziness), her publisher encouraged her to keep the name *Sand*. She signed her name *G. Sand*, then *Georges Sand*, soon dropping the final *s* in Georges. From then on she was known by that name.

Her use of a man's name, her occasional choice of men's clothing, her habit of smoking cigars and cigarettes, and her independence gave her the undeserved reputation of being unfeminine. Nothing could be farther from the truth. Her use of the pseudonym was for expediency, as was the masculine attire. (She learned that, dressed as a man, she was often admitted to places usually only accessible to men). She enjoyed smoking.

In 1832, she wrote a book called *Indiana*, and, much to her surprise, the reviews were raves and she became a celebrity almost overnight. As always, she worked very hard. (In her lifetime George produced at least 60 novels, often dealing with love and freeing women from their roles as "slaves" in their marriages. Twenty-five of her plays were produced, and essays, articles, and short stories were continually being published. She was heavily involved in the Republican cause and wrote many political pamphlets. She even started a magazine during the 1848 uprisings that brought the French monarchy down and produced the second republic. After her disillusionment caused by the autocratic rule of Napoleon III, she turned away from active involvement in politics.)

George slowly came to the conclusion that she had outgrown young Jules and their affair came to an end. There followed a succession of relationships; some were short-lived, others consumed her. She had a long, passionate, tumultuous, intimate relationship with poet Alfred de Musset. This was interrupted for a while by a liaison with Alfred's handsome, kind Italian physician, Pietro Pagello, whom she had met while she and Alfred were in Venice and at odds with each other. She also had a long, fiery liaison with Michel de Bourges, her brilliant, intellectual counsel in the notorious court case dealing with her legal separation and marital settlement. But her most famous love affair was with Frederic Chopin. George was a deeply romantic, passionate woman, always striving to find the kind of love that she craved. She had two contrary needs: a man who was a father figure on whom she could lean and, at the same time, a child-figure on whom she could lavish her strong maternal feelings. (She was unstinting with her time, energy, and compassion when her lover was ill and needed care, as was the case with both Alfred de Musset and Chopin.) This emotional conflict seemed never to be resolved.

Chopin came to Paris in 1831, having left Warsaw and its Russian Cossack barbarism. He quickly became a famous pianist and composer and was included in the group that frequented the small exclusive salons. Although he was not interested in the revolutionary ideas around him, and more concerned with his beloved Poland, he became a close friend of Liszt, who was very anxious to introduce him to George Sand. In 1836, George and Frederic met for the first time. He was a little taken aback by her masculine clothes. In 1838, at a dinner party, Chopin gave an incredibly beautiful impromptu piano performance. One of the guests was George, who was completely overwhelmed. She wrote him a simple little note in which she said they all had adored his playing. When they met again (this time she was dressed beautifully in very feminine clothes), he began to appreciate how extraordinary she was. Before long, he not only succumbed to her charms, but was astounded by George's extensive and deep knowledge of music. He realized that she was a woman of great sensitivity and deep emotion. (He was a high-strung, oversensitive, delicate young man.) His growing passion was reciprocated, and their romance became intense.

George and Frederic decided to spend the winter in Mallorca for two reasons: They had very little money and the climate was mild. (Chopin had been coughing quite a bit and needed to get away from the winter weather in Paris). Piano-maker Camille Pleyel shipped him a piano to use there. In order to help pay for the trip, Frederic promised to write 24 preludes and sell them to Pleyel for 2,000 francs. George, too, was having financial problems, and difficulties collecting the money owed her by her publisher. The couple was accompanied by George's two children and a maid. They had a difficult voyage and, when they arrived, had trouble finding adequate accommodations. Chopin developed a cold that aggravated his coughing. To make matters worse, it rained incessantly. The housekeeping load became enormous, so George had to help with that and take care of her ill lover and her children. She worked far into the night to keep up with her writing. After 14 weeks, they started back, staying in Marseilles for another 10 weeks so that Chopin could rest. George wrote to a friend, "This Chopin is an angel . . . I imagine that his is too delicate, exquisite, and perfect a nature to live for long off our fat, heavy terrestrial existence. In Mallorca, while deathly ill, he wrote music that reeked of paradise . . ."[3] Chopin was well aware of and appreciated all the devotion and care that George was giving him.

They returned finally to Nohant and the quiet of the country. She petted and spoiled him, all her maternal feelings surfacing. The problem began when she decided that physical love was bad for him and refused any attempt on his part to make love. He thus became very jealous of every man who went near her, and there were some unpleasant scenes. Still, it was a good time for Chopin, even though he preferred the social life of Paris. He had the fresh air of the country, the care of a woman who deeply loved him, the pleasure of giving music lessons to her daughter, and, most of all, the time to compose. Life at Nohant was free from schedules, and he was able to concentrate on his music. In that summer of 1839, he composed a sonata in B-flat minor, an impromptu in F-sharp minor, two nocturnes, a waltz, a scherzo, a ballade in F-major, two polonaises, two études, and three mazurkas.

When he was feeling better in the fall, they and the children, Solange and Maurice, moved to apartments in Paris for the winter. George and Frederic led separate but close lives. His apartment was near hers, and after he had spent the day giving three or four music lessons, composing, and working at the piano, he would go to the Sand apartment for dinner, to which George would invite a few special friends. Often, Chopin would play the Pleyel piano in her salon. Sometimes they would go to dinner at friends'. Chopin's friends often were straitlaced aristocrats who did not condone the presence of his mistress, and certainly did not approve of her republican ideas. George's friends were quite free-spirited. Therefore, they sometimes socialized separately.

Chopin was never comfortable concertizing publicly. He preferred the intimacy of small salons. However, his reputation was becoming so great that there was a tremendous demand for it. With George Sand's enthusiastic encouragement and moral support, her "Chip-Chip" (as she called him) agreed to perform in his first concert in eight years at Pleyel's concert hall. It was arranged that Chopin's friends would be seated in the front row and a few would be on the stage, an arrangement that evidently relaxed the pianist. He was a sensation.

Summers were spent at Nohant and winters in Paris. Friends such as Eugène Delacroix, the artist, would spend periods of time with them, pursuing their own particular interest. (Delacroix spent his time painting in a space especially prepared for him. His work there included excellent portraits of George and Frederic. Maurice idolized him as an artist and was overjoyed when Delacroix decided to give him lessons in painting.) By 1845, the relationship between the lovers began to unravel, perhaps because George was overworked, constantly had trouble making ends meet, and was growing sexually frustrated. Perhaps it also was a result of Frederic's obsessive jealousy, no sexual outlet, his poor health, and his growing dissatisfaction with country life. (In her novel, *Lucrezia Floriani*, she described the death of a romance similar to that of her own.) The final rupture came when Solange, with whom Chopin was close, decided to marry a sculptor, Auguste Clésinger. He was unstable, an opportunist, and an incurable spendthrift. Everybody warned George about him, but she would not listen, impressed simply by the fact that he was an artist. Chopin disapproved of Clésinger, and was angry that George ignored his opinion. Solange and Clésinger were married. It was a disaster, and George soon realized her mistake. Clésinger was furious at not being able to get his hands on much money, and was getting more and more in debt. He was psychologically unbalanced, aggravating this condition by his drinking. Spoiled, Solange was furious with her mother because she was convinced that she and Clésinger were not receiving all that was due them. (Even before her marriage, she had shown her jealous nature when she became resentful of her cousin, Augustine, whom George had taken into her home and made her second "daughter." And she had always been envious of her older brother.) During a terrible argument with George and Maurice, during which the couple behaved outrageously, Clésinger struck and threatened to kill Maurice and George. George threw them out of her house. Solange then told Chopin, who was in Paris, an untrue story, all of which he believed. He had chosen to side with Solange. George realized that a special relationship between Chopin and Solange had developed. Perhaps it was because they both held grudges against George. Solange told Chopin false gossip about her mother's promiscuity, which Chopin accepted as the truth. The break was irreversible. George could not forgive his siding with her daughter, and Chopin could not forgive her for being a "hard-hearted" mother. Their relationship ended in 1847. They met in March 1848 by accident, and George was gracious; Chopin was not. He wrote to Solange, "She asked me how I was. I said I was well, then I called for the concierge to open the door. I raised my hat and walked home to the Square d'Orléans."[4] At any rate, by this time, she had a new lover, Victor Borie. In April 1848, Chopin left for England. The weather during his seven-month stay was bad for his health. He returned to Paris where, on October 18, he died. George was so upset upon hearing the news that she was unable to work for days.

Life went on for George Sand. She was now free to mingle with friends without worrying about Chopin's jealous scenes. She became more involved with the theater, many of her plays being produced to great acclaim. In her private life, one lover replaced another until, in 1850, she met Alexandre Manceau, Maurice's friend. He was 32 years old; she was 45. He was an actor, and became her very competent stage manager. They fell in love, and lived and worked together. He efficiently managed all her personal and business affairs. Manceau was a compassionate man, with a talent for nursing George when she was ill (a reversal in roles). They remained together until his death in 1865.

George's remaining years were spent mostly at her beloved Nohant, writing copiously as usual (but now more about rustic life and the heart of the peasant), surrounded by her grandchildren and friends. It has been said that this was her best period with respect to her writing: "It is here that she shows her true originality and by these [works] she will chiefly live."[5] In 1876, she died, with her son, her daughter-in-law, and her daughter (with whom she had been reconciled) at her side. Her friend, Ivan Turgenev, wrote to Gustave Flaubert, "She loved both of us, but you above all, which is natural. What a heart of gold she had! What absence of every petty, mean, or false feeling! What a brave man she was, and what a good woman!")[6]

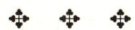

Chapter 4

Clara Wieck Schumann (1819-1896) was born in Leipzig. Her parents were divorced when she was very young. Her mother, Marianne Tromlitz, was a well-known Leipzig pianist, and her father, Friedrich, was a music teacher and businessman. He discovered in his daughter a great talent, and made her development as a pianist his main concern. Because he was autocratic, demanding, and rigid, while she was obedient, gentle, and sensitive, life was difficult for her. He spared nothing in training her, including his temper. He taught her to think of herself as an artist first, then as a woman, discouraging sewing and other "feminine" arts.

In 1828, when Clara was 8 years old and already a prodigy, she met Robert Schumann at a party. He was just 17 and graduated from high school. From the first, he was drawn to this gifted child, who was not only charming and sensitive, but who was fun and had a great sense of humor. Her father was his teacher, and he arranged to board with the Wiecks for a while.

When Clara was 9, she made her debut at the Gewandhaus. She was amazingly mature in her interpretation, possibly because her father, although somewhat reactionary in his own taste, was wise enough to allow hers to develop in her own way.

As she was growing up, Robert had his flirtations, naturally, and he became engaged to a student of Wieck's. But he then went through an emotional crisis—his second bout with mental problems (he had a nervous breakdown when he was younger). There was a history of mental instability in his family: his sister had committed suicide. He was always concerned about the possibility that he might go mad. At times he imagined that he heard sounds. He had an exaggerated fear of spaces, sudden anxiety attacks, fainting spells, and breathing problems. He and his fiancée canceled their engagement.

Then came another tragedy. His index and middle fingers of his right hand became incapacitated. He tried all kinds of remedies, none of which helped. To make matters worse, he used a mechanical device to lift his middle finger, which injured his finger even further. He changed his focus to composing, which was fortuitous for the world of music. He also became a major force in the field of music criticism. He was an excellent writer.

Music kept the friendship between Clara and Robert intact. She was impressed by his talent as a composer, and made a point of playing his compositions at her concerts. Many of those compositions were dedicated to her. Not surprisingly, when she was grown, these two friends fell deeply in love and announced their engagement. Her father was furious, thinking his plans were spoiled. He thought Robert was unstable and not suitable for his daughter. He started ugly rumors about the young man in a vain attempt to break the engagement. His behavior became so irrational that, in order to stop him, they were forced to take him to court. He was found guilty of slander and sentenced to prison. Eventually, he was released and, at least as far as outward appearances were concerned, he and Robert became friendly. Clara and Robert were married on September 12, 1840, when she was 21 years old and legally of age.

It was a wonderful marriage between two extraordinary people. Clara continued her concert career and served on the faculty of the Leipzig Conservatory, yet she always put his work ahead of hers. Although she loved him, she was somewhat afraid of him and his moods. She had the notion that a husband's career must have priority, and he, of course, agreed. This was difficult to carry out, especially since it was imperative that she spend hours at the piano practicing. She tried to avoid practicing when he was working. Aside from her career, she had the responsibilities of a large household and children. (They had eight children, although Emil died at 14 months and Ludwig was mentally impaired.) Despite her other concerns, Clara always was highly involved with Robert and his compositions, encouraging him in constructive ways. (However, she may have exerted too much pressure to get him to compose big orchestral works.) As Schumann's reputation grew, he became widely recognized as an exceptional composer and an eminent critic.

She did resume her profession, and the inevitable tensions arose because of her conflict between her professional and domestic obligations and desires. She was, after all, becoming more and more well-known and appreciated as a brilliant pianist. Life was a difficult balancing act for Clara, particularly when Robert became mentally incapacitated and unable to earn a living.

His condition deteriorated during the last 15 years of his life. On February 27, 1854, he tried to drown himself in the Rhine, but was rescued. He asked to be placed in a sanatorium and remained there for the rest of his life. For some reason, he did not seem to want to see his beloved wife and children, but he did enjoy visits from his dear friend, Johannes Brahms, who had been living with the Schumanns. Near the end, in 1856, in a letter to Joseph Joachim, a close friend and renowned violinist, Clara wrote, "Only a few words! I have been here since yesterday with Johannes . . . you will not ask me to speak of my misery, but I did receive a few tender looks and I shall carry them with me to the end of my life! Once he even put his arms round me. He recognized me!"[7] He died in 1856, 40 years before Clara's death.

After her husband's death, Clara toured as a highly acclaimed pianist, appearing regularly in England and in Russia. In 1878, she became principal piano teacher at the Hoch Conservatory in Frankfurt where she stayed until 1890. Her reputation as an unusually fine teacher grew, bringing her many famous pupils from many countries. It was considered a great honor to be taught by her.

Her relationship with Johannes Brahms is well-known. She and Robert had met him in 1853 in Dusseldorf. Schumann thought that Brahms was a genius and wrote glowingly about him in *Neue Zeitschrift fur Musik*. He insisted that Brahms move into his house and they became lifelong friends. He apparently fell in love with Clara, but realized that she was devoted to her husband. Nevertheless, they remained close friends for the rest of their lives. In terms of music, Clara and he inspired each other, both having the same preferences. She played his music publicly, especially when she returned to a full career of concertizing. As an interpreter of his music, she was unrivaled.

Her opinion about Liszt as a pianist changed through the years. She had been a great admirer of his when she was young, but grew to dislike his showiness. At one point, she refused to play at a Mozart festival because Liszt was the conductor. She felt that, as a pianist of great renown and the wife of a famous composer, she had the right to think of herself as a guardian of *pure* musicianship.

Joseph Joachim was close to both Clara and Brahms. Joachim and Clara busily pushed Brahms's music and exchanged critical evaluations concerning the music itself and its reception. (Brahms depended emotionally on his friends' opinions, because he was deeply insecure when it came to his own music.) In a letter from Clara to Joachim dated Leipzig, December 15, 1861, she wrote, "Yesterday Johannes's *Variations* (The *Handel Variations*) came out very well, and I had enthusiastic applause, curtain-calls, etc. . . ."[8] Joachim, in a letter to Madame Schumann dated Basel, November 4, 1866, wrote, " . . . Both his [Pianoforte] *Quartets* gladdened me very much, at Zurich and at Aarau . . . A man who writes like that must be noble and good!"[9]

The three musicians were faithful, intimate friends for the remainder of their lives. When Clara was 76 years old and lay dying, Joachim wrote to Brahms, "Thank God, better news has come from Frankfurt today about Frau Schumann. My head swims at the thought of losing her, but we have to get used to the idea . . ."[10] Brahms answered, "And after she has left us will not our faces light up with joy whenever we think of her? The wonderful woman in whom we have delighted throughout a long life, with ever-increasing love and admiration. That is the only way we should mourn her."[11] (Brahms, who was ill at that time, died less than a year after Clara).

Clara Wieck Schumann's influence on generations of pianists was incalculable. She felt that striving to re-create the composer's idea was more important than virtuosity. Her playing was sensitive and poetic, but based on study and knowledge.

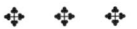

Chapter 4

Cosima Liszt von Bülow Wagner (1837-1930) is difficult to categorize. She was rigid and strong-willed, but selfless in her dedication to Wagner and his music. She was perceptive, but her perceptions were distorted by prejudices, emotions, and drive. She was highly gifted and immersed in culture. As a mother she was devoted, but she eventually left her children to focus on Wagner and his music. Cosima was a passionate woman: halfway measures were not for her. She was a magnificently powerful woman who believed completely in her ideals, yet she could be ruthless and cold in pursuing her aims. In appearance, she was tall, straight, and slim; her eyes were blue and large; her nose was long; and as a young girl, her hair was long and blond.

Cosima was the child of Franz Liszt, the great pianist and composer, and his mistress, Marie Catherine Sophie de Flavigny, Countess d'Agoult. Her parents were passionately in love with each other. They had met in 1833 (Liszt was 22; she, 28), and the countess was married at the time to a wealthy, uninteresting court official, and had three children with him. Liszt was a successful, extremely attractive, flamboyant man whom women could not resist. They both were attractive and charming. However, both were completely self-centered. She left her husband and her position in the high society of France and went to live with Liszt. They had three children: Blandine, the elder girl, Cosima (named Francesca Gaetana Cosima Liszt), and Daniel. Unfortunately, their mother was lacking in maternal feeling and apparently used her children to keep Liszt. He, however, escaped more and more into the exciting life around and in the concert hall, basking in women's adoration. He had some feeling for the children and was kind, but so utterly self-absorbed that he rarely saw them. At an early age they were placed in his mother's care and, even though their grandmother was happy to have them, they felt deserted by their parents. Their mother and father finally separated permanently in 1844. Liszt was happy to be free, but Marie was devastated and became bitter. When the children were young, they were moved from place to place and ignored by their parents; when growing up in their grandmother's house, they saw their mother only for short visits. The parents often argued about the children, but Liszt was the one who made the final decisions. Although she did not admit it, Marie was happy with the arrangement. She was able to have fun with them when they came to visit and could send them home when she was tired of them. There was a period of years when Cosima did not see her father. Because of this lack of interest on the part of her parents, Cosima developed into a determined person with the strength to pursue her goals vigorously. She discovered the wonderful world of books, and read everything she could find. At age 8 she started piano lessons, and it was apparent that she was extremely musical.

Liszt met 28-year-old Princess Carolyne Sayn-Wittgenstein in 1847. Carolyne was plain, willful, not very intelligent, and a religious fanatic (although she lived with Liszt out of wedlock). She left her child and her husband, a wealthy Polish landowner and adjutant to the Czar, and emigrated to be with Liszt. She then took complete charge of his life. She was an inferior writer who had a grandiose opinion of her talent and negatively influenced Liszt's writings. One of her first steps was to hire Madame Patersi de Fossombroni, a stern woman who had been her own governess, to take charge of Liszt's children in Paris. They were to be taken away from their grandmother and educated as princesses. The governess was a good teacher, but not warm, and certainly no substitute for a caring mother and father.

Liszt was a great admirer of Richard Wilhelm Wagner (1813-1883), who already was famous. During a visit, Carolyne and Franz convinced him to join them on their trip to Paris to see the children. Cosima was 15 years old and very impressionable. Another important meeting that her father arranged was with Hans von Bülow, Liszt's pupil, who was brilliant and talented. In spite of his caustic and sarcastic manner, Liszt admired him for his talent and his admiration of Wagner.

Carolyne and Franz transferred the children to Berlin to be cared for by Bülow's mother. This was agreeable to the older woman because she recognized that Liszt was responsible for her son's advancement. Cosima and her sister and brother were not happy, though; not only would they not have those lovely visits with their mother, but they also would not have their father with them. Cosima became more and more determined to rely only on herself.

Hans von Bülow became a famous pianist and conductor. (One of his great contributions was his influence on the interpretation of music.) Hans was hungry for recognition, yet he outwardly ridiculed the need for it. He could not give of himself emotionally, and took refuge in being condescending. He, too, lived in his mother's house at the time that the children were there, and became attached to Cosima. Both he and the young girl needed the warmth and sense of belonging to someone who had the same interests. Cosima admired his extreme commitment to music, but she was not in love. Nevertheless, they were married in Berlin on August 18, 1857.

On their honeymoon they went to visit Wagner in Zurich and stayed three weeks. Although Wagner was married to Minna (Christine Wilhelmine Planer) at this time, he fell in love with Mathilde Wesondonck, the wife of his host and benefactor. (He lived lavishly and depended on the generosity of benefactors. He felt he was entitled to this support because of his genius and felt no disloyalty in desiring his patron's wife. Even though Wagner was a small, unattractive man, he had no difficulty in attracting women and thought their adulation was his due.) He was aware of Bülow's admiration. Indeed the conductor's attention and understanding of his work were welcome. But he was not aware that Cosima was quietly and constantly observing him.

Back in Berlin, she plunged into the glamorous life of being the wife of a famous conductor, and seemed to be dedicated to her husband's career.

In 1858, they visited Wagner again. Minna was not sympathetic to her husband's work on *The Ring*, and was unhappy about his relationship with Mathilde. Finally, after much fuss, she was able to put an end to it. When the Bülows arrived, Minna and Mathilde each confided in

Wives and Lovers

Cosima. She reacted with sympathy to Richard's plight, not theirs. When she and Hans were leaving, she kissed Wagner's hand and cried. This may have been the moment when he suddenly became very aware of her.

After 22 years of marriage, Richard separated from Minna. He was still infatuated with Mathilde, and Cosima knew it. Of all his past relationships with women, Mathilde was the one she could never forget. That memory always disturbed her.

Cosima also could not forget Wagner and his genius. However, she remained loyal to her husband. She was an excellent hostess, a fine businesswoman, and his untiring traveling companion. On October 12, 1860, they had their first daughter, Daniela.

When Wagner visited the Bülows, Cosima and he took long walks and had many talks. Aside from his romantic needs, he craved intellectual companionship and, because Cosima was excited about his work on *Tristan*, she filled the bill.

They met again in Leipzig, and this time they became truly obsessed with each other. This began their passionate love. Still, she was Hans's wife, and soon had their second daughter. The next time Richard and she were together was at her home and this time their love was consummated. He was 24 years older but the age difference did not seem to matter. They had a powerful mutual physical attraction that lasted to the end.

Cosima knew that Wagner had no money and that he was always involved with women, yet she was so driven by love and her mission to serve his genius that she left her secure position as wife of a famous conductor. Her father, under Carolyne's influence, became extremely moralistic. He thoroughly disapproved when she left Hans to be with Richard. Nonetheless, in spite of her feeling of guilt and the probability of a scandal, she followed what she considered to be her "star." Cosima's youth, her unusual blond, attractive appearance, her musicality and knowledge, and, above all, her excellent listening skills attracted Wagner. In addition, he loved the fact that she was an aristocrat with diplomatic and gracious manners. (His manners were terrible.) Her devotion was irresistible.

In 1864, when Wagner's finances were at their lowest, his ardent admirer became King Ludwig II of Bavaria—a 19-year-old. As king, he was wealthy and determined to use Wagner's ideas of building Germany into a nation of greatness. As soon as he was crowned king, he summoned Wagner and arranged to subsidize him handsomely. This included a beautiful villa near the king, for use by the whole Bülow family as well. Ludwig came to love Cosima, having no idea of her love affair with Wagner. When the composer moved to Munich, the Bülows moved to Munich and Cosima divided her life between the two houses. She became her lover's secretary and counselor, kept visitors from bothering him, and in general made his life run smoothly.

Cosima gave birth to Richard's child, Isolde, in 1865. Bülow went along with the pretense that the child was his, and continued to help Wagner. It was a tragic situation for him, but he believed that Wagner's *Tristan* was a work that had to come to fruition. Perhaps, too, he felt that it was good for his career, because King Ludwig was making Munich an important music center.

Meanwhile, Richard and Cosima could not bear to be apart, but until their marriage, the pretense continued. (After his death, she destroyed and edited documents, letters, and the like that she thought would undermine Wagner's image.) She absorbed all his prejudices and ideas, to the point of preferring Germany to her native France. His antisemitism, which was virulent, was absorbed and intensified by Cosima. She became very possessive, and even chose his friends for him. She opened his mail and often dictated answers. Richard consulted her on artistic matters, having complete confidence in her because he knew that he was her mission. They both became close personally to the king, their political philosophy being almost identical to his. Eventually, however, even though he never lost faith in Wagner's musical genius and continued to help him financially, he did lose confidence in him as a man. Ludwig gave in to political pressure caused by

Wagner's participation in revolutionary political activities, and banished him from Bavaria for a period of time. Wagner settled in Switzerland. The unhappy lovers were separated.

In 1866, Minna died. Wagner was free. Cosima took her three children to live with Richard in a villa near Lucerne, Switzerland. Eva, the second child of the couple, was born in 1867.

Ludwig was devastated by his politically motivated separation from Wagner and threatened to give up his throne and live with the composer. Cosima, whom he trusted, had enormous influence on him. She persuaded him to remain king because she knew it would have been disastrous for them if Ludwig were to give up his power.

Because Bülow, in the meantime, was becoming more and more embittered, she went back to calm him for a short time. She did not want a public scandal because of Ludwig, who still had no knowledge of her relationship with Richard. They needed the king and his approval and knew that he would not have condoned their arrangement. It has been said that he was a homosexual, but believed in the code of the time: A woman must be loyal to her husband and children. She took Isolde and Eva and moved in with Wagner permanently in November 1868. She wrote to her eldest daughter and explained that her love for Richard Wagner and her commitment to his work made her leave Bülow and her two children. She had become pregnant with Wagner's third child, Siegfried, who was born in June 1869. Finally, Cosima asked for a divorce, which was granted on July 18, 1870. On August 25, 1870, Cosima and Richard were married.

Bülow became increasingly vindictive and, at first, declared that his children would remain with him (not that he was so enamored of them, nor did he spend much time with them). He finally left Munich and gave her their children. They did not see each other for 11 years. (He ultimately remarried.) Wagner assumed the role of father of five children and, surprisingly, was actually devoted to all. It was one of the few nice traits he had.

Cosima was blind to her husband's faults. She thought

he was wonderful and thought it understandable that he was arrogant and self-aggrandizing. She joined him in his hatred of Brahms, his scathing judgments of English poetry, his pretensions of being an authority on drama and politics. Even so, her tact kept things running smoothly with the king, and she was able to control Wagner's temper.

The Wagners had some interesting personal relationships. Richard and Cosima had become friendly with Friedrich Wilhelm Nietzsche, the German philosopher. Nietzsche taught concepts that included the belief in the death of God, in the superman, and the will to power. He believed in the "'natural aristocracy' of the superman who, driven by the 'will to power,' celebrates life on earth rather than sanctifying it for some heavenly reward. Such a heroic man of merit has the courage to 'live dangerously,' and thus rise above the masses, developing his natural capacity for the creative use of passion."[12] This philosophy was attractive to the Wagners. They remained intimate friends until Nietzsche began to criticize German culture. The friendship then broke.

Another close friend and colleague, Hans Richter, lived with them for several years. At first he was their copyist but he became a gifted conductor, the first of *The Ring* at Bayreuth.

Cosima had developed into an interesting woman. Even though she absorbed Richard's ideas, she had her own distinctive qualities. She was an avid reader; she could discuss philosophy with Nietzsche; a competent pianist, she could play duets with Wagner and Richter; she was a charming hostess and excellent housekeeper, a loving but strict mother, a lover of birds and nature, and sexually vibrant; and she had the ability to tame her difficult husband. She had conflicting ideas about her father. She never forgave Liszt for his neglect when she was a child, nor his attempt to make her stay with Bülow, but she loved him and was proud of him. She particularly appreciated his admiration of Wagner. Of course, his generosity and his fame were important factors, as well. She had a certain amount of compassion for him, too, because she realized that he was not a contented man. (After Wagner's death, father and daughter drew closer.)

Wagner's plan, like Cosima's, was to present *The Ring* as a unit—a German festival with the best of Germany's talent. What they needed was the place. Bayreuth was chosen because it was in an area of Germany where minnesingers sang German songs in medieval times. Also, it was in Ludwig's Bavaria, it was somewhat difficult to get to (therefore making the trip a kind of pilgrimage), it had the potential for development, and it was surrounded by natural beauty. Cosima convinced Richard to make it the site for the festival theater. They moved to Bayreuth and built an extravagant home called "Wahnfried." She had her hands on every aspect of the planning. On August 13, 1876, the festival began. It was an international event. People came from everywhere. Cosima was magnificent in appearance and an elegant hostess, entertaining important people of the world—especially important to the success of the festival. She was overwhelming, but effective. Wagner acknowledged to all that, without Cosima, this project would not have come to fruition. The festival was a great triumph. (Nietzsche came, but was disillusioned with Wagner's theatrics. To him, the festival was a flamboyant social affair. He left, and Cosima, who had missed him, never forgave him.

Ludwig, as always, continued providing his generosity and support.

During the last years of Wagner's life, Cosima was the most influential. These were the years of *Parsifal*. He felt that writing this was terribly difficult, and that he was too old, but she encouraged and supported him, always urging him on. She was exactly what he needed. The combination of these two people, both of whom had some unsavory characteristics, worked well. He was a genius and she had the necessary grace, determination, and faith in him to help. They could not bear to be separated from each other. Every night, he played his day's composition for her so that she knew almost every word and every note. "Fidi" (Siegfried), their son, was their special joy.

Richard Wagner died on February 13, 1883, and Cosima

was inconsolable. She retreated into herself and seemed to want to die, too. After about four months, she began to realize that the preservation of Wagner's work in his theater was now her mission. When there was danger that the direction of the festival would be taken from her, she rallied, and succeeded in keeping control. She chose Hermann Levi, the talented conductor, to be musical director. Cosima kept him close, but always tormented him about his being different and Jewish. He felt that he should leave, but she drew him back. Eventually, she felt she had to get rid of him, because he was a Jew and, therefore, a corrupting factor. He was succeeded by Felix Mottl, whose talent did not measure up to that of Levi. But after Levi left, Cosima was decidedly more comfortable, convinced that the productions were more "Christian" and sacred. She directed the action on the stage herself. From 1886-1906, she worked with nine conductors, the last being her adored son. He was different from his parents in that he was likable, kind, and liberal in his ideas. Unfortunately, he married an English woman, Winifred, who was extremely prejudiced (and later became Hitler's friend).

Cosima became a fierce despot, expecting all to obey her. She did things her way and was blind to new ideas, but she was successful: A pilgrimage to Bayreuth soon became the *in* thing to do.

When she became ill, she turned over the management of the festival to Siegfried, who was 36 years old. Her daughter Eve and her husband remained a great joy to Cosima and stayed near her. Siegfried was 46 when he married Winifred, who was 18. Winifred soon made it clear that when Cosima died, she and Siegfried would run Bayreuth. Cosima died at age 92 in 1930, the year unemployment soared in Germany and in which Hitler began amassing power. Cosima was buried next to her husband. Siegfried died in the same year, at age 61, and Winifred became the director of the festival. She remained director until 1944. In 1951, the American occupation forces agreed to the reopening of the festival on condition that Winifred have no part in it. Her children (who did not agree with their mother's politics and values and who had separated themselves from her) and her grandsons (first Wieland, then Wolfgang) directed the festival.

Sara Thorpe Bull (ca. 1850-1911), the daughter of a wealthy state senator in Wisconsin, was well-trained on the piano and very musical. When she was 20 years old, she met and fell in love with Ole Bull, a Norwegian violinist as famous as Joachim, Vieuxtemps, and Sarasate. Charismatic and flamboyant, with a larger-than-life personality, he captured the attention of the European and American public. He was musical, but not really at home with the classics. His most successful repertoire generally included his own compositions and arrangements, which appealed to thousands of the "common" people. Joachim said of him, "In some violinistic specialties . . . Bull could be called near-perfect. His intonation was very pure and clean, even in the most difficult runs. But he displayed an almost childish simple-mindedness and awkwardness when confronted with classical music: He was utterly unable to deal with it and had the most outlandish conceptions about its character."[13] No matter, he was the rage and in demand everywhere. His appeal seemed to reach everyone. The Russian music critic Count Odoevsky wrote, "When Ole Bull raises his divine violin, we are all conquered by him . . ."[14]

In 1870, when Bull was 60 years old and a widower, he came to America for a series of concerts. He was 6 feet tall, with a well-proportioned physique, and at this time had long silver hair. His stage presence was impressive, and, personally, he was very glamorous. When 20-year-old Sara met him, they were mutually attracted, fell deeply in love, and married. They moved to Boston, where they lived for a while. Their baby, Sara Olea, was born there. But soon Bull became restless again, and he returned alone to Norway. Typical of his *joie de vivre* was this escapade: He went to Egypt to climb Cheop's Pyramid and had someone accompany him to carry his violin. When he arrived at the summit, he displayed the Norwegian flag and joyously played one of his favorite Norwegian songs.

Sara decided it was time to join him and take charge. She and little Sara Olea settled down with him in Norway, where she managed his concerts and his everyday life. Their summers were spent at their beautiful house, which Bull built on their 600-acre estate on an island near Bergen. Their winters were spent in America. When he was 70, in 1880, they traveled back to Norway, where he became seriously ill. He died on August 17.

Sara's objective from that time on was to keep the public's memory of him alive. She wrote a book, *Ole Bull: A Memoir*, for which she collected authentic documents, and told the story of his romantic life. She completed his unfinished project of raising money to memorialize Leif Ericsson, who had discovered America, and whose statue she had placed on Commonwealth Avenue in Boston. Sara donated her husband's famous violin (called the *Gaspar da Salò*) to the Town Museum in Bergen, with the condition that no one was to play it.

Eventually, she returned to America and settled in Cambridge, Mass., where she died in 1911.

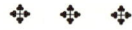

Alma Schindler Mahler Gropius Werfel (1871-1964) was a fascinating woman who helped advance the careers of some of the most creative men in music, literature, and the visual arts. She was the daughter of J. Emil Schindler, an important landscape painter of the Austrian monarchy in the Hapsburg empire. He was a member of a family of highly prominent industrialists, and sprinkled among them were some talented artists and writers. Her mother, Anna von Bergen, a soprano, gave up her career to marry Emil. She was the practical parent, a sensible, down-to-earth woman, and remained a supportive, wonderful mother all her life. Alma was close to both parents, but idolized her father, an unusually interesting, talented, and charming man. He was a captivating conversationalist, very musical, and had a wonderful voice. He spent a great deal of time with his adored daughter, and was responsible for her appreciation of all things beautiful. Because of his influence and her own impressive gift, music became an important part of her life from an early age. In fact, she began to compose at the age of 9, working on an upright piano.

Alma grew into a lovely, sophisticated young lady and was considered by many to be the most beautiful woman in Vienna. She always had been surrounded by important, creative people of Vienna and was quite comfortable with them. She had charm, intelligence, talent, and could converse brilliantly with anyone, having great confidence in herself. The one problem she had was her impaired sense of hearing, the result of measles. This did not interfere with her sensitivity to music, but she compensated for it in social situations by paying close attention to the person who was speaking to her. Of course, the men were very flattered. (Perhaps the women were, too, but she did not give much of her energy or attention to women.)

When she was only 16, the well-known artist Gustav Klimt fell in love with her, and she was attracted to him and his work, as well. He pursued her, and although she promised to run away with him, she eventually tired of his persistence. As was the case in the aftermath of most of her relationships with men who loved her, they remained friends. Max Burckhard, a famous producer and critic who was director of the Burgtheater in Vienna, was also in love with her. He took it upon himself to educate her by drawing her into the world of literature and the theater, and was responsible for her admiration of Friedrich Nietzsche's ideas.

When her beloved father died in 1892 and her mother remarried, she turned to music with a passion. She studied counterpoint and singing. Alexander von Zemlinsky, a great conductor, composer, and teacher, took her on as a student and proceeded to give her a serious education in composing. (He was the brother-in-law and teacher of Arnold Schoenberg, the illustrious composer whose new theories about the organization of music had a profound impact on 20th-century music. Schoenberg was to be a close and enduring friend of the Mahlers.) Nine of her songs were published. Alma was very attracted to Zemlinsky, and he, like the others, fell madly in love with her. Their affair and the valuable music lessons came to end after several years.

Alma met Gustav Mahler, the great Austrian conductor and composer, at a party. He was director of the Court Opera in Vienna and already famous. His background was very different from Alma's. While hers was one of privilege, elegance and ease, his was one of hard work and responsibility. His father had started to earn a living as a peddler, eventually owning a distillery in Bohemia. His mother always was exhausted by household and maternal duties. Several siblings had died, and, as the eldest remaining son, he was driven by his father to become a successful and famous musician. The family was Jewish, but when Cosima Wagner, widow of Richard Wagner, declared her opposition to a Jew being given the directorship of the Vienna Opera (probably the most desirable position for a conductor at that time), he realized that, in order to get ahead, he must convert to Christianity. He did exactly that, and was hired for that exalted role. (He already was known as a great conductor of Wagner's music.) Although he was accepted as a phenomenally brilliant conductor, his work as a composer was still unappreciated. And that was his greatest goal.

Gustav noticed Alma immediately, not only because of her beauty but also because of her direct, exciting, confident manner. She was fascinated by him, as well, even though she was aware of his having been born Jewish and despite her antisemitic feelings. All her life she had this prejudice, yet surrounded herself by, and even married, Jewish men. There was no doubt in her mind that she, as a Christian, was superior to Jews, that even though they had spirit and creativity, they needed the help of Christians to achieve their full potential. She believed they were different and did not have the "brightness" that was the birthright of Christians. And yet she always felt a close affinity to them and thoroughly enjoyed being with them.

Her conflicts apparently stayed with her throughout life, and were expressed in her diary on January 9, 1919: ". . . the Jews are at once an unprecedented danger and the greatest good luck for humanity."[15] At that time, antisemitism was on the rise, and she was particularly worried about her own relationship with them. The attraction between Gustav and Alma developed into deep love, and he proposed marriage. He explained to her that marriage with him would not be simple, because he had to be completely free to move around, and his position at the opera was not to be depended upon, all of which she understood. He composed and played vocal compositions for her, and he wrote beautiful love letters to her. A serious flaw in their relationship appeared after they became engaged, when he forbade her to compose anymore. Apparently, he was jealous of her commitment to her work and deeply involved in his own. After many tears, she agreed. In a letter to Alma, he wrote that from then on her role would be to make him happy, and his would be that of the working composer. They were married on March 9, 1902. Bruno Walter, who was on his way to being recognized as a great conductor, was Gustav's disciple, admirer, and close friend (even though 16 years younger). He wrote, "His bride, Alma Schindler, is 22, tall and slim, and a stunning beauty, the most beautiful girl in Vienna; from a very good family and very rich. But we, his friends, are very concerned by this: He is 41 and she is 22; she is a celebrated beauty, used to a brilliant life, he so unworldly and solitary . . . but their love is said to be a great one."[16] (He had described Mahler, when he first met him, as "lean, fidgety; a short man with an unusually high forehead, long dark hair, [and] deeply penetrating bespectacled eyes."[17] Although Gustav was not handsome in the classical sense, he was attractive to women, and known to have had many liaisons.)

Alma recognized his genius and devoted herself completely to him and his music. In her description of her reaction to the performance of his *Third Symphony*, she said, "My excitement was indescribable; I cried and laughed to myself . . . I was so utterly convinced of Mahler's greatness by this work that night, amid tears of happiness, I swore to him my recognition of his genius, the love that wanted only to serve him, my eternal desire to live for him alone."[18] Nevertheless, there were times when she tried to get back to her own music. But whenever she worked at the piano, he became upset at being disturbed. She started to occupy herself with copying his music. She did more and more of his manuscripts, becoming so adept that she could easily read the scores as she wrote them, ultimately becoming indispensable to him. She was required to maintain his strict schedule at home and in his profession. In addition, she was responsible for their finances, which she managed admirably, their household, and their children. (They had two children. Maria Anna, called "Putzi," was conceived before their marriage and born in 1902. She died from diphtheria in 1907, a tragedy from which they never completely recovered. Anna Justine was born in 1904, and became a talented sculptor, and, like her mother, married talented men.)

Gustav became disenchanted with his position in Vienna for several reasons—he was financially insecure, and wanted to spend more time with his family and his composing. Coincidentally, he was offered a large sum of money to conduct the Metropolitan Opera in New York City, and, with Alma's encouragement, accepted. Their financial worries seemed to be over, not only because of the new contract in America, but also because the head of the opera in Vienna, Prince Montenuovo, arranged for Mahler to receive a pension larger than that which they had expected, in addition to a large lump sum when he left. Also, Mrs. Mahler was promised a pension on the death of her husband. They left for America with hopes high.

Gustav Mahler and his wife arrived in New York in December 1907. They were extremely well-received. As was customary at the time, European conductors were only required to stay in America during the concert season. They returned to Europe in April 1908, and Gustav was to conduct. (It was the Diamond Jubilee of the Hapsburg Emperor, Franz Joseph I.) They returned to New York in November 1908, and he conducted concerts at Carnegie Hall (including his own *Second Symphony*) and opera at the Metropolitan Opera House. He was then asked to become the chief conductor of the New York Philharmonic, and happily accepted. The return to New York, where he would assume this new post, ushered in an unpleasant period for the Mahlers. To understand how this came about, it is important to know some background. The public contributed little money for these great performances. They were financed by men of great wealth (August Belmont, Andrew Carnegie, John D. Rockefeller, J. P. Morgan, Joseph Pulitzer, and George R. Sheldon among the most prominent) and administered by their wives. Mrs. George R. Sheldon was the dominant one of the 10 members who made up the powerful "Guarantee Committee of the New York Philharmonic Orchestra." The Philharmonic originally was self-governing, but ran into financial difficulties. Mrs. Sheldon rounded up financial support, and in 1909 proposed to rescue the orchestra, providing it agreed to take orders from a committee of 10 members, consisting of her friends, socialites, and three members of the orchestra. She proposed radical changes in the organization and, if accepted, promised to subsidize the orchestra for three seasons. The conductor was to be selected by the committee. Its choice was Gustav Mahler. The orchestra had no alternative but to accept the terms. The Mahlers again returned to Europe for the intervening months.

Alma was still beautiful, and men were drawn to her. Her husband was jealous, but did not overly react until he received a letter from a young man, Walter Gropius (later to become Alma's husband and a world-famous architect), saying that he could not live without Alma and implying that he wanted to marry her. Gustav confronted her with it and, though she denied any romantic connection with him, she took the opportunity to tell Gustav what was in her heart. Exhausted from all her hard work, she let out all her hurt and anger, crying that he was so involved in his own career that he neglected her. She told him that, because she was so lonely and hurt, she had really thought of leaving him, but had decided against it because he was still the very center of her life. He listened carefully, taking the criticism to heart, then decided to consult Dr.

Sigmund Freud. Through a relative of Alma's, a meeting was arranged, even though Freud was on vacation. They met in Leyden, a Dutch town, and spent four hours walking and talking. Mahler evidently was impressed by some of Freud's remarks, particularly when Dr. Freud said, "How dared a man in your state ask a young woman to be tied to him? . . . I know your wife. She loved her father and she can only choose and love a man of his sort. Your age, of which you are so much afraid, is precisely what attracts her. You need not be anxious. You loved your mother, and you look for her in every woman. She was careworn and ailing, and unconsciously you wish your wife to be the same."[19] In a letter to a pupil, Freud wrote, "I analyzed Mahler for an afternoon in Leyden. If I may believe reports, I achieved much with him at that time . . . [During] a highly interesting expedition through his life history, we discovered his personal conditions for love, especially his Holy Mary complex (mother fixation). I had much opportunity to admire the capability for psychological understanding in this man of genius."[20]

Gustav began to be more attentive, more loving, and less demanding of his wife. He began to leave love notes, instead of imperious orders. Much to her surprise, he started to become interested in the songs she had composed, and found them lovely. From then on he encouraged her work and saw to it that five of the songs were published—at about the same time as his great *Eighth Symphony*. He officially dedicated his work to Alma. He had learned his lesson well and, when they were apart for a little while, he wrote, "Almschili, if you had left me that time, I should simply have gone out like a torch deprived of air . . ."[21] He showered her with gifts and attention, and, more important, treated her with respect and deep concern. Their marriage became idyllic.

On their return to New York, they found that the situation with the committee was difficult. The wealthy ladies of the committee, ignorant about the production of concerts and music in general, were autocratic and interfering. Ultimately, their interference became intolerable. The crisis came when they attended a rehearsal that had an excellent program of which they did not approve, and proceeded to give Gustav orders. He was summoned, like an errant schoolboy, to the impressive home of Mrs. Sheldon, where he had to defend his programming and goals. The ladies criticized not only his decisions but his character, as well. Naturally, Mahler, not the easiest nor the most gracious person in the world, did not sit still for this, and a nasty session ensued. Hidden behind a curtain that inadvertently was opened was a lawyer recording all of Gustav's angry replies. They had successfully humiliated one of the greatest musical geniuses of all time.

Gustav had not been feeling well, and after that ugly confrontation, his condition deteriorated. He was diagnosed as having subacute bacterial endocarditis. He decided that he wanted to die in Vienna. After an arduous trip back to Europe, he was placed in a sanitorium in Paris, then transferred to another in Vienna. Alma was constantly at his side until he died on May 18, 1911, in Vienna. She had made a tremendous difference in his life, having given him great love, care, and encouragement, and having introduced him to her circle of artistic friends. Her knowledge, love of music, and dedication to his genius, all of which he appreciated, made her the companion he needed.

Alma Mahler was left a wealthy young widow. She and her 7-year-old daughter set up housekeeping in an apartment of their own and Alma went back to her usual activities, dressing and socializing normally, and, of course, attracting men. (Dr. Joseph Fraenkel, their friend from New York who had helped Alma care for her husband in his last days, proposed to her soon after Gustav's death). She was celebrated as Mahler's widow for the rest of her life. Her influence was felt by the power she had in giving or withholding of permission for the performance of her husband's music. One of her greatest missions remained the promotion of his works and his image. Under her guidance, the Gustav Mahler Foundation was formed.

In November of the year that Mahler died, when Alma was returning by train from Munich, where she had been honored at a premiere of Gustav's *Das Lied von Erde*, conducted by Bruno Walter, she met an old friend, Paul

Kammerer. He was a brilliant biologist and also involved in music composition and criticism. They were immediately intrigued by each other; he with her as a person generally and her position as widow of the esteemed Gustav Mahler, and she with his incredible intellect and education. He was married, so in order to be with her, he hired her as an assistant in his biological laboratory, with no salary. He became more and more in need of her, but she was not in love with him. He proved to be unstable, at one point threatening to shoot himself. Finally, Alma called his wife, explained the situation, and ended the relationship. He did commit suicide about 20 years later.

Alma Mahler was always drawn to brilliant and creative men. In 1912, her stepfather, Carl Moll, suggested that she might like the unorthodox and gifted artist Oskar Kokoschka to paint her portrait. (He was to become one of the world's foremost expressionist artists.) She met him when he came to paint Moll's portrait, and she proposed that he do hers as well. There was a violent attraction between them, and they fell madly in love. He was seven years younger than she, but experienced, handsome, a genius, and very sensual. They had a wild, passionate affair that lasted for three years. He wanted her to have his child, but Alma was superstitious about children conceived out of wedlock. She felt that her sin would be punished. He wrote, "My Alma, I love you more than I love myself . . . I must have you for my wife soon, or else my great talent will perish miserably. You must revive me at night, like a magic potion . . . I have seen how strong you can make me and what I'll amount to when this force is constantly active. You revive useless people, and I, the one you are destined for, should I go wanting?"[22] Oskar wanted desperately to marry her, and she promised him that she would after he had created a great work. He began his whirling *Die Windsbraut* (The Tempest), which is a painting of a woman (Alma) and a man (Oskar) on a cockle-shell-like bed. She is larger and asleep; he is wide awake. Alma kept putting off their marriage, and the uncertainty drove him wild. When she became pregnant, he was delighted, but she went to a clinic in Vienna for an abortion. Their relationship became prickly, and Alma was torn between wanting to leave him and wanting to stay. When World War I started, Oskar joined the military, probably mostly to escape his predicament. He sent pleading, emotional letters to her, but she began thinking about changing her life. She remembered the impetuous young architect, Walter Gropius, whom she had met before and who had written that painful letter to Gustav, and decided to find him.

Alma found out that Walter was a patient in an army hospital in Berlin, and decided to visit him. He resisted her for a while, but after two weeks, he succumbed. He proposed and she accepted. He too was a genius in his own field and founded the famous Bauhaus School. She married Walter on August 18, 1915. He was just what she wanted at that time: handsome, tremendously gifted, and Aryan, and, although she did not know him well, she thought she was in love with him. He came from an upper-middle-class German family that was very different from her own. In marrying him, she felt that she would have escaped from Oskar and the stigma of having been married to a Jew. Her one desire was to have his child and on October 5, 1916, their lovely daughter, Manon, was born.

Oskar continued to besiege her with letters, but eventually realized the hopelessness of his case. (Eventually he married, but wrote to her occasionally for years. On her 70th birthday, she received an affectionate letter from him, in which he wrote, ". . . There has been nothing like it [our love] since the Middle Ages, for no couple has ever breathed into each other so passionately . . . We'll always be on the stage of life, we two, when disgusting banality, the trivial vestige of the contemporary world, will yield to a passion-born splendor . . ."[23]

But Alma was getting restless, and when she met Franz Werfel, she fell in love again. Franz was a Jewish novelist and poet 13 years younger than she. He was not handsome, but she found him more and more attractive as time went by. Music was one of his loves, although he was not trained in it. She wanted to leave Walter, but did not want to give up Manon. She became pregnant with Franz's child, but pretended to Walter that he was the father. One day, her husband overheard her talking on the telephone with Franz and realized the truth. He behaved well, never showing his feelings, but Alma knew her secret was out. The infant, Martin, lived for only a little while. Alma was filled with guilt, knowing that this child was conceived out of wedlock.

Eventually Alma asked for a divorce, which Walter agreed to, on condition that he spend time with his daughter. (Walter later married and settled in the United States. He and Alma corresponded occasionally through the years.) She and Franz were married on July 6, 1929. They were deeply in love, but there were two problems: religion and politics. She had conflicting feelings about Jews, and he could not understand her fascist ideas. But they managed to live with these problems. He was becoming more and more famous, and life could have been easy for them. Alma's daughter Anna was grown, and Manon had become a beautiful, bright young girl. However, in 1934, when Manon was 18, she developed polio, became paralyzed, and died in the spring of 1935. Alma went into a deep depression, thinking of those she loved who had died: her father, her firstborn, her son, her husband Gustav, and now her beautiful daughter Manon.

It soon became apparent that they were not safe from Hitler and his atrocities. They decided to leave Europe, and embarked on their dangerous escape, eventually arriving in New York. Franz, who by this time was a celebrated author, and Alma, Mahler's widow and Werfel's wife, were received warmly in America. Anna, her daughter, had settled in London, and Franz's family had managed to escape. Gustav had left money in New York, so the Werfels were in good financial shape, and Alma had managed to bring manuscripts with her, as well as some of her other valuables. They headed for Los Angeles, where they settled, living near friends such as Bruno Walter and Arnold Schoenberg. Franz wrote well and happily in his new home. His book *Song of Bernadette*, which had been inspired by Alma when she came across the story of Bernadette, was taken up by the Book of the Month Club and eventually made into a movie. He continued to write until his death on August 25, 1944. They had been married happily for about 15 years.

After Franz died, Alma moved to New York City to an apartment and remained there, still involved with the creative life of the arts, until her death on Friday, December 11, 1964. At that time, there were many articles about her in the press, emphasizing her support of and fascination with geniuses, as well as all the famous men with whom she had been married or had had liaisons. In the *Dallas Daily News* it was printed that ". . . There never has been justification, in our opinion, for the claims through successive generations that Alma was merely a headhunter, a collector of geniuses. She was a vital part of their geniuses. She was involuntarily a part of a star-smitten life-force."[24]

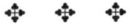

Olga Koussevitzky (1901-1975), wife of great conductor Serge Koussevitzky, was the daughter of Alexander Naoumoff, a member of the government in Tsarist Russia, serving as minister of agriculture two years before the Russian Revolution in 1917. Her mother, Anna, was a gifted writer. Olga, one of five children, was born on her family's estate near the Volga River and spent most of her childhood there. She led a life of privilege, with private schools, servants, and great luxuries. Even as a child, Olga was very creative and musical, becoming an accomplished pianist and a fine amateur artist. Her elegant sketches and witty caricatures of musicians hang in the Library of Congress.

In 1907, an important event in her life occurred: When the family was in Paris, they were invited to visit her Aunt Natalie (her mother's younger sister) and Natalie's husband, Serge Koussevitzky, who was a famous double-bass virtuoso. When Olga met him, he made a profound impression on her. He was about 33 years old at the time, and she was only about 5 or 6. This imposing man was extremely charismatic. When he left the room, the little girl felt that an important presence had left. This impression of his greatness stayed with her. When she was 12 years old and still living in Russia, she attended her first symphonic concert. The orchestra was conducted by Serge Koussevitzky, who was to become her husband years later.

In 1921, when they realized that resistance to the revolution was useless, Olga and her family escaped to Constantinople and Greece, finally settling in France with others who had taken refuge there. In 1929, her Aunt Natalie and Uncle Serge asked her to accompany them to the United States as their secretary. By then, the maestro was internationally known as the great conductor of the Boston Symphony Orchestra. Olga assumed more and more responsibilities as the years went by, especially after her aunt became ill. She acted as hostess and companion to her uncle. When Natalie died in 1942, her niece and husband went through a period of deep grief; the three had had a very close family relationship. Serge and Olga grew to depend on each other, and, on August 14, 1947, they were secretly married in Lenox, Mass., at the Koussevitzky summer home, *Seranak* (short for Serge and Natalie Koussevitzky). It was not until the couple was about to sail for Europe after the Tanglewood season that they announced their marriage publicly.

Four years later, Serge Koussevitzky died. He had been instrumental in founding Tanglewood and the teaching center, Berkshire Music Center. Olga, who identified completely with his interests, dedicated her life to working for his causes. She was a special lady, beloved for her charm, hospitality, courage, and strength, as well as for her gentle spirit. In appearance, she was delicate and frail, but she showed great strength in supporting her husband's activities when he was alive. After he died, it was important to her to keep his memory alive, and to develop the foundations with which he had been so deeply involved. Her energy seemed boundless. In 1951, she assumed the office of president of the Koussevitzky Music Foundation, which had been established by her husband in 1942, and which assists new composers by bestowing grants, commissions, and prizes. She directed the Musicians Club of

New York. From 1956, Olga served as president of the American International Music Fund, which promotes the work of living composers. She was associated with innumerable musical philanthropies, including the MacDowell Colony for creative artists and the American-Israel Cultural Foundation.

Olga Koussevitzky died when she was 77 years old in her New York apartment as a result of a heart attack. She was flown back to Lenox, and buried next to her husband. Leonard Bernstein, Koussevitzky's protégé, remarked, "How I shall miss our dear Olga—that fragile Rock of Gibraltar on whom so many of us depended for significant links with a past of love and beauty."[25] Ellen Pfeiffer wrote, "Always faithfully seated in her first-row box at BSO concerts at Tanglewood, fragile and wrapped in a lace shawl, Mrs. Koussevitzky had spent the two-and-a-half decades since her husband's death encouraging and supporting the activities which were closest to his heart. These included teaching young musicians at the Berkshire Center at Tanglewood and nurturing new American music and its composers."[26]

Mrs. Koussevitzky received many awards and honors, including the Cross of Finland, the American Medal of Honor, the Spirit of Achievement Award from Albert Einstein College of Medicine, and the Louis D. Brandeis Gold Medal. Her honorary degrees include honorary doctor of music from the New England Conservatory of Music in Boston and honorary doctor of music from Hartt College, University of Hartford.

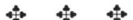

Aniela (Nela) Mlynarski Rubinstein was the daughter of Lithuanian conductor, violinist and composer Emil Mlynarski. She was born (ca. 1908) at *Llgovo*, the estate of her mother's family, which was in Kowno, Lithuania. Her gifted and famous father had been a student at the St. Petersburg Conservatory, studying violin with Leopold Auer, piano with Anton Rubinstein, and composition with

Anatoli Liadov. He served as principal conductor of the Warsaw Opera and the Scottish Orchestra in Glasgow, conducted the Warsaw Philharmonic, was appointed director of the Warsaw Conservatory, and later (1929-1931) taught conducting at the Curtis Institute of music in Philadelphia. Nela had two older sisters and two older brothers. During World War I, she and her family escaped to Russia just before Germany invaded Lithuania.

The Mlynarski family finally settled in Warsaw, Poland. Their large apartment was connected to the backstage of the opera house, a convenience for her father (and intriguing for the children). Their home was constantly filled with fascinating musicians and many relatives.

Nela, age 12, was enrolled in the same school as her sister Alina and Alina's close friend, Halina Lilpop (later the wife of conductor Artur Rodzinski). Even though Nela was four years younger than her sister and Halina, the three girls were fast friends. (Halina and Nela remained close throughout their lives.) Even at that age, and before Nela had any instruction, she danced beautifully, and was hoping to become a ballerina. She lived in a world of music, completely comfortable with highly acclaimed musicians, and absorbing knowledge and taste. Because her mother had to spend many months of the year in Lithuania trying to save her family estate, it became the obligation of the lovely and poised sisters, Alina and Nela, to perform as hostesses at the after-theater suppers. The Mlynarski children already were musically sophisticated, and enjoyed joining in critiques of the performances. It was excellent preparation for someone who was destined to become the wife of a premier pianist.

When Nela met Artur Rubinstein, he already was a recognized pianist, concertizing in many countries. She was just 18 and he almost 40 years old. He had "been around." He enjoyed women, required the finest of culinary experiences, was friends with many in high society and the art world, and was happiest when living extravagantly. He enjoyed *life*. He had come to Warsaw to play in concert with Emil Mlynarski, under whose baton he particularly enjoyed playing. The concert was a great success and, during the intermission, Nela, her sister, and her cousin entered the artist's room. He describes his first impression of her: "The tallest, who was very blond, showed great vitality and charm . . ." [27] He looked only at her.

After concertizing in a few other cities in Poland, he returned to Warsaw and visited her at her home. She danced to his accompaniment of a Chopin mazurka, and she told him her dreams of becoming a ballerina. Soon they fell in love. He said, " . . . She was the image of what I always loved and admired so much in Polish women . . . she was beautiful, slim and very well-built, a small fine face with the bluest eyes, like turquoise, an irregular nose, small, beautifully shaped ears, a fine forehead crowned by a mass of dark blond hair. Her most striking feature was her long slender neck, which gave her a proud bearing . . ."[28] He wanted to marry her, but was afraid of the fact that she was beautiful and so much younger, and would be pursued by other men. In fact, he had conflicting feelings about marriage in general. He asked her to marry him, but then asked her to wait. She agreed. Later, when confessing her love to Halina, her friend said, "He's a ladies' man, Nela." She replied, "I don't care. I love him."[29]

Rubinstein continued on his concert tour, happily looking forward to a letter from his beloved. But Nela did not want to be the first to write. When he did not hear from her, he began to worry about her feelings for him. Soon he was scheduled for another tour starting in Warsaw. Unfortunately, a former paramour of his insisted on going with him, even though she saw that he was uneasy about it. Because they both had been invited to a party at the British embassy, they arrived together, only to meet Nela and her father. Artur had some explaining to do, but he finally convinced her that all was well. She told him about the pianist Mieczyslaw Munz, who wanted to marry her. He again told her of his love, his desire to marry her, and of his plan to tour in South America the following year. He explained that, after he had enough money to support her in the style he thought was appropriate, they would marry. He confessed to being a spendthrift, and promised to be more responsible in the future. She again agreed to wait for him.

He went on his tour and actually began to economize. But because of a lack of understanding, their relationship came to a standstill. Nela had not received a letter from Artur, was hurt, and would not initiate the correspondence. And he, in his pride, was waiting for her to write first. While in Buenos Aires, he heard that Nela had married Munz in Warsaw. Artur was miserable. During the winter of 1927-1928, Nela had met the young virtuoso pianist, who courted her in a whirlwind romance and whom she married shortly after. The newly married couple, along with Nela's mother and father, went to the United States, where Munz was a professor of piano at the Curtis Institute in Philadelphia. He had a heavy schedule of teaching, concerts, and recitals. Fortunately, the young wife was occupied with her parents, particularly her father who was not at all well. (He had decided to accept the offer to teach conducting at the institute, because he was no longer physically able to conduct). It was not long, however, before Nela realized that the marriage was a mistake, and decided to divorce Munz. She returned to Europe to pursue her studies in dancing.

Just about this time, Artur Rubinstein was the guest of honor at a party that Halina Lilpop, Nela's friend, also attended. He said to Halina, ". . . And so I am looking for a wife, a Polish girl . . . I want one heart, a faithful, loyal, Polish heart."[30] Halina told him about Nela's marital situation. During the 1931-1932 concert season, Artur returned to Warsaw to perform. While there, he attended a concert, where he met Nela again. It was as if no time had passed. After the concert, they went out to dine and to dance, at which time Nela asked, with a smile, "Well, would you marry me now?" To which he replied, "Certainly, you should know that."[31] Because she was not yet divorced, there was a long period of courtship, in which Nela accompanied Artur on some of his concert tours and in which they were separated because of their different activities. (She returned to Dresden to her studies or visited her family in Warsaw; he continued to meet his commitments). Finally, her divorce was granted and they were free to marry.

Nela met Artur in Paris, and they announced their engagement. Parties were given by friends of the great pianist, and she was accepted wholeheartedly. Her training and experience in society equipped her beautifully for her role in his life. She was completely at ease with everyone and was admired for her elegance, sophistication, and charm.

With Nela's help, Artur Rubinstein had approached the moment of truth. He realized that he had relied too heavily on his innate musical gifts and not practiced diligently enough. He explained his shortcomings in his earlier playing this way: "When I was young, I was lazy. I had talent, but there were many things in life more important than practicing. Good food, good cigars, great wines, women . . . When I played in the Latin countries— Spain, France, Italy—they loved me because of my temperament. When I played in Russia there was no trouble because my namesake, Anton Rubinstein, no relation, had conditioned the audiences there to wrong notes. But when I played in England or America, they felt that because they paid their money they were entitled to hear all the notes. I dropped many notes in those days, maybe thirty per cent, and they felt they were being cheated . . . I was spoiled and I admit it."[32]

Abram Chasins said, "At long last he met the right woman, Aniela Mlynarski, a sensitive beauty with good hard sense. When they married during the early thirties, after Rubinstein had batted around the world since the turn of the century, he began to assume the full responsibilities and disciplines of a serious musician and performer. For five years, he buckled down to the hardest work he had ever done."[33] Rubinstein, in discussing this later, said, "Was it to be said of me that I *could* have been a great pianist? Was this the kind of legacy to leave to my wife and children?"[34]

Because of the long waiting period in Paris for a marriage license, they were married in London in July 1932. Nela's life was about to become filled with all the excitement that her husband generated. Aside from her extraordinary ability to adapt to this frenetic, glamorous life (her husband had enormous energy and drive), she was equipped with attributes that made her particularly helpful to Artur. She understood the problems of a concert career and helped him to cope. She was a superb cook, in addition to being a capable and charming hostess (and he was one of the world's gourmets). She was a warm, down-to-earth person, adding stability to their family life. (They had four children: Eva was born in Buenos Aires, Paul in Warsaw, and Alina and John in the United States.) She was independent in her thinking, deciding what was best for her family and herself, not only concerning herself with her family's physical welfare, but handling finances and arrangements. There were times when she had the wisdom and the courage to let her husband proceed on tour by himself. (It usually was when she was needed elsewhere.) Nela was adventurous, yet competent. She flew in an airplane and drove a car before Artur did, encouraging him to do the same. Being the wife of a famous performing artist is always a juggling act. Her friend, now Halina Rodzinski, the conductor's wife, said, "Few realize that how a woman performs as an artist's wife is an art, one unfortunately not taught at any university, academy, or conservatory. There is so much to know and to do, things for which one's entire life is a preparation and a continuous schooling. On the surface, being the wife of a conductor appears glamorous . . . But in short order this glamorous life develops a tedium of its own. There is so much of *it*, and so little time for one's self. And paramount is the constant demand that one be a happy and loving wife . . ."[35]

In 1937, the famous manager Sol Hurok offered Rubinstein a tour of 20 concerts in America. He had not been well-received there 14 years earlier, and had vowed not to return. However, Hurok convinced him to accept, and Nela, who had always dreamed of this moment, was overjoyed. They found that the musical climate in the United States had improved considerably. There were many new and excellent orchestras, generously supported by a growing number of lovers of classical music; institutions of higher education had added fine music departments; and summer music festivals were springing up all over. Artur's concerts proved to be hugely successful and the Rubinsteins and the American public became an item. They soon became American citizens. They had one home in Paris and one in California, still making long tours elsewhere, including the Orient and Australia. They also kept an apartment in New York City, because of Artur's frequent trips there. In winters, he was usually in the East and Midwest, and in the summers and during vacations he was back home in California.

During the Nazi occupation, their Paris home was taken over by the Germans. They spent the war years in Brentwood, near Los Angeles, surrounded by old friends who had fled Europe and by new friends, many of whom were famous Hollywood stars (Nela and Artur loved the movies). They happily settled in, but were worried about their friends and relatives in Europe. (Members of Artur's family who had stayed in Lodz and Warsaw had been killed horribly by the Nazis.) When the war in the Pacific broke out, Nela became active at the canteen in the military camp nearby, and spent one hour each day in a designated booth on the alert for signs of enemy planes.

After the war, they became concerned about Palestine and the Jewish refugee problem attributable to British policy. Those in power in Britain (many of whom were antisemitic) were anxious to please the Arabs, and seemed callous to the plight of the Jews. This began Artur's commitment to the state of Israel. He gave concerts every year to help its orchestra; he gave a chair of musicology at the Hebrew University in Jerusalem; and he established the Artur Rubinstein Piano Competition, among other philanthropic activities.

The other immediate concern of the Rubinsteins was their house in Paris, which was still occupied by probable collaborators. On investigating the situation, they found that no one wanted to help them regain their house. After a long period, the couple who lived there decided to get a divorce and move out. Although the tenants had not paid any rent, the Rubinsteins had to give them about $3,000 to get them to leave. After much reconstruction and redecorating, the Rubinsteins moved back in. When they returned to California, Nela decided that it was time to buy a larger house there, and found a small estate on Tower Road in Beverly Hills. They all loved living there, but after seven years, they accepted an offer for the house and moved to New York. Their time was divided between Paris and New York, with frequent trips to Israel.

In 1958, Nela and Artur decided to visit the Mlynarski home in Warsaw, where many of Nela's family members had returned. It was with great relief that she found that Warsaw had been completely rebuilt and life was full and thriving again.

When Artur was in his early 80s, he developed macula degeneration in both eyes. He gave his last concert in London at Wigmore Hall when he was in his late 80s. Nela, of course, remained completely devoted to him. She taught him the joys of radio and encouraged him to write a sequel to *My Young Years*, a memoir of his early life. In 1973, he had hired a young Englishwoman, Annabelle Whitestone, to make concert arrangements and accompany him on his tours. When he decided to write *My Many Years*, he asked her to help him type, organize, and edit it. He became close to her, and by the time he was 90, he was dependent on and grateful to her for making life enjoyable. When he was 92, he said, "Now suddenly, Miss Whitestone has revealed to me all the glorious chamber music of Mozart, Haydn, and Beethoven with all sorts of combinations of string and wind instruments of which I have never even heard . . ."[36] And, "Thanks to the devotion of Miss Whitestone . . . I have been able to visit again my beloved Venice and Rome and even Israel."[37] In an interview when he was ninety-five, he told of his deep love for Annabelle. One can imagine Nela's feelings.

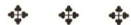

Galina (Pavlovna) Vishnevskaya Rostropovich (1926-) was born in Leningrad, but when she was six weeks old, her parents sent her to live with her father's mother. She lived with her grandparents, an aunt, and an uncle. Her mother was young and beautiful, but wild and irresponsible. When her father was not at home, her mother would have other men visit her. Actually, the only time that Galina lived with her parents was when she visited them in their dacha outside Leningrad when she was 4 years old. Her few memories of them focused on their indifference to her, her mother's passion for singing, her father's rich, dramatic tenor, and her own love of singing. (She was told that, when she was 3 years old, she had voice tones that were amazingly mature for a child.) One night her parents had a violent quarrel, after which they decided to separate. She was asked to choose between them; She chose her father, who immediately sent her to his mother in Kronstadt, a small fortress town two hours by boat from Leningrad. The little girl was withdrawn and cold at first, but soon their devotion and warmth reached her, and she was able to relax and have deep feelings for others.

Galina grew to love her grandmother and her grandfather. They were very good to her, perhaps even pampering her. Their home was in a building of communal apartments where there was no privacy and no secrets.

Her schooling was rather ordinary, but she loved to read, which helped her make up for deficiencies in the curriculum. The one activity that always interested her was singing. It was in the early years in school that she met her first singing teacher, a man who was madly in love with music, and he introduced her to the joys of performing. When she visited her mother for her 10th birthday, she was given a gramophone and a record album of the opera *Eugene Onegin*. This was the start of her love affair with opera; at this point in her life, her career was chosen, her path was set. She began to devour works written by Tolstoy, Pushkin, Lermontov, and Balzac, among others. In addition, she studied ballet and drama for two years. This was a world to which she could escape when she could not bear life around her. Stalin, who was at the height of his power, had started his terrible purges. Everyone was under pressure to *love* Stalin. Turning in your friends, neighbors, or even family members who dissented became the thing to do. It was, to say the least, an unpleasant time.

Her father was an ardent communist, and had participated in the suppression of a rebellion in 1921 in which he killed his own people. Galina always felt that this affected him for the rest of his life. Drinking vodka was a national pastime that destroyed members of her family. Her father took to drinking, which made him very mean. Although he was educated and intelligent, he was ruined by vodka, his passion for the Communist party, and his guilt about its methods. Occasionally, he remembered Galina and would have his mother bring her to see him, but this did not happen often. In 1941, he invited his 14-year-old daughter to spend her vacation with him. The Germans advanced at a time when her father was out of town. Alone, she managed to get on a bus and traveled night and day to safety. It was a time of great bloodshed and deprivation. People were starving. Her parents were of no help. Her mother had a new husband and had settled in the eastern part of Russia. Her father, that great fighter for communism, had a civilian job in Kronstadt and was living with his mistress and her children. He stole food for them, but paid no attention to his own family which was in great need.

In 1942, her grandmother died. The last opportunity to be evacuated occurred soon after. The family left, but Galina, who was in a state of depression, decided to stay where she was, alone and with almost no food. Her father decided to leave Kronstadt with his mistress Tatyana and her children, but not to take Tatyana's old grandmother with them. Without any thought of the consequences, he brought her to Galina and left. The old woman died soon after, and Galina again was completely alone. She stayed there in a daze, getting weaker and weaker. Spring arrived, and a team started to search for survivors. They found her in bad condition, and took her to a government barracks, where she gradually recovered. Her job there was to watch for flares, fires, and explosions. Although she was physically cared for, her artistic life was empty. But when it was discovered that she could sing, she was called upon to perform at the Navy Officers' Club. This was the first step back into the world of music. She continued this work for a year and a half, until the Russians broke the blockade of Leningrad, which is where she went after receiving a discharge.

Galina was determined to get on with her career. At first she was hired as an assistant lighting technician at the Vyborg Palace of Culture. She was able to study and attend concerts. In 1944, she met and married a sailor, George Vishnevsky, but this was a mistake and they parted. She was accepted into the Leningrad District Operetta Theater, and quickly became one of their soloists. Here she learned the ropes of performing on stage. Mark Ilich Rubin, a violinist and the director of the operetta troupe, fell in love with her and they married. He was 40 and she was 18; the difference in age and experience gave her a sense of security and family. She gave birth to a son, who died at two and a half months.

Just about this time, her father's new wife (he had several) visited Galina and said he had been arrested and convicted for telling a joke about Stalin. His sentence was imprisonment for 10 years. Although by this time she felt nothing for him and was not affected emotionally by his plight, that he was in prison would, if known, affect Galina's career. This secret kept her on guard and apprehensive. In filling out forms, she wrote that her father was declared missing in action during the war, praying that this lie would not be discovered.

The situation with respect to the music world was terrible. Leaders of the party, who generally were musically ignorant, were the ones who made the decisions about the merit of music and of musicians. Their judgment was based strictly on whether or not the ideals of the party were served. Stalin and the Communist Party were to be glorified. Sergei Prokofiev and Dmitri Shostakovich, geniuses both, were objects of vilification. Great works were buried for years. One had to tread carefully.

Galina continued to rise in the world of opera. She studied voice with Vera Nikolayevna Garina, who, at 80, was still able to demonstrate techniques of singing. She helped improve her student's voice to an incredible degree in a short time, so that Galina was soon ready to sing the important arias in the great operas. She was accepted into the world-famous Bolshoi Theater in Moscow, becoming one of its top prima donnas. As soon as she became famous, officials from the Ministry of Culture insisted that she attend and sing at government receptions and other events. These were usually held at embassies, the Metropol restaurant, and, for more important events, in the Kremlin in St. George's Hall. It was supposed to be an honor, but for Galina it was degrading. By the time the artist would be called on to perform, the men would be drunk, crude, noisy, and boisterous. These men were of the large, privileged, ruling class, with special luxuries about which the ordinary citizen could only guess.

Things went from bad to worse when Stalin died. Salaries and benefits, which had not been great even for the leading singers, were cut. In spite of all the honors, Galina and Mark still lived in a communal apartment and with few luxuries.

At a reception she was introduced to one of the greatest cellists of this century, Mstislav Rostropovich, who was recognized as an exceptional talent. He accompanied her home, flattering her outrageously. By this time, she had been married to Mark for 10 years. Sometime after this meeting, she was sent to Prague, Czechoslovakia, to sing in *Eugene Onegin*. At her hotel, she again met Rostropovich (called "Slava") who invited her to join him for dinner. Thereafter, they were inseparable, both completely involved in the other, magnets irresistibly drawn to each other. Later Slava said, "It was love, an explosion of love. I was happy to be alive!"[38] After four days, they decided that, when they returned to Moscow, they would marry.

Meanwhile, the Ministry of Culture sent Galina from Prague to Belgrade, Yugoslavia, to perform. She was to accompany the government delegation, which included Nicholas A. Bulganin, Nikita S. Khrushchev, and Anastas I. Mikoyan. There, at the Soviet embassy she met Bulganin, chairman of the Council of Ministers (chief of state), and Khrushchev, general secretary of the Central Committee of the Communist Party. Bulganin fell for Galina, and proceeded to shower her with flowers and attention. (This was to be a long-term infatuation on his part. His feeling for Galina was known by powerful members of the government, who were careful not to offend her.)

As soon as she returned to Moscow, she told Mark about Slava. Mark tried to dissuade her, but Galina knew that Slava was the man with whom she wanted to spend the rest of her life. She left Mark and joined Slava. Because her marriage had never been officially registered (she and Mark were married during the war, when no one had the time or the patience for paperwork), she did not have to obtain a divorce. Slava and she were married at the Registry of Acts of Civil Status in 1955. It has been a difficult marriage, partially because of his "roving eye," but a long-lasting one; they are devoted to each other. At first, they shared a two-room communal apartment with his mother and sister. Within the year, they were able to buy a four-room apartment that they did not have to share. At first, they could not obtain a permit to live there because each Soviet citizen was only entitled to a living space of nine square yards (not including the housemaid). Galina was pregnant, and therefore they were entitled to 27 square yards, but the apartment was 100 square yards. However, on the New Year's Day 1956, Bulganin arrived to celebrate with them. This visit became known at once, and the permit was delivered to them the next day. Their first daughter, Olga, was born on March 18, 1956. Their second daughter, Elena, was born on June 22, 1958. (Both daughters are musically talented.)

Galina was a fighter, accustomed to triumphing over adversity. She had learned the hard way to stand up for her principles and her rights. Slava was an idealist, somewhat naive, with tremendous enthusiasm and energy. Together, they made a great team, both dedicated to the beauty of music and the integrity of musicians. This was especially important at a time when the Soviet world of the arts was deteriorating rapidly. Galina was acknowledged in opera circles as a great singer, the Bolshoi's top soprano. Slava was an internationally celebrated cellist. In the late '60s, he began to be appreciated as a conductor. One of his first successes was conducting *Eugene Onegin* at the Bolshoi Opera with his wife in the role of Tatyana. In addition, he was a fine pianist, often accompanying his wife in recitals. They both were sent on tours to many countries, including the United States. (Although they were paid large fees in these countries, the money, except for a small amount given them for expenses, was turned over to the Soviet government. They did manage to bring back some material things, however.)

Aside from their great talents, their most impressive contribution was their bold fight for artistic freedom. The Central Committee, in 1932, had decreed that all creative artists' associations be dissolved. To replace them, large arts organizations, such as the Composers' Union, were formed by the party to control the artists. At a time when ordinary people were starving in the Soviet Union, the government treated artists with special rations and other luxuries so they would serve as contented propagandists for the Communist Party. The reign of terror was at its height, and it was particularly dangerous to disobey the powers that be.

Dmitri Shostakovich, a composer of genius caliber, was an important example of the treatment received in the USSR at that time. When his opera, *Lady Macbeth*, was criticized as Formalist and "noise," he fought back. He wrote an article in which he said, "In the past, I have been subjected to powerful attacks from critics, mainly for Formalism. I did not accept those reproaches then, nor do I accept them now. I have never been a Formalist, and I shall never be one. To defame any work as Formalist on the grounds that the idiom of that composition is complex and sometimes not immediately understandable, is to be unconscionably frivolous."[39] He had become famous internationally, and his music was performed by the finest orchestras and under the batons of the greatest conductors; yet, the party proceeded to cut him down to the size that they decided was appropriate. Mediocrity, not elitism, made those in authority comfortable. They began a systematic campaign to tear him down. He did not respond verbally or in writing, but into his compositions he poured all his deep emotions about the tragic loss of freedom for the individual. His *Fifth Symphony* communicated everything he wanted to say. (Fortunately, those in charge did not understand the underlying message of his work.) By this time, he had learned to lie to the members of the party about its meaning, and the symphony was accepted.

Yet, in 1948, the Central Committee came out fully against formalism, accusing not only Shostakovich but others, including Sergei Prokofiev. (The term *Formalism* seems to have been a catch-all term to be used for convenience.) The works of these brilliant composers were banned for a few years. They were not allowed to teach at the conservatories for a while, and were, in fact, deprived of a decent income. Although Shostakovich continued to compose with great success, and much of his music was performed to enormous acclaim outside of the USSR, he received very little of the royalties, the bulk of it going to the state.

He and Rostropovich became fast friends, and in 1954, Slava introduced him to Galina. From then on, they were all close. Galina and Slava fought for him and, when needed, helped him financially. (He returned all that he had borrowed.) In 1958, when the First International Tchaikovsky Competition in Moscow was organized, he was made chairman of the steering committee. The attention the outside world focused on this event forced the party to pay homage to their great musicians. A decree was issued in which the Soviet leaders admitted that they had been wrong to persecute these gifted people. Throughout the years that Galina and Slava were in Russia, they both worked to help Shostakovich in every way possible.

Another dear friend who was the recipient of their love and support was Alexander Solzhenitsyn, the famous writer. Slava had met him in 1968. Solzhenitsyn was very ill, and lived in a village where he had a damp little cottage and very little else. He was about to be expelled from the Writers Union, an act that would take away his rights. Slava and Galina invited him to stay with them in a guest cottage on grounds near their dacha. He gratefully accepted. He had written his first novel, *One Day in the Life of Ivan Denisovich*, which made him famous throughout the Western world. At first, it was well-received by Soviet authorities, but they soon realized the effect that his writing was having on the people. He had awakened their consciences. He also wrote *The First Circle* and *Cancer Ward*. He was not able to get *Cancer Ward* published in his own country but it was published and distributed widely in the West. It dealt with the typical party bureaucrat, and, of course, all the bureaucrats saw themselves in this role and did not like the image at all. In 1970, the author won the Nobel Prize, and attacks on him became even more pronounced.

Slava told Galina that he was planning to send a letter in defense of Solzhenitsyn to the newspapers *Pravda, Izvestia, Literaturnaya Gazeta*, and to the publication *Soviet Culture*, and Galina warned him that this would really arouse the anger of the party against them. Slava offered her a divorce, in name only, so that she would not have to share in the reprisals. But she refused the divorce, and they worked together on the letter, and continued trying to get *Cancer Ward* published. Needless to say, the letter was not published in the Soviet Union, but the foreign press was glad to print and distribute it. He had written about the Soviet censorship of the arts, the limiting of individual freedom, and the power over the arts held by people with little if any knowledge of the arts. The mind-set of Soviet officials was illustrated in his account of the following event: When on tour in Vienna, the couple dined with Vladimir Semyonov, the head of the Soviet delegation to the disarmament commission. With his connections and power, Galina thought he might certainly be able to help. She brought up the subject of Solzhenitsyn. After much conversation, Semyonov asked, "Does he love Lenin?"[40] She realized immediately that it was of no use to discuss it further.

Solzhenitsyn was sent into exile in 1973. In 1984, after the Rostropoviches had left the Soviet Union, they received a letter from him. He said, ". . . Without your protection and support, I simply would not have survived those years

Wives and Lovers

. . . And you tended my solitude with tact, you didn't even tell me of the growing constraints and harassment you were subjected to. You created an atmosphere I would never have dreamed possible in the Soviet Union . . . You paid a cruel price for it, especially Galya, who lost her theater forever . . .[41]

By protecting and befriending Solzhenitsyn, the Rostropoviches had antagonized the party, and from that point on it was all downhill. The first indication that the persecution had started occurred when a film about Galina was canceled. Slava was removed from the Bolshoi, and not allowed to accept foreign tours. Moscow orchestras were instructed not to engage him to conduct, nor to allow him to perform in solo concerts in their halls. This humiliation gradually escalated for him to the point that he was forced to accept offers in the provinces, a terrible step down for him. Galina was not targeted as drastically. She was still in demand at the Bolshoi and received the highest award in the Soviet Union, the Order of Lenin. However, her name was never mentioned in the media in her own country.

After a year of this treatment, Rostropovich told a Western journalist about it. His friends became aware of their plight. When the San Francisco Symphony, conducted by Seiji Ozawa, went on tour to the Soviet Union, the cellist was invited to play. He played so joyously and beautifully that Galina realized that it was necessary for his soul to leave so that he could perform with great orchestras in a free atmosphere, and with wonderful audiences. She finally said to him, "Slava, . . . Enough! I have no intention of pretending any longer that nothing is going on. Sit down and write to Brezhnev, requesting permission for the whole family to go abroad for two years."[42] While waiting under the greatest tension for permission to leave, Sen. Edward Kennedy's secretary called to say that the senator had told Leonid Brezhnev that the American people were very upset about Slava's situation and that he hoped that Mr. Brezhnev would expedite his departure. They found out later that Leonard and Felicia Bernstein, who were Slava's friends, had called the senator when they heard he was going to Moscow, and suggested that he intervene in order to help the renowned cellist. Brezhnev agreed and the Rostropovich family left for the United States where Slava was scheduled to receive an honorary doctorate of music at Harvard University. Galina was 47 years old and in her prime. It was 1974.

They settled in the United States and continued their careers. They live in Washington, D.C., New York, Paris, and Lausanne. In 1977, Slava was appointed music director of the National Symphony Orchestra in Washington, D.C. He and Galina also became members of the faculty at the prestigious Curtis Institute of Music in Philadelphia.

In March 1978, Slava and Galina were informed that their citizenship had been revoked by the Soviet government. This was a big shock to them. In spite of everything, they still loved their country. However, when Gorbachev came to power, their citizenship was restored. In 1990, Mstislav Rostropovich was invited to give a series of concerts in his native country and he accepted.

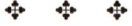

Felicia Montealegre Cohn Bernstein (1922-1978) was born in Costa Rica. She was the oldest of three sisters. Their mother was Clemencia Montealegre, who was Costa Rican, a devout Catholic, and from a long line of aristocratic ancestors. Their father was Roy Elwood Cohn, an American, the son of a Jewish father and an Episcopalian mother. When Felicia was two months old, the family moved to Santiago, Chile, where she was raised. Her father was a mining engineer and the head of the American Smelting and Refining Company. As a result, her family life was one of privilege and luxury. Felicia learned to speak several languages at home, and was educated in a convent school run by British nuns. When she was 21, she decided to choose citizenship in her father's country, and pledged her allegiance to the United States at the embassy in Santiago. She had really wanted to study acting, but her parents did not approve. Instead, she studied music and, when she was 23, was sent to New York to study with a great pianist and friend of the family, Claudio Arrau. He believed she had exceptional talent, and was guiding her toward a concert career. Hers had been a structured, ordered life and, when she arrived in New York in 1945, she was ready for adventure. She enrolled for an acting course at the New School in New York City and assumed the name Felicia Montealegre (her mother's maiden name).

In February 1946, Mr. Arrau invited her to accompany him to a performance of the *Brahms Concerto I*, in which he was to be the soloist with the New York Philharmonic Orchestra, to be conducted by Leonard Bernstein. After the performance, her teacher and his wife had a reception at their home in Forest Hills, N.Y. Leonard Bernstein also attended the party. She had seen him conduct at the City Center, and was extremely impressed. She told friends that she was going to marry him. When they met at the party, they immediately became absorbed in each other. From then on, they were an item. Felicia had an apartment on Washington Place near Lenny's, which was on West 10th Street. They saw each other regularly at first, but their courtship was not smooth. Lenny was torn between his homosexual and heterosexual desires, and between his conflicting needs for freedom and for a stable, traditional marriage with children. (It is not clear whether or not Felicia knew of his sexual inclinations at that time. Perhaps she knew and did not want to cope with the problem.) His emotional ups and downs made her unhappy. In addition, Lenny had a hectic schedule and did not stay in steady communication with her, adding to her insecurity.

Felicia had decided soon after arriving in New York to stop working toward a career as a concert pianist and to concentrate on becoming an actress. It was not long before she was recognized for her talent. She was described by several who knew her as a beautiful, elegant, and intelligent woman, forceful in a quiet way, yet friendly and frank, with a wonderful sense of humor. Stephen Sondheim said, "She had exquisite taste. She was a class act."[43] Felicia was anxious to work in films and, in 1946, she went out to Hollywood with Lenny. (He had been asked to write a score for a picture.) While they were vacationing in

Mexico, they announced their engagement. They truly loved each other, but other factors drew them together as well, and made marriage to each other a worthwhile goal; Bernstein knew that it was good for his career to be married, and Felicia knew that being married to this incredibly brilliant, famous, well-connected musician would certainly help her career. The wedding was set for June 1947, but they had no specific date. Felicia stayed in Hollywood, while Lenny went on his conducting tours in the United States and with his sister Shirley in Europe and Palestine. He was not due to return to the United States until June. June came and went. In July, Felicia found out, probably from Shirley, that Lenny was going to be at Tanglewood for the first concert on July 24. She arrived there, stayed with Lenny in a cottage at the Blantyre estate, and was introduced to everyone as his fiancée. It was difficult for her, nevertheless. There was uncomfortable jockeying for position with his sister and with his former teacher and current assistant, Helen Coates. Leonard constantly found fault with Felicia. At the end of the summer, the engagement was ended; no one seems to know all the reasons. There were one or two reconciliations after that, and they remained friends, but she began dating again, as did he.

By 1949, she had become well-known as a television actress, receiving excellent reviews and commanding high fees. In 1950, when she was understudying Eva Gabor in a Broadway play, she met a handsome and fine actor, Richard Hart, who was playing opposite Gabor. She fell madly in love. (Shirley, who had become her friend and had kept in contact during this period, thought he resembled Lenny.) Although Richard was married and had three children, he and Felicia began to live together. The one unpleasant aspect of their life together was that he was a heavy drinker who sometimes became violent when drunk.

In the spring, Lenny went on tour in Israel and Europe for several months. Shirley, who was in New York, kept him up-to-date with news of Felicia. He wrote back to her, "How strange that you should have written just now of Felicia! Ever since I left America, she has occupied my thoughts uninterruptedly, and I have come to a fabulously clear realization of what she means—and has always meant—to me. I have loved her, despite all the blocks that have consistently impaired my loving-mechanism, truly and deeply from the first . . . I would marry her tomorrow . . ."[44] He went on to say he was jealous of Hart, who he felt was wrong for her, and that he had written to apologize for his treatment of her during their engagement. He asked for news of her. Felicia, though, was very much in love with Hart and planned to marry him when he became free.

In 1951, Lenny and Shirley returned by ship from another tour in Europe. When they arrived in New York in January 1951, Felicia met them at the pier, and they all went to have drinks at a friend's house. While there, she checked her telephone messages and found that Hart was in a coma at the hospital. She rushed to be with him, and a few hours later, he died in her arms. The media reported that he had died of a massive heart attack, but there was a persistent rumor that he had committed suicide. He had been very ill with cirrhosis of the liver, but had continued drinking. Shirley advised Lenny to help Felicia through her mourning. The couple grew close again. He had planned to take a year off and spend it composing in Mexico. He departed, and Felicia went to Europe. She knew that he wanted to marry her and she soon decided in her own mind that she would accept. But she wanted to prove her independence first, knowing that he was completely involved in his work in Mexico.

Bernstein began to vacillate again, but on June 4, 1951 Serge Koussevitzky, the great conductor of the Boston Symphony Orchestra who had guided him and greatly helped his career, died. Lenny located Felicia in Europe, telling her of his need for her, and she arrived home in July. She immediately headed for Tanglewood and Lenny. After a few days, they announced their engagement. He was still ambivalent, but, with the help of his brother Burton, Lenny finally realized that Felicia was very important to him. Felicia was everything he was not: elegantly cultured, fluent in several languages, perfectly at ease in society, always tastefully groomed, with a calm demeanor, keeping her feelings to herself. She also had the admirable ability to face difficulties and to make decisions. In contrast, Lenny was wildly emotional, often overly demonstrative, showing his emotions without inhibition, exciting and excitable, interested in everything and everybody, impulsive and unpredictable, with very little sense of moderation. His music and his career were his first priorities. Their contrasting traits balanced their life together. Despite these differences, they had many goals and beliefs in common, which they each expressed in a different way. They made a fascinating combination. They loved each other, but the doubts in each of their minds were still there. Nevertheless, on September 9, 1951, they were married by two rabbis in Temple Mishkan Tefila, of which the Bernstein family were members. (Felicia had converted to Judaism.) The young couple then drove to Mexico, where they stayed for several ecstatic months, finishing his sabbatical year there.

It was a good marriage in the beginning and their family grew nicely. On September 8, 1952, their daughter Jamie was born, and they were overjoyed. Lenny's doubts about the marriage dissolved. Felicia soon went back to acting, although her husband's career and the family came first in her life. They had moved to a nine-room duplex apartment in the Osborne on West 57th Street in New York City. It was across the street from Carnegie Hall. They hired a nurse for the baby. Helen Coates, Lenny's former piano teacher and now his assistant, lived and had her office in the same building. Felicia had decided that she would manage their household and personal affairs (and even cut her husband's hair), organize their entertaining, and listen to Lenny's plans and concerns, sometimes advising and cautioning him when she thought it necessary. At times, she would act as his prompter or critic. Later she had important speaking roles in some of his performances. Although she joined him on his travels, she had some career commitments of her own in New York. They both enjoyed traveling together; they had fun and had none of the family problems that arose at home. In New York, his sister and brother were in and out of the house all the time (Lenny was close to them and included them whenever he could.) The baby had a nanny, preventing Felicia from spending much time with little Jamie, and Shirley, Burton, and Lenny had their inside humor and Bernsteinian ways. For these reasons, Felicia felt alone, and first she resented not having Lenny and Jamie to herself. But as time went on, she became a vibrant part of the Bernstein family. They all enjoyed and appreciated each other.

On July 7, 1955, Felicia gave birth to their son, Alexander Serge. In 1961, the family moved to a large duplex apartment on Park Avenue. The lower floor was the family's living quarters. The penthouse floor had a library and elegant rooms for entertaining as befitted their exalted status. Felicia furnished it tastefully. She had developed a passion for hunting for bargains in antiques and contemporary pieces. At the same time, she had started studying painting and sculpting. Her career seemed not to occupy her as much as it had, although she occasionally went back to acting. She concentrated on her family, entertaining, Lenny's career, painting, and music. Then came Nina, their third child, on February 28, 1962. The family was complete.

Felicia was a steadying influence on Lenny. She had some strict standards that he needed. He depended on her for her loving care, guidance, common sense, taste, and moral support. In return, he deeply loved and admired her. However, she may have unwittingly caused an incident that involved the group called the Black Panthers and caused him problems. Felicia was an ardent member of the American Civil Liberties Union. She and her husband held the same political beliefs (Lenny campaigned for Robert Kennedy, they were both against the Vietnam War, and Felicia campaigned actively for Eugene McCarthy). Felicia thought the amount of the bail set for the Black Panthers was unfairly high, and that they were being held too long (10 months) before their trial. But the Black Panthers were a revolutionary and violent group, and the public was appalled by them. Felicia decided to raise money for the Black Panthers by having a meeting at their home on Park Avenue. Unfortunately, she made the mistake of serving cocktails and canapés and turning it into a party. There were 90 guests.

Tom Wolfe, the writer, was there and wrote an article about it for *The New Yorker*. This became part of his book *Radical Chic and Mau-Mauing the Flak Catchers*, in which he showed the incongruity of the Black Panthers mixing with a "rich, chic" crowd in a room with butlers and maids. Charlotte Curtis, who was society editor of *The New York Times*, also reported about it. It became a famous event that angered Jews in the United States and in Israel because of the Panthers' extreme antisemitism and anti-Zionism. It also landed the couple on J. Edgar Hoover's list of subversives. Lenny, much to his credit, never mentioned the fact that it was his wife's idea, and forever afterward, the term "radical chic" was identified with him. Felicia never again came out publicly for her causes but worked for them unobtrusively. (One of her major causes was Amnesty International in Chile. Others were Israeli student scholarships, the Church World Service, and a boys' school in Greece). Later, when Felicia died, Lenny accused the Federal Bureau of Investigation of harassing them with hate letters and press articles. For three years, he repeatedly tried to get information under the Freedom of Information Act, but was not successful. He said he was well aware that his phone was tapped by the F.B.I. and the Central Intelligence Agency.

Because of his increasingly frequent and less discreet homosexual relationships (of which even his children were becoming aware), Felicia finally gave him an ultimatum, demanding that he give up these liaisons or leave. (In earlier years, her art teacher, Daniel Schwartz, had asked her why women stay married to homosexuals. She said she could not understand making so much out of the issue of sexuality, and that there were other things about her husband to which she was very attracted. She intimated that she had had boyfriends [not necessarily affairs] and that was life. Schwartz thought she was covering up her true feelings, but that she enjoyed the kind of life that had opened up to her through her marriage.) Evidently, she now had suffered enough hurt and embarrassment. In 1976, she discovered that Lenny was having a serious affair that could threaten her marriage. He responded to her ultimatum by leaving her to live with his lover, Tom Cothran.

Nevertheless, Lenny still loved Felicia and was riddled with guilt. He was unable to get along with Tom. In fact, it became apparent that perhaps Felicia was the only one who could deal with his eccentricities and self-indulgence. He engaged Felicia to perform in a concert at Lincoln Center, and, a month after that, with much persuasion on his part, they were reconciled. They had moved to a 12-room apartment in the desirable Dakota on Central Park West and 72nd street in New York City and had a weekend home in Fairfield, Conn. They appeared to be happy, but Felicia was not. She not only had terribly upsetting marital problems, but had developed cancer and was in the process of coping with that. She had had a mastectomy in 1974. She was able to regain her health to a large degree, but, in July 1977, found out that she had lung cancer. She was very ill and in pain, and Lenny spent every available moment caring for her. In November she had an operation to remove the pericardium.

In January 1978, despite the danger and her baldness from chemotherapy (she wore a Russian fur hat to hide it), she journeyed to Vienna to be with Lenny for his revival of *Fidelio*. In February, Lenny gave a party at the Hotel Sacher in Vienna for her 56th birthday and the anniversary of their meeting. After traveling with him to Milan, she flew back alone to New York to continue her chemotherapy. In her last months, Lenny bought her a house in East Hampton, Long Island, so that she could look out at the ocean. She moved there three weeks before her death. Because she had recently returned to the Catholic church, the Monsignor Puma drove out to hold a mass in her bedroom. Felicia died on June 16, 1978, with her husband and her sister-in-law Shirley at her bedside. Lenny was devastated and never fully recovered. After she died, he said, ". . . I had fantasies about Felicia, and guilt about whether I was in any way responsible . . . and does science know, how does medicine *really* know that cancer can't be caused by some great agony, some great emotional stress . . . You can't know. I mean, such a deep-rooted guilt at the death of your most beloved person in the world which, for me, she was. The only person in the world, unique. The most beautiful, the most gracious, the funniest, the smartest; she could also be the most vulgar, she could be the most racée, a wonderful mother, a marvelous wife and companion. Irreplaceable . . ."⁴⁵

He mourned deeply for her. It was not until the following Christmas that he was able to find some enjoyment in life. After Felicia's death, Leonard Bernstein had no one to control him. He became extremely self-indulgent, leading a wild, unorthodox life, until he died in 1990.

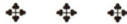

Marta (Martita) Montañez Casals (1937-), a gifted cellist, was married to Pablo Casals, the great Spanish cellist and conductor.

Casals left his beloved Catalonia in Spain at the end of the Spanish Civil War in 1939 when the dictator, Francisco Franco, and his fascist supporters entered Barcelona. He settled in Prades, on the French side of the Pyrenees, and continued to work toward the return of the Spanish republic. He had been giving benefit concerts to raise funds for the Musicians' Committee to Aid Spanish Democracy, an organization of which he was honorary chairman. The committee included Albert Einstein, Serge Koussevitzky, and Virgil Thomson. When Casals arrived in France and saw the terrible plight of the Spanish refugees, he began organizing aid for the flood of refugees who were confined in horrendous camps. (France was under the rule of fascist Daladier.) He continued to give as many benefit concerts as possible in the unoccupied zone of southern France and in Switzerland. Prades was his home for 17 years, throughout World War II, and afterward. Through it all, he continued doing all he could to help his countrymen. So passionate was he in his opposition to the Franco regime in Spain that he refused to appear in countries that, under the Non-Intervention Agreement, recognized the fascist Spanish government. (Because of his admiration for President Kennedy, he made an exception and appeared at the White House in a concert of chamber music in 1961.) Casals vowed that he would not return to his own country until democracy was restored.

Alexander Schneider, the Russian-American violinist, conductor, and teacher, and Mieczyslaw Horszowski, the brilliant Polish pianist, had persuaded their close friend, Casals, to come out of retirement and commemorate the 200th anniversary of Johann Sebastian Bach's death with a festival in Prades. In 1950, the first Prades Festival took place. Casals was the music director and conductor; "Sasha" Schneider supervised the arrangements and was the concertmaster; the soloists were violinists Joseph Szigeti and Isaac Stern, and pianists Horszowski, Rudolph Serkin, and Eugene Istomin. The proceeds went to help the Spanish refugees. The program was a stupendous success, so much so that it was decided that it would become an annual event.

Pablo Casals and Martita met at the second Prades Festival in France in 1951. She was a lovely 14-year-old-cellist. Casals was a 75-year-old celebrity. Her uncle, Rafael Montañez, brought his niece from Puerto Rico to attend that second Prades Festival. He was a friend of the Defilló family (Casals' mother, Pilar Defilló, had been born in Puerto Rico when it was under Spanish rule), and asked to visit the great man. Casals was charmed by the young girl even then. After the festival, Montañez and his niece returned to their home in Puerto Rico. Three years later, her uncle wrote to Casals, bringing him up-to-date on Martita's music studies (she had been at the Mannes School in New York with Professor Lieff Rosanoff, who had been a student of Casals' in the early 1900s). Montañez suggested that Martita go to Prades to study with the master. Casals agreed.

When she arrived, Casals saw that the teenager had blossomed into an intelligent and beautiful woman with a lively personality and a great sense of humor. Martita stayed at the house of a Catalan family that he knew. Her lessons were a joy to both. She was, according to Casals, one of the best pupils he ever had—disciplined, talented, and easily and totally able to absorb his teaching. Although she applied herself seriously to her work, her bright outlook and happy personality lightened the atmosphere. Casals felt responsible for her, but she was, in fact, self-sufficient and helpful to him. With her great facility for languages (soon conquering Catalan), she was able to assist him with his correspondence. She became his driver, chauffeuring him to his friends. Very soon, they were inseparable. In 1955, when he was about to leave her to teach his annual master classes in Zermatt, he realized that he needed her with him always. She, too, acknowledged her need to be with him, and they traveled there together. He proposed marriage to her, saying that he understood that he was an old man, but he loved her and wanted her to be his wife. She happily accepted.

Casals had been involved in several romances in his youth. In 1906, he had an affair with a Portuguese cellist, Guilhermina Suggia, a student of his. Although they were not married, she appeared on concert programs as Mme. P. Casals-Suggia. They parted in 1912. In 1914, he married a singer and member of a socially prominent family, Susan Metcalfe. In 1928, they separated, and in 1957 were divorced. He also had a long, deep relationship with Madame Capdevila, a widow, who left Spain and lived with him for many years in Prades. They were so devoted to each other that, when she died, he brought her back to Sant Salvador, Spain, to be buried near his beloved mother.

But his love for Martita was like no other he had ever experienced. He said, "I have cause to thank God for much that has happened in my long life. I have enjoyed much good fortune and much happiness. But the years I have shared with Martita have been the happiest years of my life. I was blessed in my childhood to have a mother like my mother, and I have been blessed in my old age to have a wife like Martita. . . . Martita is the marvel of my world, and each day I find some new wonder in her. I am aware that I am no longer exactly a youth, but if I speak of her in words perhaps expected of young lovers, it is because that is how I feel about her. Perhaps, indeed, because I have lived longer than most people, I have learned more than most about the meaning of love."[46]

Before they were married, they visited Puerto Rico with Enrique Casals, Pablo's brother. Casals enjoyed everything about it. They visited his mother's birthplace and discovered that, not only had Martita's mother been born in the same house his mother had been born in 60 years earlier but both had been born on November 13. These were good omens for the couple. Casals decided to settle in Puerto Rico, and Martita was delighted.

Gov. Muñoz Marín asked Casals to establish an annual music festival, and he enthusiastically agreed. Sasha Schneider accepted the assignment of organizing it. Just before the first concert, Casals suffered a heart attack. Because people had come from all over to attend, and, as a tribute to the maestro, the concert was performed, with Sasha conducting from the concertmaster chair. The festival was a huge success.

Martita was at his side throughout his recovery. She kept his spirits up, took charge of all his affairs, including correspondence, welcomed visitors, made appointments, and protected him in every way she could.

When he had almost recovered, they married. They had a simple ceremony on August 3, 1957, and moved into a little house in Santurce, outside of San Juan, on the ocean. Theirs was a busy life, but each day was started with a morning walk together. Martita was involved in all her husband's activities, including the founding of the first Puerto Rican symphony orchestra, the Puerto Rico Conservatory of Music, of which he served as president, and the Festival Casals. Aside from all her other activities, she became the cello teacher at the conservatory. From 1960 on, they spent every summer at Marlboro, Vt., at the music festival, where he conducted master classes. Martita organized all their travel together to lessen the strain for her husband. She was devoted to protecting him. Typical of her care was the following incident: She knew President Kennedy and Casals had a great mutual respect for one another. When the American president was assassinated, she tried to keep the news from her husband, warning his guests not to mention it to him. He learned about it that evening, and was so shocked that for hours he was unable to speak to anyone.

After a number of years, Martita and Pablo had a country house built near the village of Ceiba on the coast, 50 miles from San Juan, called *El Passebre* (The Manger), named after the oratorio Casals had composed. They spent their weekends there, often accompanied by their close friends, Rosa and Luis Cueto Coll. They loved their time there, high on a hill overlooking the ocean.

On October 22, 1973, after 16 years of marriage, Pablo Casals died. Martita became director of the Festival Casals, president of the Puerto Rico Symphony Orchestra, and president of the Puerto Rico Conservatory of Music. Her loving devotion and his own causes made him productive in his last years.

On February 15, 1975, Marta Casals married the renowned pianist and their dear friend, Eugene Istomin. After her marriage, she resigned as president of the Festival Casals and, in 1980, became the artistic director of the Kennedy Center of the Performing Arts in Washington, D.C. When she learned that elections in Spain had granted home rule to the Catalans, Martita gave permission in 1979 for Casals' body to be taken to Spain to be buried.

Chapter Five

Inspired Teachers

Most great musicians teach, although not all of them well. This chapter highlights distinguished teachers whose fame is based chiefly on their success in guiding and inspiring students.

Isabella Vengerova (1877-1956) was born in Minsk, Russia. She belonged to a prominent family that had settled in Kiev. She had always been exceptionally musical, and had studied piano privately with the great Theodor Leschetizky; at the St. Petersburg Conservatory with renowned pianist Annette Essipov; and with Joseph Dachs at the Vienna Conservatory.

She became an instructor at the St. Petersburg Conservatory in 1906, and a professor there in 1910. She remained in that position until 1920. After performing on tour in Russia and Europe for three years, she decided to live in the United States. She arrived in 1923 and made her debut with the Detroit Symphony Orchestra in 1925.

Madame Vengerova was offered a professorship at the prestigious Curtis Institute in Philadelphia in 1924, when it had just been founded. She accepted, becoming one of the most important members of the faculty. Curtis was particularly oriented toward the solo artist, the "virtuoso." The faculty had as its members well-known musicians at the top of their fields. In 1950, in recognition of her great contribution as a piano teacher, she was given an honorary doctor's degree.

Isabella Vengerova was physically imposing. She was very wide but not tall, and inspired fear and awe in her students. Shouting, stomping, scolding, sarcasm, and chair-throwing, were all business as usual, as far as she was concerned. Her teacher, Leschetizky also had been a terror. He used to listen under his pupils' windows or outside their doors to hear if they were doing what he had taught them. Madame, in turn, constantly checked on her pupils to see if they were following her instructions. She was interested primarily in beautiful tone, and was strict about hand positions. She had definite ideas about wrist action, and emphasized slow practicing and clean pedaling.

Leonard Bernstein wanted to study with Madame very much, having heard that she was the greatest piano teacher in America, but he had a difficult time adjusting to her style of teaching at first. When he was asked at his first lesson to play a Bach fugue for her, he said, "She stopped me after a few bars and said, 'Why are you kicking the pedal? Why is the pedal down at all? You're playing Bach . . .' She scared the living daylight out of me, so I left the lesson absolutely trembling!" The next week he went back and played a Beethoven sonata, and was afraid to use the pedal. He quoted her as saying, "Doesn't it say *piano*? Doesn't it say *legato*?" "Yes," answered Bernstein, "but I was afraid to put the pedal down. . . ."[1] In describing her method (which he admired), he said that one of her important goals was to make him produce a singing tone, as she had been taught by Leschetizky. He called her a "slave driver," but knew he needed someone who would make him work hard. Although she seemed fearsome, in actuality, she was fiercely protective of her pupils. She was secretly softhearted and deeply involved in the careers of her students. She usually started her day on schedule, but became so involved in her pupils that she was drastically off schedule by the end of the day. The length of the lesson usually depended on how close it was to a performance.

Her home and studio was in New York City. She had a large apartment on the 11th floor of a building on 93rd Street, between Broadway and West End Avenue. Her summers were spent in the Adirondacks. As an emigré, she was active in the Russian emigré community, and was a close friend of Rosina Lhévinne, who taught piano at The Juilliard School. They both came from the Russian school of playing and understood each other's aspirations. Another close friend was Vladimir Horowitz.

She was ill for a long time before she died. However, as always, she was interested in everything going on. Her bedroom became a hub for visiting friends and colleagues. Her phone kept her in contact with the rest of her world.

Isabella Vengerova was a great teacher of fine pianists. In addition to Leonard Bernstein, her famous students include Gary Graffman, Samuel Barber, and Lukas Foss.

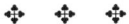

Rosina Lhévinne (1880-1976) was born in Kiev, Russia. She was part of the "golden age" of pianism. Anton Rubinstein, Josef Hofmann, Alexander Scriabin, and Leopold Godowsky were some of the great artists she heard as a child.

Rosina graduated from the Moscow Conservatory in 1898, having won the coveted gold medal. That same year she married Josef Lhévinne, a brilliant and famous pianist. She continued her career, appearing in such places as Vienna in 1910, St. Petersburg in 1911, and Berlin in 1912; she and her husband remained in Berlin during World War I. (Josef was interned there during the war, but was allowed to continue his profession.)

In 1919, the couple went to the United States, where

Josef concertized with major orchestras, playing in recitals and appearing with his wife as a duo. (Abram Chasins said that in the Debussy-Ravel *Fêtes,* played by Josef and Rosina Lhévinne, "duo-pianism realizes ultimate standards of taste and technique, of coloristic beauty and stylistic precision."[2]) They established their own music studio and taught at the Juilliard Graduate School in New York (from 1922). Madame Lhévinne wrote, "Our years of teaching were a great source of pleasure for us both, and one reason for this was that we were both in some ways flexible . . ." However, she said, "Once I taught one of his students while he was away on tour. When he returned, he gave the student a lesson. There was a phrase about which we evidently disagreed, and when the student played it 'my' way, he asked: 'What idiot taught you that?' The answer was, 'Mrs. Lhévinne.' But that was the exception that proved the rule. We did not always agree, but we generally respected the other's opinion."[3] She decided to devote herself to his career, at the same time developing a reputation for herself as one of the most influential teachers of her time. Among her students at room 412 at the Juilliard School were John Browning, Van Cliburn, Misia Dichter, and Garrick Ohlsson.

Her method of teaching was derived from Anton Rubinstein's method, and often was referred to as that of the "Russian piano school." It was an interpretive approach, very different from that of the German school. (The German school of piano playing has been described as "one of scrupulous musicianship, severity, strength rather than charm, solidity rather than sensuosity, intellect rather than instinct, sobriety rather than brilliance. It is a school that stresses planning and leaves nothing to chance."[4]) Rosina Lhévinne's roots were in the 19th century romantic repertoire.

Madame Lhévinne was a determined and serious teacher with definite ideas, yet she was always open to interpretations other than her own. Nevertheless, there were limits beyond which she would not allow a student to go. She never corrected for the sake of correcting; rather, she built up a student's confidence and enthusiasm, so that his or her personality remained intact. She strove for a singing quality and, of course, great technical facility. Her students' lives always concerned her, to such a degree that she sometimes would interfere "for their own good."

Rosina Lhévinne died in Glendale, Calif. on November 9, 1976, at the age of 96.

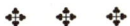

Estelle Liebling (1880-1970) was born in New York. She was a gifted soprano who studied with Mathilde Marchesi in Paris and with S. Nicklass-Kempner in Berlin. She sang at some of the great opera houses, including the Dresden Court Opera, the Stuttgart Opera, the Metropolitan Opera House in New York, and the Opéra-Comique in Paris, as well as with some of the major orchestras in the United States, France, and Germany.

Her talent as a teacher led her to the Curtis Institute in Philadelphia from 1936-1938. From there she went to New York City, where she taught for many years in her studio at 145 West 55th Street. Her most famous pupils were Beverly Sills and Amelita Galli-Curci.

Madame Liebling was a chic, elegant, imposing woman with a great sense of humor. A wealthy woman, she was married to Archie Mosler of the Mosler Safe Company. As with most great teachers, her interest in her most talented students was not limited to music. She emphasized in her teaching the ability to conduct oneself well in society. (See Chapter 7, Beverly Sills).

Estelle Liebling was famous for writing cadenzas, and published a book on the subject called *The Estelle Liebling Coloratura Digest* in 1943.

At age 90, even though she was ill, she still attended Beverly Sills's opening nights, after which she would give her valuable evaluation. She died in September 1970.

Olga Hickenlooper Samaroff (1882-1948), pianist and teacher, was born in San Antonio, Texas. Her grandmother, a concert pianist, and her mother taught her when she was young. She then studied in Paris with Delaborde. She was the first American girl to be admitted to the Paris Conservatoire. After returning to the States, she studied in Baltimore with Ernest Hutcheson, then went to Berlin to continue her studies with Ernst Jedliczka. At some point, Olga changed her name to "Samaroff." She felt that the name "Hickenlooper" did not suit a concert pianist. She concertized with many orchestras in the United States and Europe, and gave recitals with Kreisler, Zimbalist, and other well-known violinists. She was known to be a specialist in the works of Johann Sebastian Bach, playing his keyboard music on the concert grand.

In 1911, Olga married Leopold Stokowski, and gave up her career as a concert pianist. However, they were divorced in 1923, and she went on with her own career. She worked as the music critic for the *New York Evening Post* (1927-1929), and taught at the Philadelphia Conservatory and the Juilliard School of Music in New York City (1924-1948). Many of her students had successful careers, including Rosalyn Tureck, Eugene List, William Kapell, and Alexis Weissenberg. She wrote and published some excellent books, *The Layman's Music Course* perhaps being the most outstanding.

The Samaroff Fund has supported fine young talent, including, at one point, Van Cliburn.

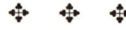

Nadia (Juliette) Boulanger (1887-1979) was one of the most eminent teachers of music composition in history. Her influence on American music is felt even today.

When Nadia was born, Paris was a small, busy city. Montmartre, where her family lived, was an area of Paris featuring an assortment of artists' studios, farms, mills, and brothels. *Demi-mondaines*, women of questionable reputation, frequented Montmartre. At that time, social classes all over France were quite distinct. Aristocrats considered manners and appearance to be all-important. Most of their income was derived from rent and investments, certainly not from work. Members of the bourgeoisie modeled themselves after the aristocracy. They admired moderation in all things, including dress. To be correct, it was considered essential that each household have a salon in which to entertain, with a piano, paintings, and other beautiful appointments. And it was important that every home have at least one servant. Each lady of the house had a weekly "at home" day during which she received visitors. A rigid protocol of behavior was followed. The more distinguished the guest list, the more distinguished the hostess appeared. Excluded from this class were women of the theater, including musicians, who were grouped with the *demi-mondaines*. To keep one's reputation as a member of the bourgeoisie, a woman must not appear in public alone, and was to be protected at all times. The father arranged for his daughter's marriage, and the mother or governess managed her education. Of course, the father had the ultimate legal authority, and made all the final decisions.

Nadia's paternal grandparents were of the bourgeoisie. Her grandfather, a cellist, had taught at the Paris Conservatoire. Her grandmother, in spite of the stigma attached to women who were entertainers, had been a star at the Opéra Comique (much to her parents' consternation). Nadia's father, Henri Alexandre Ernest Boulanger, entered the conservatory at age 16, studying piano and composition. He went on to win the prestigious Prix de Rome and became known as a composer of choral music, a choral director, and a teacher, At the age of 57, he became a professor at the Paris Conservatoire. In 1869, he received the Legion d'Honneur.

In 1874, he went to Russia to perform. Raïssa Ivanovna Myschetsky saw him conduct and followed him to Paris, where she enrolled in his voice class at the Conservatoire. She had a beautiful contralto voice, but she was not very talented musically. However, Ernest fell in love with her, and they were married. She had won no awards, which may explain her driving ambition for her daughters. Raïssa was a brilliant, imperious, exciting, excitable beauty. Although she had been married before (possibly so she could emigrate), she never talked about it, giving everyone (especially her daughters) the impression that her background was that of Russian nobility (there is no indication that this was true).

Nadia was raised as a Roman Catholic, and her religion was always important to her—although she believed deeply in the right of others to practice their own faiths. The family lived in Montmartre, the center of "sin." Yet the area had other attractions, including an exciting circus, wonderful entertainers, and fine artists. The bourgeois home life of the family was very circumscribed; although social status was important, the emphasis was on music. Raïssa's "at home" day usually was filled with distinguished people, such as Gabriel Fauré, Charles Gounod, Jules Massenet, and some wealthy friends. Raïssa, according to the fashion, had her own room in which Nadia slept. She was completely involved in every aspect of the child's existence, even though Nadia had a governess. They had a piano and a harmonium in the house, but Nadia initially fought any interest in music, saying that she wanted to become a doctor.

Nadia's mother was extremely loving, but an exacting and severe disciplinarian. She required that her daughter study constantly, and be completely obedient. Compliments were definitely frowned upon. The child was taught early on that she was not to marry. The family was comfortable financially, but her parents did not feel they had enough money for a dowry. More important, Ernest was much older than Raïssa; therefore, Nadia was expected to take care of her mother when her father was gone.

When Raïssa became pregnant with her second daughter, Nadia was 5 years old. The fear of losing her mother's love to the new baby may have ended her rebellion against music. From this point on, she applied herself to her music studies with a vengeance and loved it. It was quickly discovered that she was very talented.

Raïssa always demanded and got the best. She was

haughty and proud, but she made a point of instilling in Nadia the quality of humility. The child worked hard and competed successfully with students much older than she. But whenever she was complimented, her mother emphasized that she must not be self-satisfied This created an insecurity that always would conflict with her ambition and pride in her work. Nadia actually was a bold, assertive person with definite ideas. She was extremely intelligent and gifted, and knew it. Her mother's training in humility, however, stayed with her, creating self-image problems all her life. Evidently, she did not resent her mother's control over her, believing this attention was an indication that Raïssa really cared about her.

In 1893, Nadia's sister, Lili, was born. Her father made Nadia solemnly promise that she always would be responsible for Lili's care—an oath she always honored, sometimes at her own expense. At age 7, she was told that she must take on adult duties and vigorously pursue her music studies. Lili shared the bedroom with her older sister and her mother, observing and learning quickly and easily. She was charming, pleasant, and lovely, whereas Nadia was emotionally volatile, forceful, and ungainly. Yet they were always close. Lili quickly absorbed what Nadia had taken a long time to learn. Unfortunately, at age 3, she had developed Crohn's disease, then called "intestinal tuberculosis." Her health was precarious from then on and her older sister felt responsible for her care.

At 9, Nadia entered the Paris Conservatoire, being particularly talented in piano and organ. She was one of the youngest students. She also studied privately (composition with Gabriel Fauré and organ with Charles Marie Widor). The strain of this work in poor light affected her eyesight, and she had to wear glasses from then on. When her father died in 1900, her mother, because of French law, had to share decisions about her children with a male coguardian, their close friend William Bouwens van der Boijen. This was perfectly acceptable to all, and the family continued to function properly. Nadia began winning prizes almost immediately upon attending the Conservatoire. The training she received and her association with some of the greatest musicians of the time had a positive impact on her career. She was beginning to receive well-deserved recognition, but, as usual, her mother deflated her: "You are quite pleased with yourself, aren't you? But are you certain that you did all that you could?"[5] In addition to the pressure of her work, she had to find a way to support her family. There was some money, but Raïssa lived in high style, and Lili was not well. When she was still in her teens, Nadia began to teach. She knew that her role was to serve her sister and mother and that she was never to marry. Lili and Raïssa, of course, could not be expected to work. As a teacher, she was strict and demanding, but very concerned about her students. She had begun to earn money, but women were paid only half as much as men in teaching jobs.

In 1904, after winning top prizes at the Conservatoire, she met Raoul Pugno, a 52-year-old pianist, organist, and composer of great renown. He had a large appetite for everything: women, food, drink, and the arts, especially music. Physically, he was enormous. He admired Nadia's talent and adopted her as his favorite protégée. They worked together constantly, in performance on the organ and the piano, as well as in composition. The writer Gabriele D'Annunzio, who knew them both, said, "The music of this Nadia Boulanger exalts and stuns me. Her collaborator, Raoul Pugno, is the magician of the keyboard; but the soul of the score is Nadia . . . This union of two musicians brings to pass successfully something never seen before; it's certainly the first time that a virgin has inseminated an old impotent."[6] After 1904, Nadia and her family spent summers near Raoul Pugno's grand estate in Hanneucourt-par-Gargenville. In Paris, they moved to a residence only one block away from Pugno's home. There was much gossip about the relationship between this famous man (married with children) and Nadia. No question it was intense. His protégée became the object of his attention (and he was known to have ignored his wife). Therefore, people assumed they were having an affair, especially because they often worked alone together. But perhaps not. It is quite possible that to her he was a father figure. In any case, she never discussed the subject. Their collaboration and concert tours lasted until Pugno's illness and death in 1914. Nadia was desolate when she lost Pugno. He had supported all aspects of her career and life, even encouraging her conducting activities at a time when women did not usually conduct. His name alone had attracted big audiences to their joint recitals and concerts. She was now on her own.

She continued to study and perform. Despite her obedience to her mother, she was an independent woman, supporting controversial causes, ignoring the gossip about Pugno. Because Pugno had attracted all kinds of celebrated musicians to his home, Nadia was immersed in a world of fine music and interesting people. She became completely comfortable in this environment. Madame Boulanger entertained regally and extravagantly in her salon, bringing these fascinating and important people into her sphere. (At that time, Paris was filled with great artists. Serge Diaghilev had brought in his Russian Ballet. Composers and performers such as Serge Rachmaninoff and Feodor Chaliapin enjoyed meeting their colleagues and others at the salons. Princesse Edmond de Polignac's salon (see Chapter 2) was perhaps the most famous.

Nadia performed more and more. She tried for the prestigious first grand prize of the male-dominated Prix de Rome in composition, but failed. Women had only recently been admitted. In 1908, she made international news. She had entered the Prix de Rome competition again, but did not follow composing regulations and antagonized those in charge, including Camille Saint-Saëns, who was furious. He and others wanted her disqualified. The press took up the issue from both sides. France's minister of Public Instruction decided that her work was to be evaluated solely on its value as music. She became a finalist and won second grand prize. The feminists made much of the fact that she was a woman, and she emerged a heroine, particularly because the jury was all-male. Saint-Saëns was vindictive long after. Nadia still was not satisfied because she had not won first prize.

Lili was tall, slim, lovely, chic, and had a natural

talent for composition. She, too, aspired to win the first grand prize of the Prix de Rome competition. She did not have to earn a living, and had the time to concentrate solely on her composing. Nadia had missed the first prize for the fourth time. After studying music seriously for only three and a half years, Lili, at age 19, entered the competition for the first time and won the first grand prize—a gold medal, four years of study at the Villa Medici, and a monthly cash allowance totaling 30,000 gold francs. In addition, the winner was promised a public performance of her works. The first woman admitted to the Villa Medici, Lili became internationally famous. Even though Nadia was well-known in her own right, increasingly recognized for her teaching and, to a lesser extent, for her performing and conducting, she must have suffered when her sister won. But she never admitted it, always helping Lili in her career.

By her early 20s, Nadia was a professor of piano at the Conservatoire Femina-Musica, a prestigious position, and also taught at the Conservatoire National. She was close to her students, especially the most talented, and they remained devoted to her. Nadia was unusual in that she became a mother figure to her students, and she exposed her students to all schools of composers. Igor Stravinsky greatly impressed her (she remained his supporter and friend for life), but she introduced her pupils to the music of others, including Arnold Schoenberg, who was Stravinsky's arch rival at that time.

Lili progressed quickly as a composer, even though she was not well and was in and out of sanitariums. She became more admired as a composer than her sister, and was elegant and fashionable. (Nadia continued to dress conservatively, and had the image of an "old maid.") Lili's music was published, giving her a better financial return than that of her sister. But Nadia received more and more acclaim internationally, as a teacher of great talent and charisma. She had an astounding number of successful prodigies.

Then came World War I. Nadia and Lili became deeply involved in war work. They organized the Comité Franco-Americain du Conservatoire National de Musique et de

Déclamation, a committee led by influential Americans and Frenchmen, many of whom were well-known musician friends of the two sisters. They were the only women in the organization, listed as secretary-founders. The purpose was to provide food, clothing, and money to families, to write letters from home, and to send informative newsletters to composition students who had been called up to serve their country. However, by 1917, Lili had grown very ill and, on March 15, 1918, she died. Nadia said, "The greatest influence on my life was the one of my sister, Lili. When she was born, I had the impression I had been honored by a responsibility that I must guide, protect her. . . . Very soon she was such an unbelievable personality that she became my guide. She was so pure and inaccessible to any kind of temptation . . ."[7] Nadia mourned her sister for the rest of her life. She continued to work for the recognition of all Lili's compositions, playing her sister's works in her concerts and bringing attention to them whenever she could.

When the United States entered the war as France's ally in 1917, an organization called "American Friends of Musicians in France" was founded. Walter Damrosch, the great conductor of the New York Symphony, was the president. The plan was to create an orchestra of French musicians. Harry Harkness Flagler paid the expenses of a six-week tour of the troops. At the time, Nadia was secretary of Comité Franco-Americain, and probably contributed to or originated the suggestion that a music school for Americans be founded in France. This was the ideal time. The French were grateful to the Americans for their help in the war, and Francophilia among the Americans was at its height. (Wealthy American heiresses married French nobility, American artists of all kinds based their activities in Paris, and many other expatriates settled in the city.) Armistice was declared, and the project for the school gained momentum. Nadia was much admired by Damrosch and the others, both as a musician and as one who had been helpful to Americans. They were instrumental in arranging concert tours for her in the United States, something she had always wanted. She was invited to appear with

Damrosch and the New York Symphony in 1925. Aaron Copland had been commissioned to compose an organ concerto for her to play.

But it was as a teacher that she was truly famous, and it was considered a coup to have studied composition, harmony, and orchestration with her. In addition to serving on the faculty of the Paris Conservatoire from 1909, she taught at the École Normale de Musique in Paris from 1920, established an innovative series of children's concerts there, and was appointed as a teacher of composition in 1935. She also taught privately, with students eventually coming from all parts of the world.

The American Conservatory at Fountainbleau became a reality. In 1921, Nadia joined its faculty and was recognized as the most honored and respected teacher there. From 1920 to 1940, the best American composers were her students. In 1950, she became the school's director. Among her American students were Aaron Copland, Roy Harris, Walter Piston, Virgil Thomson, Marc Blitzstein, Elliot Carter, Samuel Barber, Roger Sessions, and David Diamond. Copland expressed the exhilaration derived from her explanations and revelations about the art of composing. Later, Harold Schonberg, the music critic, reported that Copland described his studies with her as "the most important musical experiences of his life." Schonberg added, "Boulanger became the teacher of virtually every important American composer of the period from 1920-1940 . . . So numerous were her students, that it was said every American town had two things—a five and dime, and a Boulanger pupil."[8] One of her main principles was that of *la grande ligne* (the long line in music). Her ability to accept new ideas was passed on to her students. It was important to her to arouse the interest of her students in the experimental music of the 20th century, as well as the classical and traditional music of the past. Nadia said, "When I teach, I throw out the seeds. I wait to see who grabs them . . . Those who do grab, those who do do something with them, *they* are the ones who will survive. The rest, *pfft* !"[9] Copland, who continued to communicate with her for the rest of her life, said, "One must not forget that mademoiselle's intelligence went beyond the subject of music. She was a superior person, knowledgeable about literature and other arts. Altogether, you had the warmth of her personality, the extensive musical knowledge, and a first-class intellect. The feeling in her Paris studio was of being at the center of what was going on in the artistic life of Paris . . ."[10] Because of their devotion to her, a group of her students began calling itself the "Boulangerie," and it was considered an honor to be part of this organization.

Nadia did not hesitate to use her social connections to further her students' careers. In Paris, she had her own salon, where discussions about art and other intellectual matters were the norm. One was likely to meet Aaron Copland, Igor Stravinsky, Erik Satie, Maurice Ravel, Serge Prokofiev, members of *Les Six*, and the Ballets Russes, as well as people such as Pablo Picasso, Ernest Hemingway, and Gertrude Stein. Her favorite students were invited and, of course, the social intercourse was of great value to them. In the summers, she invited a group of them to her home in Gargenville to get to know them better and observe their social behavior, which was important to her. Other members of top Parisian society invited the students to their mansions and châteaus. This not only gave the Fountainbleau students great opportunities, but awakened French socialites and nobility to the value of supporting the school.

Nadia and her mother threw New Year's Eve dinner parties and lavish fancy dress balls to which her special students received invitations. (Aaron Copland met Walter Damrosch at one of these occasions. The conductor heard one of his compositions and arranged to program one of Copland's works at a New York Symphony concert, with Nadia conducting.) Nadia was often invited to the formal musicales of Princesse Edmond de Polignac, where she met prospective aristocratic patrons for her protégées. She became a close friend and recipient of the generous patronage of the princess. (Upon the princess's death, Nadia received a 500,000-franc legacy.) This friendship was rather strange; the princess was flamboyant, her homosexuality known to all, while Nadia was conservative and discreet. But when it came to the socially select, Nadia waived any objections to their behavior. (In fact, politically as well as socially, she was a dedicated Royalist.)

In 1930, she met another member of the Polignac family who was important in her life. Marie-Blanche, Comtesse Jean de Polignac, niece of the princess and daughter of Jeanne Lanvin the couturière, was beautiful and had a lovely singing voice. Among her projects of support was taking charge of Nadia's performing clothes (always simple and almost always black), made at the elegant House of Lanvin. The count became Nadia's patron, particularly in the performances in which his wife participated. The member of the Polignac family who did the most for Nadia was Prince Pierre of Monaco. He named her his chapel master, and she held this position when his son, Prince Rainier, became the reigning prince. Her relationship with the prince, his wife, Princess Grace, and their family was special; the royal family was warm and supportive until the end of her life.

Raïssa Boulanger suffered a long and debilitating illness, and by the time she died in 1935, Nadia was exhausted. She was now alone, except for her friends. It took her quite a long time to recover, but in a year or two she was able to resume her active life. On a tour to the United States in 1938, she was the first woman to conduct the Boston Symphony Orchestra. In 1939, she was the first woman to conduct the New York Philharmonic. Her schedule, which was incredibly full, included many lectures.

During World War II, she began to teach at the Longy School of Music in Cambridge, Mass. She had left France in 1940, when France surrendered to Hitler, and lived with Winifred Hope Johnstone and her sister, both admirers of Nadia. Winifred Johnstone became her liaison in the United States. Schuyler Chapin, a student of hers at the Longy School of Music, assisted her in various capacities, such as page-turning and organizing lunches. He reported that, at one point, she suggested that his talent did not lie in performing or composing, but in management. This started him in the direction in which he ultimately was highly successful, one of his well-known positions having been general manager of the Metropolitan Opera. During this time, she taught at Radcliffe College, Wellesley College, and at the Juilliard School. In addition to her other attributes, she was considered a superb choral conductor.

In 1946, Nadia returned to her beloved France. She was welcomed back as a true celebrity. She continued to receive well-earned honors everywhere, including honorary degrees and decorations by various countries. Her career continued, even though she was going blind.

Nadia Boulanger died on October 22, 1979, after a long period of illness during which she slowly became frail and incapacitated. Leonard Bernstein, who had studied with her briefly and impressed her tremendously, had a close friendship with Nadia that lasted to the end of her life. He was with her when she was close to death. Bernstein said that Nadia was almost in a coma when he heard her say something in a strong voice. Bernstein asked her, *Vous entendez la musique dans la tête?* (Do you hear music in your head?) . . . Instant reply: *Tout le temps. Tout le temps.* (All the time. All the time)[11]

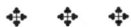

Dorothy DeLay (1917-   ), the most revered and respected violin teacher of this generation, was born into a musical family in Medicine Lodge, Kans. Her mother was a pianist and her father, who played the cello, directed the curriculum for the Kansas public schools and was a local superintendent. At age 4 she started violin lessons. In 1933, she attended Oberlin College and studied music and psychology at the University of Michigan. In 1937, she went to The Juilliard School to do graduate work. Six men influenced her with respect to music: At the University of Michigan she studied with Michael Press, a student of Leopold Auer, who was Jascha Heifetz's teacher; and at Juilliard her teachers were Hans Letz, Felix Salmond, Raphael Bronstein, and Louis Persinger (who was the head of the violin department at that time and who taught well-known violinists such as Isaac Stern and Yehudi Menuhin). The sixth man was Ivan Galamian, with whom she was professionally associated.

DeLay married fiction writer Edward Newhouse in 1941, but she still concertized. In 1946, after her second child was born, she began teaching in Juilliard's precollege division. Galamian then took her on as his assistant. He was an excellent teacher but a strict disciplinarian, putting fear into the hearts of students. Although she had great respect for him, DeLay's philosophy was quite different. She has always believed in involving the pupil in decisions. Individuality is important to her, although her students all tend to have a similar clear tone. Her goals—aside from perfecting technique and working out interpretations while expressing the composer's intent—are to teach violinists to express their own personality and temperament, to avoid rigidity, to have confidence, and to be relaxed. She wants the violinist to fully enjoy performing.

She involves herself in the lives of her pupils, trying to guide them so that their paths are easier and richer. She is concerned about everything that affects them: their practice schedules, career arrangements, and personal problems, for example. Anything to help the student. Itzak Perlman, who is handicapped because of polio, was taught by DeLay to drive a specially equipped car. She helped him work out a method of carrying his violin case (a handgrip is on his crutch) and urged him to have a more active social life. She recognized his extraordinary talent when he was just a teenager, at a time when nobody felt he could manage any career that involved traveling. She thinks it is of prime importance to live as normal a life as possible and to study other disciplines in order to broaden one's view.

From 1948 to 1970, she was associated with Ivan Galamian at Juilliard and at Meadowmount (Galamian's school in the Adirondacks in the summer). In 1970, she decided to teach on her own. She told him that she had accepted a position at the Aspen Music Festival that summer. Galamian was highly insulted and they never spoke again. He tried to have her discharged from

Juilliard, but was unsuccessful. When comparing his rigidity in teaching and treatment of his students, and her sweet, understanding, wise approach, it was inevitable that many students would prefer her.

Although she has taught many of the great violinists, she also has taught many, other fine musicians who have become part of an orchestra or chamber group, either of major proportions or small community size. Involving talented musicians in the community is one of her top priorities. Her husband has said that he feels her biggest contribution has been the education of those many musicians who have gone on to be members of an orchestra or other group, or of a conservatory faculty.

This remarkable woman has not only been teaching at Juilliard, but also at the University of Cincinnati and the Royal College of Music in London. She gives master classes in other countries as well. Her famous students include Perlman, Schlomo Mintz, Cho-Liang Lin, Nadja Salerno-Sonnenberg, Nigel Kennedy, Midori, and Gil Shaham. She is known for her genius in knowing about and teaching performance on the violin and for her tact. With all her grandmotherly demeanor, she is definitely a worldly woman and quite fierce when it comes to furthering the career of one of her "little babies." She arranges auditions with conductors, and manipulates situations so that important people in the field will have an opportunity to hear these talented young people play. However, she will only do this for those she considers worthy. She does not think contests are important. Instead, she emphasizes preparing her students to perform well on stage, to project well, and to present themselves to the best advantage. She always is open to new ideas, always ready to learn from others.

In October 1994, she received the National Medal of Arts, awarded by President Clinton. She was described by the White House as "the world-renowned teacher of the violin, the first woman, and the most influential in her field."

❖   ❖   ❖

Helen Coates (ca. 1900-1989), Leonard Bernstein's piano teacher, came from Illinois and settled in the Boston area. Her mother and she lived together in a house on The Fenway. She had studied with Heinrich Gebhard, the most prestigious teacher in Boston at the time, and was on the way to a career in piano performance. However, she decided that she preferred teaching, and became Gebhard's assistant. Helen was described as tall, well-educated, and straitlaced. She never married.

When Lenny, at age 14, asked Gebhard to teach him, he was sent to study with Miss Coates. Gebhard, according to a friend, secretly thought the boy was not talented enough, but Helen immediately realized that Lenny simply needed special work on his technique, which had been inadequately developed by his previous teacher. She proceeded to work with him on this. It was apparent to her that this brilliant student was gifted and easily bored, and she cleverly designed interesting work that would challenge him and allow for creativity. Time was of little consequence to her, because of her enthusiasm for his talent, and she generously gave him additional help with some extra musical studies that he was interested in—piano scores of operas, in particular. In order to give him extra time, she scheduled his lessons at the end of the day. They most often lasted two or three hours. She was young enough to understand some of his problems, and old enough to give him the benefit of her experience. Helen could not resist being drawn into his life, feeling almost maternal toward him. She realized he was an exceptionally talented young boy with great potential, and that he must be protected and nurtured. She was, in fact, the first person to recognize Lenny's talent. He developed a great affection for her, and appreciated her worth as a teacher and a person, thereafter making her his valued confidante, and sharing his excitement about music and his career. (It was an interesting relationship, given the facts that their personalities were in direct opposition and they were 18 years apart in age).

Helen Coates remained close to him during her whole life. Even when he went on to study with Gebhard (who finally acknowledged that he was an exceptionally talented young man and took him on as his student), to take music courses at Harvard, then to work with the famous Isabella Vengerova at the Curtis Institute in Philadelphia, he continued to write newsy letters and articles to Helen, keeping her well-informed. She would respond, sometimes sending brownies or some little present. Often she would write to encourage him when he was feeling down or to give him advice on practical matters. Letter-writing was not his mother's forte, and Helen happily assumed that role. Whenever he could, he would arrange to send her tickets to attend one of his performances. She was present at his conducting debut at Harvard, and from then on encouraged him in his conducting career, as well as in his composing and piano playing. After he conducted the Curtis Orchestra in Wagner's *Tannhäuser* and Brahms' *Third Symphony* at the end of his first year at the institute, he wrote to Helen, "It is the most glorious thing one can do, and I haven't calmed down yet . . . I've got the bug in earnest now . . ."[12]

In 1944, Lenny asked her to became his administrative assistant, a position originally occupied by his sister Shirley (see Chapter 8). She agreed and resigned from her position at the Dana Hall School in Wellesley, Mass. She arrived in New York within two days and went to work. In order to do her job well, she enrolled in a typing course. She was energy personified, and loved taking care of all the details of his career. Since she was discretion itself, he confided in her about his personal life. She handled his finances, traveled with him, acted as his secretary, and made arrangements for concerts, auditions, and other events. In this capacity, she was in a position of power, being the one to decide who could or could not reach Lenny. Because he hated to say no and she was good at it, she acted as the intermediary he needed. Even when his future wife, Felicia Montealegre, would call and ask to speak to him, Helen often would refuse to disturb him if he was resting. She remarked at one time that, if Lenny ever married, his wife would just have to understand that his music comes first. (Eventually, she and Felicia got along well, each respecting the other's sphere. When the couple was married, Helen moved to the same apartment house with a separate office, so she would be available. She understood that his wife would give his work first priority.)

There is only one occasion worth noting in which there was any unpleasantness between Helen and Lenny. After having worked devotedly for him for six years, he suddenly discharged her. At that time he was trying to renew his relationship with his ex-fiancée, Felicia Montealegre, who was in love with Richard Hart and well on the way to becoming a success as an actress. Lenny was aware that Felicia had objected to his reliance on Helen and that she had felt Helen's disapproval when they were engaged. Lenny might have been trying to show his independence from Helen, or perhaps he was becoming irritated by her involvement in his affairs. In any case, Helen, who received the letter of dismissal while she was abroad taking care of some of his business, returned to New York and angrily replied by letter (he was back in Europe). She stated that she had no idea that he resented their relationship. She said it was because of his dependency on her, and his desire to turn over to her the handling of the details of his career and his personal life so that he would not have to be bothered, which drew her into every aspect of his life. As for his personal affairs, she pointed out that it was he who drew her into his private life. Lenny realized that she was right and that she was indispensable, a selfless and devoted friend. Within a few days, he apologized, and she was again his assistant with all the powers she had before. But it took her a while to recover from the hurt and anger. From then on, their friendship was strong and filled with affection.

Ms. Helen Coates died in 1989 at age 89. Bernstein organized her memorial and wrote this poem:

> "Goodness" you would say, "goodness gracious!"
> And you departed with grace as you were meant to.
> You remain, all the same, just as you were meant to;
> In a million mysterious, graceful ways.[13]

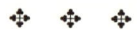

Phyllis Smith Curtin (1921-), in her mid-70s, is still a glamorous woman, always dressed tastefully, even when wearing casual clothes, and has a warm and irresistible personality. She is highly intelligent and sensible. She has a sincere desire to teach young singers and to help them achieve success in the best sense of the word. Ms. Curtin has succeeded in two careers. A great singer and diva for more than three decades, she now has an international reputation as one of the great singing teachers. She was born December 3, 1921, in Clarksburg, W. Va. Her parents were E. Vernon and Betty R. Smith.

She received a B.A. degree from Wellesley College in 1943, majoring in political science. (She believes, even now, that a well-rounded education will broaden a singer's perspective.) At the same time, she studied at the college with Olga Averino, who was a Russian soprano specializing in the music of Ravel, Rachmaninoff, and Schoenberg. She taught Phyllis to be independent in her decisions about singing and performing. After graduation, Phyllis began to sing in and around Boston. For three summers she studied with Boris Goldovsky in Tanglewood's opera program. When she realized that her singing had weaknesses, she faced it honestly and decided to study with the teacher whose students she admired for the beauty of their voices. He was Joseph Regneas, and his teaching style suited her. He was the last teacher with whom she studied, but she was ever alert to ways in which she could improve. She said, "Throughout my entire singing career, I was always listening to my colleagues, noticing what worked for them and what did not, from the technical point of view. I was interested in technique, not as an end in itself but as a support for what I wanted to do. You should go for everything you can imagine artistically, and the technique must be adequate to service it. My teaching was also an important part of my performing career. . . . I found that being able to explain . . . made it easier to understand for myself. My classes at Tanglewood have kept me at the absolute center of what it means to be a singer. That's why I never had a vocal crisis in my entire career."[14]

In 1946, Phyllis Smith married Phillip Curtin. The

couple had one daughter, Claudia Madeleine. The marriage did not last.

Phyllis spent many summers at the Berkshire Music Center in Tanglewood as a student (in 1946, she sang there in Benjamin Britten's *Peter Grimes*, which received great reviews), becoming more and more appreciated as a fine and knowledgeable opera singer. She made her recital debut at Town Hall in New York City in 1950, and her opera debut at the New York City Opera in 1953. She has sung with leading orchestras and opera companies all over the world, including the New England Opera Company, the New York City Opera, the Teatro Colón in Buenos Aires in 1959, and the Vienna State Opera in 1960-1961. She made a successful debut at the Metropolitan Opera Company in New York City on November 4, 1961, and at La Scala in Milan in 1962. She performed in recitals and operas throughout the United States and in many foreign countries. In 1965, she became an artist-in-residence at the Tanglewood Music Center in Lenox, Mass., during the summers. She remained dedicated to its aims, becoming an important member of the vocal department and eventually establishing a master class. She took possession of an old farm building on the grounds of Tanglewood and began her classes there. This program became popular, with the "Phyllis Curtin Seminar" occurring every summer. Hundreds of young singers applied for the course. Only 30 are accepted each year. She has had to limit the attendance of each student to three successive summers. Her method has been to have a student sing a song with an accompanist, after which members of the class are asked to critique the performance, in that way learning from others' mistakes as well as their own. As a teacher, she discussed voice placement, production, timbre, expression, phrasing, etc. One of her biggest problems has been finding time enough to work with each of these gifted young singers.

One of her main goals has been to teach students to be individuals, not imitators of "superstars." The baritone Sanford Sylvan, one of Ms. Curtin's students, said, ". . . She forces you to question all the old habits that creep in through tradition—you may want to adopt some of them

Inspired Teachers

in the end, but you cannot accept them absolutely."[15] Her positive experience with the New York City Opera taught her that, ideally, a company has creative *individuals* who respect each other and work together as a team. Another important point that she tries to get across to students is that each singer must not only understand proper breathing and technique, in general, but must know the composer's whole score, rather than merely his or her own part.

Ms. Curtin's excellent influence has been widespread. She went on to become the head of the voice department at Yale University, then dean of the School of Fine Arts at Boston University. She has taught master classes in Beijing, Moscow, and Canada, as well as in the United States. She has been an important member of the National Council on the Arts. An impressive and lovely woman, she has contributed much, not only as a fine performer but as a superb music educator.

Chapter Six

Patronesses in the United States

Elizabeth Sprague Coolidge (1864-1953), called "Patron Saint" and "Lady Bountiful of Chamber Music," was responsible for establishing in the United States the performance of high-quality chamber music. It has been said that she was the most important patroness of music in the 20th century. At age 52, she started her philanthropy in the field of music. When her parents died in 1916, she inherited their fortune. Her family had been in the wholesale grocery business in Chicago.

Elizabeth had been a pianist and had studied music composition. Her father was one of the sponsors of the Chicago Orchestra, and she had played with it under its founder, Theodore Thomas. After she married Dr. Frederic Shurtleff Coolidge (her husband was a surgeon), she organized musicales in her home, becoming known as an important patroness who truly cared about the performers and performances she supported. She continued this for 40 years or more.

Mrs. Coolidge had a summer home in Pittsfield, Mass., and a winter home in New York. In 1918, able and enthusiastic, as usual, she established, with the help of cellist William Willeke, the Berkshire Festival of Chamber Music at South Mountain, in Pittsfield. She had a concert hall built called "the Temple of Music" and had some cottages constructed for the performers. With her guidance and support, the Berkshire String Quartet was created, new works were commissioned, and prizes were given. Among the composers were Ernest Block, Sir Edward Elgar, Manuel de Falla, Roy Harris, Paul Hindemith, Ottorino Respighi, Arnold Schoenberg, Ernest Toch, and Anton Webern. When William Willeke died in 1950, Sally, his wife, became the artistic director. She established the Young Audience Concerts, which consisted of 30 or more concerts performed for more than 20,000 children in western Massachusetts and New York.

After seven years, Mrs. Coolidge transferred the festival to Washington, D.C., where she was instrumental in having a small concert hall built for chamber music. This is the Coolidge Auditorium in the Library of Congress.

The Elizabeth Sprague Coolidge Foundation was established in 1925. Its purpose was to enable the music division of the library to conduct music festivals, to have extension concerts at educational institutions, to broadcast chamber music, to present prizes, to commission works, and to help further musicology at the library.

Among the many gifts given by Mrs. Coolidge were large contributions of money for a music building at Yale University, the establishment of a tuberculosis hospital, and a school for physically handicapped children in Pittsfield.

In 1932, she created the Elizabeth Sprague Coolidge Medal, given for special musical contribution to the cause of chamber music.

For her contribution to education, she was given honorary degrees at Yale University, Smith College, Mills College, Mount Holyoke College, Pomona College, and the

University of California. In addition, she was decorated by foreign governments for her contribution to the culture of their countries.

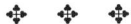

Mary Louise Curtis Bok Zimbalist (1876-1970). In 1974, this tribute to Mrs. Zimbalist appeared in the 50th anniversary issue of *Overtones* at the Curtis Institute of Music in Philadelphia: "For most of its fifty years, every concert, assemblage, and gathering at the Curtis Institute was graced by Mary Louise Curtis Bok Zimbalist, a presence so evocative and responsive that it lives in thousands of memories across the United States and in other lands where Curtis artists make music and fulfill the promise of their unique education. To walk into the Institute, to sit in its concert hall or be among its students, is still to hear the low speaking voice, to see the smiling eyes slightly slanted in mysterious intelligence and wit, to feel oneself in the presence of a loving heart and a mind of steel. Ideals are empty matters without the will and energy and realism to implement them. Mary Louise Curtis Zimbalist possessed those powers beyond the great material inheritance which enabled her to use them fully.

"She was gentle. It would be impossible to imagine her other than calm, wise, gracious, understanding, tolerant, a lady of exquisite taste and poise: a woman of enormous strength and determination. Her response to every interest and occupation was constructive. She loved music; in her character, to love meant to build and to serve. She had a sound musical education, and her keen mind reflected all her tastes—wide reading, a lifelong sense of scholarship, a searching, constantly widening intellect, a practical turn of thought beyond philosophical reflection and the gift of drawing out the best in people. She grew, and her remarkable sense of values grew all the years of her very long life.

"To a fascinating degree, the Curtis Institute personifies the character of its founder. She combined a sense of quality, uncompromising and austere, with profound generosity and kindliness. Every Curtis graduate and student who has passed through the tough competitive auditions and exacting disciplines of entrance and study and performance, to receive his or her Curtis education tuition-free, has felt the two hands of the founder. Her pride in the school, in its students and graduates, and the joy she took in them kept her always a vivid participant in their lives and careers. Her gift for friendship was wide, varied, eagerly shared. She had congenial interests with the likeliest and also with quite unlikely people, always encouraging them to be themselves. Her vision was grand, but her ways endearing. She was a great woman. For her we can quote the son of Sir Christopher Wren, who engraved over a door of St. Paul's Cathedral this tribute to his father, the architect: 'If you seek his monument, look around you.' And we add: Listen too. For the Curtis Institute, the United States, and many other countries echo the creation of the white-haired lady whose wisdom, warmth, and strength live on in the world's best music."[1]

Mary Louise Curtis, who was born in Boston, was the daughter of Cyrus and Louisa Curtis. Cyrus moved his family to Philadelphia, where he felt he could establish his publishing company. Both parents, who had fine singing voices, loved church music and helped found many choir groups. It was not long before Cyrus became an important publisher, his first success being *The Ladies' Home Journal* (his wife was the first editor). At that point, they were able to afford an organ and a piano in their home and Mary began to study music seriously. When she was enrolled in the Ogontz School for Young Ladies, music was her major field.

Mary's mother decided to retire as editor and proceeded to search for a successor. She finally decided that the perfect person for the job was Edward W. Bok, a journalist originally from The Netherlands, who had come to her attention because of his ability as an editor and his talent in advertising. He became the new editor of *The Ladies' Home Journal*. Both Cyrus and Edward had known poverty, and both had been newsboys. They were ideally suited.

Mary and Edward fell in love and were married in 1896. They had two sons, Curtis and Cary. Edward was a man of deep feelings and concern for others. He was especially troubled by the plight of women. In New York, he had headed the Bok Syndicate Press and developed a full page of reading material for women. When he became editor of *The Ladies' Home Journal*, he established departments devoted to advice and information for women. He was committed to women's suffrage and other causes, one of them being the importance of keeping cities clean. Mary shared his commitments, and together they were impressive in their good works and philanthropies.

When her mother died in 1910, Mary realized that her life needed further personal commitment and depth. Her father understood this and introduced her to Mrs. Samuel Fels, who in turn introduced her to the Settlement Music School on Christian Street. This school was founded for culturally and financially deprived children. She gave money for a new building (completed in 1917) and became involved in the children's musical development.

By 1923, she realized that the very talented had no place to continue their training. That is when she decided to create the Curtis Institute of Music for those who were making music their profession. She started the endowment with a gift of $500,000, and increased it as time went on. (After consulting with her sons, the total endowment became $12 million in 1927.)

It opened in 1924 on property off Rittenhouse Square. Originally, the structures had been the George W. Childs Drexel mansion, the Edward A. Sibley house, and the Theodore H. Cramp mansion. (Another building was added later.) The first director was Johann Grolle, the principal administrator in the Settlement Music School. He was succeeded by William E. Walter, well known in the business world. An advisory council made up of influential people such as Josef Hofmann, Leopold Stokowski, Felix Adler, Marcella Sembrich, Edward W. Bok, Cyrus H. K. Curtis, Edward A. Ziegler (assistant general manager of the Metropolitan Opera), and Ernest Urch (from the Steinway Company), was formed; and an incredibly distinguished group of musicians made up the faculty. Dorothy Thompson wrote from Salzburg, "It is strange that here in Salzburg, 7,500 miles from America, where Max Reinhardt's musical and theatrical festival has assembled so much international talent and art interest, Philadelphia should be on so many people's tongues. However much or little may be known about Philadelphia's wealth, industries, and commerce, all European lovers of art know of the Philadelphia Orchestra, the [Philadelphia] Forum (founded by Edward W. Bok), and the Curtis Institute."[2]

By 1927, Leopold Stokowski enlarged the Curtis orchestra to 85 musicians, and Mrs. Bok asked Josef Hofmann to be the third director. They announced that there would be no tuition fee, starting in the 1928-29 season. There would be full scholarship, and only students who were outstanding in music, who had a special talent, and admirable personal characteristics, would be admitted. In 1929, Emil Mlynarski (Artur Rubinstein's father-in-law) was appointed the conductor of the opera productions and of the Orchestra of the Curtis Institute of Music.

In 1930, Mrs. Bok's husband died. Soon after, her father became seriously ill, and died in 1933. Her sons were married, so she devoted herself completely to her life's project. Whenever school was in session, she was there to work. In the summer she lived in Rockport, Me., where she and her husband had a house. In the late '20s she began to invite some of the members of the Curtis faculty to summer there and teach some of the exceptional students. Carlos Salzedo established the Harp Colony in the next town of Camden. Rockport became a mecca for fine musicians from all over.

When Josef Hofmann resigned as director because of the demands of his performance career, Mrs. Bok took over the reigns of Curtis. In 1939, she appointed Dr. Randall Thompson as the fourth director. In 1941, Efrem Zimbalist, the great violinist who was on the faculty, was appointed director. He and Mrs. Bok agreed that a small student body with emphasis on the relationship between teacher and student was the best way to proceed. Even now, there are only about 170 students and about 75 faculty members.

The Curtis policies are unique in several ways:

1) It is the only conservatory in the Western World that is tuition-free; acceptance is based on auditions.
2) The term of a student's stay is determined by his or her teachers.
3) The enrollment is very small, just enough to make up the orchestra and the opera department, plus a small number of students of keyboard instruments, composing, and conducting.
4) Each student must study with an important teacher (there is no preparatory division, although the very young will receive extra lessons)
5) Students must be under 20 years old.
6) Teachers are gifted performing musicians who do not depend on their income from teaching, so that the school is free to accept students strictly on merit.
7) Each piano, conducting, and composition student is loaned a Steinway piano while at Curtis.

Among the heads of departments were Josef Hofmann and Rudolf Serkin in the piano division; Efrem Zimbalist, Leopold Auer, and Carl Flesch in the violin division; Marcella Sembrich, chair of the voice department; and Leopold Stokowski, Artur Rodzinski, and Fritz Reiner, all chairs of the conducting department. The faculty included Samuel Barber, Leon Fleisher, Gary Graffman, Seymour Lipkin, Mstislav Rostropovich, Galina Vishnevskaya (Rostropovich), Wanda Landowska, Mieczyslaw Horszowski, Isabella Vengerova, and many of the principal players of the Philadelphia Orchestra. Students there included Leonard Bernstein, Samuel Barber, Lukas Foss, Eugene Istomin, Gary Graffman, Gian-Carlo Menotti, Jorge Bolet, Boris

Goldovsky, Jaime Laredo, Anna Moffo, Ned Rorem, Peter Serkin, Benita Valente, Richard Goode, Ju Hee Suh, Pamela Frank, and Rose Bampton.

Mr. Zimbalist and Mrs. Bok became romantically involved, even though he was somewhat younger, and were married in Rockport in 1943. Their respective children were present. (Mr. Zimbalist had been married to singer Alma Gluck, who died in 1938. He had a daughter, Maria Zimbalist Bennett, a son, Efrem Zimbalist Jr., and a stepdaughter, Marcia Davenport.) The couple remained devoted to each other and totally committed to their goal at Curtis. Mr. Zimbalist retired in 1968, and was succeeded by Rudolph Serkin, who served as director until 1976. John de Lancie served from 1977-85. Pianist Gary Graffman has been director since then. Mrs. Zimbalist worked as president of Curtis until 1969, when her health began to falter. At that time, her son Cary became president. In Rockport each summer, she and her husband were enthusiastic members of the audience of the Bay Chamber concerts. Because of her influence in awakening the public to the need for supporting the study and performance of music, these concerts attracted some generous benefactors.

She received many honors and degrees, including those from University of Pennsylvania, Williams College, the National Institute of Social Sciences, Colby College, Temple University, Combs College, and Bowdoin College. The Polish government conferred upon her the Chevalier's Cross, the Austrian government bestowed the Order of Merit, and she received the Gimbel's "Woman of the Year" award.

About five years before her death, her health began to deteriorate seriously, and at age 93, she died. Her funeral was in Philadelphia, attended by a great many who loved and were grateful to her. The Curtis String Quartet played music that she had particularly loved. Many of the students, members of the faculty, and staff, when asked, told of their fond memories: of her intense concern and warmth (she always made sure that the students had the proper instruments, warm clothes, money for recitals, and anything else they needed for their well-being and careers), of the traditional Wednesday afternoon teas, and the annual Christmas party (the first having been held in 1925).

Not only had she dedicated herself and her energies to the Curtis School, but she also was a board member of the Philadelphia Orchestra, and chairman of the board and main supporter of the Philadelphia Grand Opera Company. Her philanthropies included other cultural institutions, the United Way, the Red Cross and hospitals, and relief for those unemployed during the Great Depression. She bought the Burrell collection of Wagneriana and brought it to the United States.

Alumni of Curtis have gone on to brilliant careers, many winning coveted awards. Of the American and Canadian orchestra members, 231 have been trained at Curtis, 55 hold principal chairs. In the "Big Five" American orchestras (Boston, Chicago, New York, Philadelphia, and Cleveland) 30 percent are alumni of Curtis. (Of the members of the Philadelphia Orchestra, almost 50 percent are from Curtis.) Thirty-nine voice students have gone on to the Metropolitan Opera, a remarkable figure, considering that only a small number are accepted in the program.

Gary Graffman, the present director, has vowed to keep Mrs. Zimbalist's philosophy alive. One change that is in the offing is a program for obtaining public financial support. It has become apparent that the income from Curtis is not enough, as confirmed by Mr. Graffman and A. Margaret Bok, the founder's daughter-in-law, who has taken over the Bok role and is a power on the board of trustees.

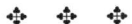

Gertrude Robinson Smith (1881-1963), the leading figure behind the founding of Tanglewood, was a summer resident in the Berkshires in Massachusetts. She was a member of a well-known New York family. Her father, Charles Robinson Smith, was a lawyer on Wall Street and a director of Allied Chemical. Gertrude was raised in great luxury at 1 Sutton Place, Manhattan. Her mother, a beautiful woman and member of high society, was descended from Richard Mather, one of the first settlers in Massachusetts (and grandfather of Cotton Mather). There also was another daughter, Hilda, who married the grandson of Harriet Beecher Stowe. The salon at their home on Sutton Place and frequent trips to Paris provided the setting for the girls' rich education in the appreciation of music.

In appearance, Gertrude was plain—a stocky woman—who showed no interest in marriage (her companion for 40 years was Miss Miriam Oliver). She was a close friend of many creative people, including Edith Wharton, Gertrude Stein, Sarah Bernhardt, Anne Morgan (daughter of J. P. Morgan), and Nadia Boulanger.

During World War I, she and Edith Wharton, both of whom had a strong feeling of duty to help those less fortunate than they, campaigned to raise money for medical equipment, ambulances, and surgical motor units to send to France. She started an Ice Flotilla Committee to raise money for ice-making machines for Allied field hospitals. At that time, she traveled back and forth to France to observe and make sure her contributions were being used to the best advantage. She was tireless and fearless, flying over the front lines in small, unsafe planes.

After the war, she continued her good works. Another of her projects was the Vacation Association, which helped girls who worked in the city vacation in the country in the summer. She had developed into a powerful, determined, and competent woman, dedicated to helping others.

The family had an estate of 115 acres near Stockbridge, Mass. She asked for and received a small part of the estate for her own cabin, which she shared with Miriam Oliver. They did most of the construction of "The Residence" themselves, with the advice of Daniel Chester French, the sculptor.

When she was 53, Gertrude was approached by Dr. Henry Kimball Hadley, conductor and composer, who had the idea for summer concerts. They both agreed on three concerts for the following summer. He went to New York to line up an orchestra, while Gertrude began organizing supporters in the area. Two of her first major supporters were her friends, Mrs. Owen Johnson and Mrs. William

Fulton Barrett. At the start, she was able to get 64 influential, wealthy women to make up the membership of the Berkshire Symphonic Festival, Inc. Gertrude was named president, and Elizabeth Sprague Coolidge was honorary president. The first concert was scheduled to take place on Saturday, August 25, 1934. The New York Philharmonic-Symphony, which was playing at Lewisohn Stadium in New York City in July and part of August, was engaged by Hadley to play at the Berkshire festival.

In 1935, the concerts were continued, and the orchestra increased from 65 to 85 members. Miss Robinson Smith and her committee worked hard to publicize and raise money for the festival. She said, "It is high time that America had its own Salzburg, and we are taking a step in that direction. The people of the Berkshires are prepared to receive and serve visitors from all over the United States."[3]

Because of a scheduling conflict caused by the New York Philharmonic-Symphony's commitment to the Lewisohn Stadium concerts (run by the strong and competent Mrs. Charles "Minnie" Guggenheimer), and because Hadley had resigned as conductor, the board members decided to engage Serge Koussevitzky and the Boston Symphony Orchestra. Koussevitzky usually went to Europe in the summer, but Miss Robinson Smith convinced him to accept. He advised her to hire his friend and well-known critic, Olin Downes, to give a preconcert lecture before each performance. After his lectures, Mr. Downes would stay on to review the concerts (usually enthusiastically) for *The New York Times*, in this way arousing great interest in the festival.

In the first two years, when the concerts were held on Hanna farm, there was no shelter, although a circus tent was rented in case of rain. The board and the conductor were interested in a permanent site for a pavilion. As luck would have it, Mrs. Gorham Brooks (Rosamund Dixey Brooks) offered her estate, Tanglewood (originally "Highwood"), to the Boston Symphony Orchestra. It had been bought by William Aspinwall Tappan in the middle 1800s. In 1936, Mrs. Brooks (later Mrs. Andrew H. Hepburn), the granddaughter of Mr. Tappan, and her aunt, Miss Mary Aspinwall Tappan, agreed to contribute the property to the orchestra. The offer was accepted and architect Eliel Saarinen was hired to design the pavilion. Gertrude would have preferred that the property be donated to her group, rather than the orchestra. Later she asked why it was decided in that way. Mrs. Brooks (now Mrs. Hepburn) answered, "I thought about it, and since the Berkshire trustees are a more or less changing group of people and the Boston Symphony is a thing that had been established for fifty years, I thought they were a capable, conservative crowd, and I thought their motives were entirely uncommercial and entirely to further art . . ." Mrs. Hepburn explained that she thought the orchestra officials were more experienced, and should be in charge of the festival as well, "just as when a child reaches a certain age it is wise to afford him the proper advantages away from his parent." Needless to say, Gertrude was not thrilled with this attitude, and replied with typical sharpness: "Yes, but you don't want him kidnapped."[4]

A fortuitous event occurred that greatly helped Gertrude and her fellow fund-raisers: During a concert on Thursday evening, August 12, 1937, a violent storm interfered with the all-Wagner performance. Thunder, lightning, and torrents of rain descended on the audience of about 5,000 people. Miss Robinson Smith spoke to the audience at intermission, saying, "This storm has proved conclusively the need for a shed. We must raise the $100,000 to build it."[5] That very evening, $30,000 was pledged. The goal of building a pavilion was changed to that of constructing a shed (which would cost less) and this dream was well on the way to becoming a reality. The Boston Symphony owned the land, and Berkshire Symphonic Festival, Inc. owned the Shed. (Of course, this naturally led to some tension between the two organizations.) Maestro Koussevitzky started a summer school on the grounds for talented musicians, and this added to the enormous cost of running the Berkshire Music Center and the concerts.

On October 4, 1945, after a period of conflict between the orchestra and Gertrude Robinson Smith, she and her board sent a telegram to the officials of the Boston Symphony Orchestra, informing them of their decision to give the Shed to the orchestra. In 1950, Berkshire Symphonic Festival, Inc. came to an end. As a gesture of gratitude, Gertrude was given the permanent use of Box #1 in the Shed, and her great contribution was acknowledged publicly.

After 1945, Miss Robinson Smith spent most of her summers in France. When she was in her 70s, Charles Munch became the conductor, at which time she returned to her home in the Berkshires and again became a force at Tanglewood. In October 1963, when she was in her 80s, she returned to New York, where she died. A plaque in her memory that is on the Shed and the Gertrude Robinson Smith Conducting Award are reminders of her importance to Tanglewood.

Lila Bell Acheson Wallace (1889-1984) of the Lila Wallace–Reader's Digest Fund, Inc. (originally the Lila Acheson Wallace Fund, Inc.) and her husband, William Roy DeWitt Wallace, founded and developed the *Reader's Digest* in 1922.

Lila was born in Virden, Manitoba, Canada. Her father was the Reverend T. Davis Acheson, a Presbyterian minister. Her mother was Mary Huston Acheson. The family moved to the United States when the children were young, settling in small Midwestern towns where the reverend preached.

Lila spent her high school years in Lewiston, Ill., then continued her education at Ward-Belmont School in Nashville, Tenn., and the University of Oregon in Eugene. After receiving her bachelor of arts degree, she taught English in the high school in Eatonville, Wash., and helped manage a YMCA summer home. During World War I, the YMCA took on the project of helping women who were working in factories. Its aims were to improve their working conditions and to help them cope with managing their lives. Lila's job was to organize recreational centers for them in the East. After the war, she continued in social work under the auspices of the Labor Department in industrial centers. She created programs that included classes in music, other arts, languages, and homemaking. She worked very hard to persuade canning factory owners to build schools and recreational facilities for migrant workers. In 1920, she came to Minneapolis to establish a YMCA for industrial workers, and there she and DeWitt Wallace began their romance.

DeWitt came from a devout family that believed in academic excellence; monetary success did not interest them much. (His father was Dr. James Wallace, Ph.D., D.D., LL.D., a professor and later president of the Presbyterian college, Macalester.) DeWitt was not content to follow in his father's footsteps. He was brilliant, intensely curious, and an avid reader. (His wife later reported that he would read anything he could get his hands on), but he was particularly fascinated by magazine articles because of their emphasis on current events and subjects. He never did receive his degree at the University of California at Berkeley, preferring to acquire knowledge firsthand by working. He worked at jobs that gave him the experience needed for his future career of publishing, editing, and marketing. DeWitt had the absolute conviction that a "little magazine" containing condensed articles would provide knowledge of every kind to those who wanted to learn and to get ahead. He was convinced that it would be well-received. He spent every available moment perfecting his condensing techniques, reading about every topic that interested him and writing synopses of the articles. But he was not able to interest anybody in backing his new idea.

DeWitt had attended Macalester College (in St. Paul) with Barclay Acheson, Lila's brother. When he saw his friend's beautiful sister Lila at the Acheson home in Tacoma, Wash., during Christmas vacation, he felt that he had met the girl of his dreams, but was told that she was engaged. Later, after he had served in the infantry in the Great War and been discharged, he heard that Lila was working in New York and had not married. He sent her a telegram, urging her to return. She accepted a temporary job in St. Paul, and the romance was off and running. DeWitt proposed on their first date; Lila accepted on the second. When he showed her his sample magazine, she fell in love with his project, calling it a "gorgeous idea." In 1921, as fate would have it, he was fired from his position in the publicity department at Westinghouse Electric in Pittsburgh and, at that point, decided to start his own business and sell subscriptions directly to readers by mail.

Lila and DeWitt were married on October 15, 1921, in New York. In writing to his family about his wife, he said, "I know no girl who has the perfect qualities she has to make me a happy wife. I don't think she will ever become restless. She can content herself being alone in the daytime, is a friend of reading and improving her mind, loves music, loves to take hikes, actually enjoys to keep house, has very good taste, is economical, has never been sick, is very easy to look at, is thoughtful, considerate & *affectionate* . . ."[6] With borrowed money they started their magazine, *Reader's Digest*. DeWitt (known as "Wally") had 52 percent of the stock; Lila had 48 percent. Their first office was under a speakeasy in Greenwich Village at #1 Minetta Lane. In order to pay the printer, Lila sublet one room and shared their kitchen and bath with another couple. They both worked hard and long, writing to possible subscribers. They were tireless in their reading and in condensing the magazine articles that went into their first magazine. Five thousand copies of the first edition were printed in February 1922. Very soon, they found they had enough subscribers to pay for the next issue. In September of that year, they moved to a garage apartment in Pleasantville, N.Y., where they continued their work. Later her husband said, "I have the perfect wife. In the beginning, she was willing to undergo the strictest economy and to live in very simple conditions. When I married Lila, she was young and lovely and she enjoyed parties and people. I brought her to a $25-a-month garage apartment in Pleasantville, and we just worked all the time and never went out—but she knew it was what I wanted to do."[7] Their timing was perfect for this kind of publication: Self-improvement was in vogue as the key to advancement. The magazine caught on, and by 1930, circulation grew to more than 1 million; by 1939, 3 million; and by 1979, 30 million. It also became one of the largest publishers of books and recorded music.

In 1939, Lila and DeWitt moved the offices to a large complex in Chappaqua, N.Y. It incorporated Lila's excellent ideas for design and furnishings, and was modeled on the governor's palace in Williamsburg, Va. She had an office of her own at the headquarters, often suggesting an idea for the magazine and selecting the artwork. Her taste and knowledge of art and design served her well when she took it upon herself to design and decorate *High Winds*, their magnificent 22-room Norman-styled house in Mount Kisco. Both their offices and house were filled with paintings by great artists, selected and purchased by Lila. In 1973, when she was 83 years old, Lila and her husband officially retired, although DeWitt kept in close touch with the policies and the editorial staff. She and DeWitt lived well but quietly, entertaining small groups, attending concerts or the theater, traveling, and pursuing their individual philanthropies. Their devotion to each other was legendary. Because they had no children, their plan was to use much of their money to benefit others. Each had his or her own fields of interest.

Mrs. Wallace established her own fund, which was incorporated in 1956 with the following specific goals: 1) improving the cultural life of communities, building audiences for the performing, visual, folk, and literary arts; 2) increasing adult literacy; and 3) developing urban parks. To get an idea of the activities of the fund with respect to music, mentioned here are a few of the grants awarded in 1992: $2.5 million to the Chamber Music of America, New York City; $1.85 million to the Association of Performing Arts Presenters, D.C.; $1.4 million to the Wolf Trap Foundation for the Performing Arts, Vienna, Va.; $7 million to the Smithsonian Institution, D.C., for Americas's jazz heritage; and $1.3 million to Dance USA. At the end of 1993, the fund's assets were $8 million. She was a trustee of the Juilliard School for 12 years, contributing much of the funds needed for programs, endowing chairs for extraordinary teachers in the fields of music and drama, and providing funds for well-known artists to perform and teach. She endowed chairs at the Metropolitan Opera, the New York Philharmonic, and the Chamber Music Society; and sponsored new works at the New York City Ballet and the New York City Opera. One of her very worthwhile philanthropies was the establishment of a foundation for Martha Graham (see Chapter 9) and her dance group. She was the chairman of its board of directors.

Other examples of her major contributions were: 1) to the Metropolitan Museum of Art in New York City, more than $50 million (there is a wing, named for her, exhibiting 20th-century art. She also arranged to have fresh flowers in the niches of the great hall, in perpetuity. Because of Mrs. Wallace, the museum was able to present its beautiful collection of Egyptian art, for which she had a special love); 2) for the restoration of Claude Monet's studio and gardens at Giverny, France; 3) for the purpose of saving, moving, and restoring Boscobel, an historic mansion of unusual beauty in Garrison, N.Y. (it is now a museum of decorative arts); and 4) to the New York Zoological Society to construct the *World of Birds* at the Bronx Zoo. Her philanthropies, although mostly centered in the New York area, are widespread.

DeWitt died at age 91, on March 30, 1981. Lila died three years later. In her last years, she established, in the New York Community Trust, funds that continue to distribute financial support for designated purposes.

Alice Tully (1902-1994) was the daughter of a New York Republican senator, William J. Tully, and of Clara Houghton Tully. She was the granddaughter of Amory Houghton, the founder of Corning Glass. Her cousin, Arthur Houghton, was a founder of Lincoln Center. When she was 8 years old, she was taken to her first opera, *Hansel and Gretel*, and this deeply impressed her. But when she heard Josef

Hofmann at a piano recital at Carnegie Hall, she knew that music would be her career, in one way or another.

When she was 17, she began studying music seriously. She persuaded her parents to let her study voice in Paris. Her teacher was Jean Périer, who prepared her for her debut in 1927, at the age of 26, with the Pasdeloup Orchestra of Paris. Alice loved Paris, and lived there from 1922 until 1938, making trips back to America to perform in recitals. In 1935, Miss Tully made her American debut at the Manhattan Opera House. In 1936, she made her Town Hall debut.

When she returned to the United States to live, she decided that she wanted to learn to fly, which she did with great enthusiasm. She was a member of the Women Flyers of America. Later, she became a Red Cross nurses' aide, remaining in this work until two years after the end of World War II. All this time she was still engaged in her singing career, but in 1958, she decided to end this aspect of her life. She felt her voice did not measure up to the standard she wanted, nor was she as committed to her singing as she had been.

In 1959, she inherited a fortune and devoted herself to full-time philanthropy. While living in Paris, she had acquired exquisite taste and tremendous knowledge in the arts, having developed a special interest in 18th-century culture. Her philanthropies also touched the areas of medicine, education, and wildlife preservation. But her emphasis was always on music. The institutions that benefited most from Alice Tully's interest and support are the New York Philharmonic, the Metropolitan Opera, the Juilliard School, the Metropolitan Museum, the Pierpont Morgan Library, the Institute of Fine Arts at New York University, and the Alliance Francaise. She was responsible for the founding of the Musica Aeterna chamber orchestra, which performed at the Metropolitan Museum. She was a member of a committee, called the Lincoln Center Emeriti, which dealt with crucial issues that concerned the Lincoln Center for the Performing Arts.

Because of her vision, support, and commitment, the Alice Tully Hall for the performance of chamber music was constructed in Lincoln Center. Both she and William Schuman, who was president of Lincoln Center at that time, agreed that Alice Tully Hall should be the home of a resident chamber music group, named the Chamber Music Society of Lincoln Center. Miss Tully was chairman of the Chamber Music Society's board of directors, and involved in almost every aspect of its construction, policies, and organization. In fact, she was so involved that, during the construction, she took it upon herself to visit the American Seating Company. With her was Charles Wadsworth and Edward, a friend of hers who was 6 feet 3 inches tall. She had her friend sit down and stretch out his legs, and that became the way the distance between the rows of chairs was decided.

The founding artistic director, Charles Wadsworth, and Alice Tully, the founding chairman, collaborated for years, and were completely in tune with each other. He had met her in Italy in 1961 at the Spoleto Festival, with which he had been involved for a few years and had directed some of its concerts. She never missed his Noonday Concerts which featured music for instruments and voice. Having spent some time together in the informal atmosphere of the festival, they developed a special friendship and understanding. Later, when they were informed by William Schuman that they would be working together at Alice Tully Hall, they were both delighted. Although Mr. Wadsworth had complete authority when it came to artistic decisions, he had great respect for Miss Tully's musical judgment, and often consulted her. Everyone admired and respected her. Laurence Dow Lovett, chairman of the Chamber Music Society, said in 1992, ". . . Miss Alice Tully's commitment to the idea [of Alice Tully Hall] was crucial and made our founding possible. She was our chairman during the society's first 20 years; her wisdom and leadership helped us grow and thrive. . . . If her many contributions to other important institutions have resulted in even a fraction of the benefits that we have experienced, then we must recognize that there is hardly an area in the cultural life of this city that she has not touched and changed for the better . . ."[8] Alice Tully Hall opened in 1969.

Miss Tully also built and supported work retreats for musicians, donated scholarships, established grants, contributed to music libraries, commissioned music compositions, donated instruments, and supported new music. She has received many honors, including the National Medal for the Arts. France honored her by making her an Officer of the Legion of Honor.

Charles Wadsworth said of Alice Tully, "Alice's great dignity and elegance is coupled with a wonderful sense of humor that includes an enjoyment of the healthy, earthy variety as well as the graceful bon mot qualities of character that form a marvelous combination." On another occasion he said, ". . . Because of her passionate commitment to music and her concern with the individual, she has touched more lives than can be counted . . ."[9]

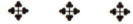

Elizabeth Nitze Paepcke (1902-1994), with the help of her husband, Chicago industrialist Walter Paepcke, founded the Aspen Institute and the Aspen Music Festival in Aspen, Colo. Her father, William A. Nitze, was chairman of the romance languages department at the University of Chicago. Elizabeth studied painting at the Art Institute in Chicago, worked as an interior designer and stage designer, and was active in philanthropies that bolstered Chicago's cultural life. When she married, her husband, too, became interested in the arts, and she convinced him that in business it was important to use talented, artistic designers instead of the usual commercial artist. This combination of art and commerce influenced other projects in their lives.

Elizabeth was beautiful, with a memorable smile and lovely blue eyes, but she never felt that this was important. Instead, she concentrated on her vision for the arts. Everyone who knew her was impressed with her strength of purpose and will, softened by her gracious manner.

In 1939, when at her ranch in Colorado, Elizabeth arranged a ski outing for her house guests. They reached the top of Aspen Mountain and were all astonished at the incredibly beautiful view. In 1945, they returned to Aspen and realized that it would be the perfect area for a ski town full of the finest of cultural activities. The idea was to combine opportunities for physical recreation with those for feeding appetites for culture. With the help of her brother, Paul Nitze, who was the arms-control advisor for the country, Robert Hutchins, president of the University of Chicago, and other friends, the plan came to fruition. They attracted interesting people such as Albert Schweitzer and Thornton Wilder. Because of the Paepckes' strong work ethic, moral discipline, and feelings of obligation to society, Aspen became a haven for those who wanted a healthy and culturally oriented life.

Walter died in 1960, before the advent of drugs and other manifestations of the disintegration of their vision. Elizabeth became more and more disappointed. In the 1970s, the City Council, which was fighting against the growth of the town, moved out to Maryland. In the 1980s, Aspen was inundated with people flaunting wealth and glitz, spoiling the original concept; Elizabeth was devastated. The town, however, still honors Elizabeth Paepcke as a woman of great integrity, taste, and foresight.

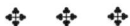

Six women were primarily responsible for the dream of the Hollywood Bowl coming to fruition:

Artie Mason (Mrs. Joseph) Carter is called the "mother of the Hollywood Bowl." A piano teacher from Missouri, she went to Vienna with her husband (a physician) and, while there, studied with the great Theodor Leschetizky. They then returned to America and settled in Hollywood. She was petite, feminine, and did not have a great talent for business. But she was charming, dedicated, and had a genius for holding the whole project together. She was responsible for establishing the world-famous Easter Sunrise Services and the Symphonies Under the Stars.

Florence Behm (Mrs. Leiland Atherton) Irish is called the "crusader for the Hollywood Bowl." From 1926 to 1945 she was completely involved in every aspect of the Bowl organization. A strong, imposing, practical woman, she was also warm and energetic, and loved everyone. Born in Los Angeles, she was the eldest daughter of Ada and William Behm, and was a third-generation Californian. Her father engineered the foundation construction of the original Philharmonic auditorium. Her years growing up were spent on a large ranch belonging to her grandparents. The whole family was musical, and Florence took music as well as elocution lessons. When she was grown, she studied business administration and business law, and was fluent in Spanish and German, all of which were powerful assets in her projects. Her husband, Leiland Atherton Irish, was a musician and successful businessman. In 1912, they moved to Hollywood, where she became active in various organizations. Those active in the Hollywood Bowl project turned to her to carry on Mrs. Carter's work. For 15 years, she was the guiding spirit of the Bowl. As general chairman and director, she provided great leadership.

Christine Wetherill Stevenson was the driving force for the founding of the original Theater Arts Alliance and the purchase of the Hollywood Bowl property. Her father was the head of the Pittsburgh Paint Company. She was extremely wealthy, and a great patroness of the arts. Her husband's wealth came from the munitions business, which was upsetting to her. She arrived in Hollywood in 1918 and, possibly because she wanted to make amends for the war's destruction of the arts, she became interested in furthering the arts, using her influence to bring leading artists to Hollywood. She believed in reincarnation, and was active at the western headquarters of the Theosophical Society in Krotona, high above Hollywood. There, she conceived the idea of outdoor presentations based on the lives of the great religious leaders of the world. Mrs. Stevenson started the financial drive for the amphitheater in the dell. **Mrs. Chauncey D. Clarke**, another dedicated patroness of the arts, worked with her.

Patronesses in the United States

Dorothy Buffam "Buff" (Mrs. Norman) Chandler was born in Illinois and moved to California at age 1. Her parents were pioneers in Long Beach, where her father became mayor, head of the board of education, and helped develop Long Beach Harbor. He founded a prestigious chain of department stores. Dorothy, who was the youngest, loved music and athletics. She was tall, blond, energetic, and had great stamina. She also was strong-willed. After graduating from high school as her class valedictorian, she went to Stanford University, then she studied journalism at the University of Southern California. She married Norman Chandler, the eldest son of Harry Chandler, publisher of the *Los Angeles Times* and one of the important figures in the original organization of the Bowl. Norman later became the publisher of the *Times*. Dorothy was a born executive, and was responsible for the Bowl's reopening and its preeminence. The Hollywood Bowl is the summer home of the Los Angeles Symphony Orchestra. She brought together supporters from the music, financial, social, and civic worlds. Later, she raised more than $13 million to create the Music Center in downtown Los Angeles.

Myra Hershey provided much of the land, selling a portion of her property for the low price of $20,000.

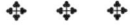

Among the many women who have supported the Metropolitan Opera in New York City, **Eleanor Robson Belmont,** the wife of financier August Belmont, was one of the most important. It is clear that, when that institution was not able to plan a season celebrating its 50th anniversary, Mrs. Belmont started an intensive fund-raising drive to establish a guarantee fund. During that time, Mrs. Belmont and two other supporters devoted themselves completely to this cause, and practically lived at the opera house for months. The other two were Cornelius Bliss, who represented the box holders of the Committee for Saving the Metropolitan Opera, and who was the father of Anthony A. Bliss (future general manager and president of the Metropolitan Opera), and Lucrezia Bori (the great lyric soprano who served as the chairman of the committee). The necessary money finally was raised.

In May, Eleanor became the first woman member of the Metropolitan Opera board. She started the Women's Metropolitan Opera Club, members of which were entitled to use the grand tier boxes and the Metropolitan Opera Club on Saturday nights. (That night was selected because it was informal and, therefore, easier for women to attend.) The purpose of the club was to fill "a need for the women who enjoy and love opera, but who do not feel they can afford the regular subscription and who heretofore have not cared to attend alone."[10] There were two classes of membership: $30 for 12 performances or $15 for six. Mrs. Belmont's stated mission was that the people of New York "look upon the opera as theirs, that the people should look upon it as an integral essential part of the life of the city."[11] She founded and became the chairman of the Metropolitan Opera Guild in 1935.

As a young girl, Eleanor was an actress, and was said to have inspired George Bernard Shaw's *Major Barbara*. After her marriage to August Belmont in 1910, she left her stage career and became active in philanthropies concerned with music and other worthwhile causes. This was a lady of dignity, beauty, intelligence, excellent judgment, devotion to the democratization of the opera, and with a great love of opera itself. She was a loyal supporter of Rudolph Bing when he was general manager. Her "Annual Giving Program," run by her National Council, was of great help to him.

Since her death, the Belmont Fund has continued to provide money for grants to help young musicians.

Friends of Mrs. Belmont who are notable for their work in support of the Met:

Mrs. John Barry Ryan (Margaret Kahn Ryan) was the daughter of Otto Kahn, the powerful and wealthy investment banker. He was one of the leaders in the development of the Metropolitan Opera, chairman of its board in

1911, and president of the board in 1918. He was called "America's foremost patron of the arts" by *Time* magazine.[12] Otto Herman Kahn (1867-1934) was from a Jewish banking family in Germany. Musical recitals were held often in his home and he developed a passion for music, particularly, and the arts generally. He went into the family profession of banking for which he had been trained and was well-suited, then going on to London to become a British subject. In 1893, he came to America to the New York office of the banking firm for which he worked. He married Margaret's mother, who was a member of a very prominent American Jewish banking family. It was not long before he became a partner of Kuhn, Loeb, one of the powerful Wall Street firms.

In 1903, Jacob Schiff, the senior partner of the firm, recommended that Otto become a member of the Metropolitan Opera's board of directors. It was exactly the kind of position for this cultured, knowledgeable, and astute young man, and he accepted. He bought up the shares of other stockholders, and, in 1911, became chairman of the board and, in 1918, president. He ran into one obstacle that he was not able to overcome for a long time: Although there was no apparent antisemitism on Wall Street, it was prevalent uptown in high society. Jacob Schiff, an American citizen since 1870, senior partner of Kuhn, Loeb, was refused a box of his own at the Metropolitan Opera. That was also true of the power behind the Met, Otto Kahn. They and others like them had to lease a box. Otto, as chairman of the board, was entitled to use the director's box, but that was not what he wanted. Finally, after much subtle campaigning, he was offered a box of his own. It was an event prominently reported by the New York press.

This was the atmosphere in which Margaret grew up. She was surrounded by cultural advantages, sincerely loved music, and came to appreciate the importance of presenting it to the public. She worked hard to develop financial support for the Met, and she contributed heavily herself.

Appearing in the *New York Times* on April 18, 1995, was an announcement about Margaret Ryan: "A concert in memory of Margaret Kahn Ryan is to be given at the Metropolitan Opera House on Thursday at 5 P.M. Mrs. Ryan served on the Met's board from 1956 until 1981, when she became an honorary director. She worked on fund drives for the company, and her personal donations enabled the Met to offer new productions of several operas, including *Don Carlo* and *Cosi Fan Tutte*. Among those taking part in the concert, which is free and open to the public, are the mezzo-sopranos Marilyn Horne and Frederica von Stade, the soprano Hei-Kyung Hong, the tenor Paul Groves, several members of the Metropolitan Opera Orchestra, and James Levine, the company's music director. . . ."[13]

Mrs. Lewis Douglas, a strong leader on the board of the Metropolitan Opera, was responsible for bringing organization to its fund-raising. She was deeply involved in its problems, and when the Met was in financial trouble in the 1966-1967 season, she raised an additional $3 million over the losses of that year, then another $500,000 to reduce the deficit in the working capital.

Mrs. John D. Rockefeller Jr. (Martha Baird Rockefeller) was a big contributor to the Metropolitan Opera and a close friend of Rudolph Bing, the general manager. When she died, she left $5 million for an endowment fund. The Rockefeller family already had decided that the Rockefeller Foundation would take a financial interest in the performing arts (John D. Rockefeller III was the family representative), but her bequest was her own.

Mrs. Ogden Phipps, another prominent supporter of the Metropolitan Opera, was an active and influential member of the board.

Mrs. Albert Lasker and **Mrs. Frederick K. Weyerhaeuser** joined Mrs. Belmont and her friends in raising and contributing funds necessary for the splendid productions at the Metropolitan Opera House that Mr. Bing presented.

Mrs. DeWitt Wallace (see separate section in this chapter)

Other notable patronesses in the United States:

Rosalie J. Leventritt, wife of Edgar M. Leventritt, in whose honor the Leventritt Competition was founded in 1939, was the guiding force of the competition. She was from Birmingham, Ala.

Mrs. Leventritt was an elegant, lovely, and sweet lady with a good sense of humor and a shrewd mind. She had always been interested in encouraging and supporting gifted young musicians in every way. Not only was she involved in the competition, but she also helped established the Marlboro Festival in Vermont and the Casals Festival in Puerto Rico. Her great friends were the Adolf Busch family, the Serkins, the Menuhins, George Szell, and others of stature in the world of music. Her warmth and hospitality made her home on Park Avenue in New York City a gathering place for friends and colleagues.

The Leventritt Competition was one of the most prestigious, yet it was not well-known by the general public. It had a discreet image, and was quite unusual in its agenda. It offered no cash prize, but the winner was asked to play with the top orchestras. If the jury felt that the contestant was not mature enough at the time to embark on a career of playing with these orchestras, it was not obligated to award any prize. It also was possible to award more than one winner. The jury was made up of people such as George Szell, Rudolph Serkin, William Steinberg, and Gary Graffman. Some of the winners were Eugene Istomin, Alexis Weissenberg, Kyung-Wha Chung, Pinchas Zuckerman, and Van Cliburn. It was sponsored and run by the Leventritt family.

Catherine Filene Shouse (Mrs. Jouett Shouse) was the power behind the founding of the Wolf Trap Farm Park for the Performing Arts in Vienna, Va. It is the first national park dedicated to the performing arts. The Wolf Trap Foundation, originally created by the secretary of the Interior, manages the artistic and educational programming, as well as the Wolf Trap Opera Company, the Wolf Trap Orchestra, and some master classes. The philosophy, inspired by Mrs. Shouse, is to appeal to differing tastes. In October 1994, she received the National Medal of Arts. It was presented to her by President Clinton at the White House.

Mrs. Charles Sprague-Smith, who was from New England, was the power behind the Bach festival of Winter Park, Fla. It started as a vesper service in 1935. She became interested and active in gathering funds. The musicians ran the festival, but she established the rules: There was to be no applause and only music by Bach. It has changed since her day. Other music is played, there is a larger orchestra and choir, applause is allowed, and admission tickets are sold.

The park, "Stern Grove," site of the Stern Grove Midsummer Music Festival in San Francisco, was donated by **Mrs. Sigmund Stern** in memory of her husband. Her goals were to give people the opportunity to hear the best in music and to give musicians employment. Since 1928, it has been co-sponsored by the San Francisco Park and Recreation Department. Concerts are free. The average attendance is between 15,000 and 19,000 people.

Of the wonderful women who have taken upon themselves the burden of furthering fine classical music in this country, **Anne Ratner** is one of the most remarkable. Appearing in *The New York Times* on June 16, 1995, was her obituary: The heading was "Anne Ratner, 90, Patron of Musicians." The article went on to say:

> Anne Ratner, a music patron who kept alive the idea of the music salon, died on Saturday at her home in Manhattan. She was 90.
> Ms. Ratner put on concerts by first-rate artists in the

living room of her Riverside Drive apartment. Among those who appeared, often more than once, were the Emerson and Juilliard Quartets, the singers Arleen Auger and Cecilia Bartoli, and the pianists Richard Goode, Jeffrey Kahane and Andras Schiff. Appearance at these evenings became somewhat of a status symbol among musicians, and they often served as showcases for emerging talents.

Ms. Ratner, who organized these evenings by herself, asked each person in the small audiences for at least $30, but personal profit was not on her mind. Ms. Ratner was born in Russia and reared in Williamsburg, Brooklyn. She studied the piano and in 1929 married Hyman Ratner. After her husband died in 1960, she taught at the League Center for Seriously Disturbed Children in Crown Heights, Brooklyn. The salon concerts—up to 18 per season—developed through her work at the center and served as benefit events for the center and for Camphill Village, a community in Copake, N.Y., for mentally handicapped adults.

She is survived by two daughters, Molly Finn of Manhattan and Judy Pitt of Leonia, N.J.; two sisters, Rebecca Jarmon of Forest Hills, Queens, and Mina Gudeon of Sunrise, Fla.; a brother, Saul Kamen of North Hills, L.I., eight grandchildren and three great-grandchildren.[14]

Mrs. E. D. Gillespie and **Miss Frances A. Wister** did much for music in Philadelphia.

Mrs. Lenore W. Armsby was a significant patroness in San Francisco.

Clara Bauer was deeply involved in the support of the Cincinnati Conservatory.

Fanny Raymond Ritter was a great advocate for the support of composers, concerts, opera series, educational institutions, and festivals.

Maria Longworth Nichols Storer was instrumental in founding the Cincinnati May Festival, which focuses on major choral works and operas.

Ellen Battell Stoeckel established the Norfolk Music Festival in Connecticut at her estate, which was donated for that purpose. This festival was the first summer music festival in the United States. The Yale concerts are played there in an acoustically excellent music shed.

Ella May Smith was the dynamic president of the outstanding and philanthropic music club in Columbus, Ohio.

May Garrettson Evans was an important supporter of the prestigious Peabody School of Music in Baltimore, Md.

Janet Schenck, an admirable philanthropist, founded the excellent Neighborhood Music School in 1917 in New York City. Eventually, it became the Manhattan School of Music.

Harriet Gibbs Marshall worked for and contributed to the Washington, D.C., Conservatory.

Adella Prentiss Hughs helped found the Cleveland Orchestra and Severance Hall in Cleveland, Ohio.

Ima Hogg was a powerful force in the Houston Symphony in Texas.

Helen H. Taft, with the able help of her fellow patronesses, **Bettie Fleischmann Holmes and Annie Sinton Taft,** was the leader of the Ladies' Musical Club in Cincinnati, Ohio. This club was devoted to the Cincinnati Symphony Orchestra.

Mary Howe and **Marjorie Merriweather Post** led the Friday morning Music Club in its support of the National Symphony Orchestra in Washington, D.C.

Eleanor N. Sanger (Mrs. Elliot M. Sanger), a member of the Naumburg family, was a founder of WQXR in the New York metropolitan area.

Jean Tennyson, whose husband, Camille Dreyfus, was chairman of the Celanese Corporation of America, was an ardent supporter of opera and opera singers, including Beverly Sills and Mary Garden. She was an important contributor to the San Francisco Opera.

In the mid-1940s, in Center Harbor, N. H., **Mrs. Heidy Speilter** and **Mr. and Mrs. J. Edward Kurth** formed the New Hampshire Music Festival with New York musicians.

Mary Hale of Alaska, active patron of the arts, had Julius Herford and Robert Shaw come to Alaska and direct Anchorage's chorus and symphony. This developed into the Alaska Festival of Music. In 1984, the festival established a permanent home in Anchorage at the Alaska Performing Arts Center.

In 1992, the Cincinnati Symphony was in a state of crisis but was saved by two important "angels." **Patricia Corbett** (age 85), wife of the deceased J. Ralph Corbett, managed to obtain for the arts more than $33 million through a family foundation; and **Louise Nippert** (age 83), wife of the deceased Louis Nippert, one of the owners of the Cincinnati Reds, gave an undisclosed, but very large, amount. Fifteen million dollars was added to the orchestra's endowment.

For information about the following women, please see Chapter 9: Martha Graham:
Irene and **Alice Lewisohn**
Rita Morgenthau
Edith Julia Isaacs
Katherine Cornell

Chapter Seven

Creative Administrators

Clara Damrosch (1869-1948), pianist and co-founder (with her husband, David Mannes) of Mannes College, was a member of one of the greatest and most exciting dynasties in the American world of music.

Her grandfather, Leopold Damrosch, was an eminent conductor and violinist. He arrived in New York City from Germany with his wife Helene (who was a fine, professional lieder singer), his sister-in-law Marie von Heimburg (who was a professional chorister), and his children. Leopold made his conducting debut in America with the *Arion Society*, which he developed into a superb group. He then went on to conduct the New York Philharmonic, found the Symphony Society in 1878, conduct the first major music festival in New York, successfully tour with his orchestra in the West, organize the German Opera Company, and conduct the Metropolitan Opera. He and his wife had the spirit of pioneers, which they instilled in their children. They had been deeply involved with the cream of the musical world in Europe (Liszt and Wagner were numbered among their friends), and soon were closely involved with the great musicians in New York City. It was not long before they became part of the wealthy and powerful German society that individually, and as a group, was committed to having great German music performed. (At the time, in the 1870s, the Germans dominated musical life in the United States.) Among their friends were Andrew Carnegie, Theodore Steinway, Elkan Naumburg, and Gustave Schirmer. Although they were dependent on these people, who were their patrons and patronesses, they never compromised their standards in music.

The whole family was intensely musical, ambitious, and a force in the development of the German tradition of music in America, particularly in New York City. Clara's brother Frank, the oldest of the children, was a conductor and teacher. He was instrumental in founding the People's Singing Classes (which became the People's Choral Union), the Musical Art Society, and the Institute of Musical Art, which became affiliated with the Juilliard School in 1926. *The New Grove Dictionary of Music and Musicians* (1980) gave Frank full credit for the evolution of this great institution when they said, "The Juilliard School of Music, a conservatory of international reputation, was begun by Frank Damrosch in 1905 as the Institute of Musical Art."[1]

Clara's brother Walter was the next oldest. He became an internationally celebrated conductor (and was less well-known as a composer and educator). He was the conductor of the New York Oratorio Society, the New York Symphony Society, the New York Philharmonic Society, and the Metropolitan Opera. He organized the Damrosch Opera Company and the American Expeditionary Force bands. He was the musical adviser to NBC and the conductor of the NBC orchestra in weekly music appreciation programs. After World War I, he became the president of American Friends of Musicians in France. Through his war work in France, he was accepted by the French musical world. He founded schools for bandmasters in France that, in 1921, were succeeded by The American School at Fountainbleau, dedicated to bringing American musicians to France to study with French musicians who had been trained at the Paris Conservatoire. Nadia Boulanger (see Chapter 5), who had worked with him, was a force there and had enormous influence on the music of American composers.

Clara and her sisters had exactly the same opportunities for studying as their brothers. She became a fine professional pianist. Her younger sister, Elizabeth, taught singing and piano and lectured occasionally. Her elder sister, Marie, also was trained musically, but did not go on with her career.

The children had regular music lessons from other professionals, but at home it was required that they play regularly for their father. The standards were very high. Much was expected of them, but they seemed to thrive on this diet. Their house was filled with the great musicians of the day. (Anton Rubinstein and Pablo Casals were among those who made music in their home.) On Sunday afternoons, particularly, there was usually chamber music played, along with piano-violin sonatas, and piano trios. Clara's taste and interests developed rapidly in the direction of chamber music. When she was older, she wrote, "The creative beauty and mastery of the great composers fulfilled my religious needs. No sermon can be worthier of God or realize the inner truth better than the immortal works of Bach or the exquisite purity of Mozart."[2] She declared that she did not have this spiritual experience with orchestral works of composers of the romantic school.

As a young girl, Clara seemed to be attracted romantically to violinists. (This probably was to be expected, considering the fact that she adored her father, who was a violinist.). She ultimately married violinist David Mannes, with whom she developed a successful career in piano-violin duo performances.

When Leopold died in 1885, Helene moved the family to a small apartment on West 34th Street, near the Metropolitan Opera House. Clara was 17 years old. Walter and Frank were in charge of the financial decisions, but Helene was still the center of the family. Although money was a problem, and even though Clara and her sister Ellie were still in school, Helene decided to send them to Germany for one year of music study. She was able to finance this by chaperoning and teaching six young women who wanted to study in Dresden. The nine women left for Germany in September 1888. The rest of the family was completely supportive of the situation, which was highly unusual in that the education of the daughters in a family usually was sacrificed for that of the sons. This experience was invaluable for Clara, who, at the age of 20, had become a pianist of professional caliber. When the women returned to the United States, they found that Walter was to be married to Margaret Blaine, the daughter of Secretary of State James G. Blaine. Frank had already married Hetty Mosenthal, and Marie had married Ferdinand Wiechmann. Helene, her sister "Tante" Marie, and the two unmarried girls moved into a smaller apartment on West 72nd Street. Frank and his family lived in the same building, and Walter and Margaret lived two blocks away. They continued to be a closely knit clan.

Clara began to teach, and soon became self-supporting. She was somewhat lonely. (Ellie had left to marry Harry Seymour.) Chamber music was her love, but at that time, it was not possible for a woman pianist to develop a career in that area of music. But one evening, David Mannes, who played violin in the New York Symphony Orchestra, came with a friend to call at her home. It was obvious that he was very much taken with this young lady. As they were leaving, on an impulse, Clara invited David to come to play some pieces of chamber music with her. He immediately accepted.

David's family had immigrated from Poland, had very little money, and settled in a rough section of New York City. His parents were Orthodox Jews, yet encouraged independent thought. (Clara's father was Jewish and her mother was Lutheran; neither practiced his or her religion. It has been reported that Leopold was baptized in the Lutheran church when he was married to Helene. Clara and the other children evidently had no real identification with any religion.) David separated himself from his religious background, but never from his family. His devotion was to music. He discovered his love for the violin when he was very young, and made himself a one-string violin from a cigar box. His parents were impressed with their son's potential, and managed to buy him an inexpensive violin and to pay for some lessons. However, his lack of exposures to great music kept his talent from developing rapidly. Added to these frustrations were his physical problems. As a child, he had suffered a serious accident in which he was badly burned, and from which he never fully recovered. For the rest of his life, he was subject to debilitating depressions.

Leopold Damrosch was his idol. One evening, the great man's son Walter attended a performance in a theater in which David happened to have a solo. The conductor was impressed. Walter was looking for violinists for his new symphony orchestra and hired David. He was given a contract, and the young man's life was changed. He went on to become concertmaster of the orchestra, and had the kind of musical experiences of which he had always dreamed.

At rehearsals of the Oratorio Society, he became attracted to a woman who sang in the alto section. It was Clara. He arranged to be invited to her home, and that was the beginning of their romance.

In 1897, Clara went to Berlin to study piano with the great Ferruccio Busoni, and David went to Berlin in order to study violin with Carl Halir. He had rearranged his travel plans so that he might sail to Europe on the same ship as Clara. They saw each other in Berlin, and after four years of courting, he proposed and was eagerly accepted. They were married on June 4, 1898, in her sister Ellie's house in Middle Granville, N.Y.

The young couple moved to an apartment in the same building that housed Helene and Tante as well as Frank, his wife and children, and his wife's relatives. All their apartments were close. David had never wanted to manage his financial affairs, and had turned everything over to his mother. Now that he was married, Clara managed the practical side of their marriage. She taught in the apartment, and David sublet a studio in which he had students. He was already an important violinist in the New York Symphony and had other interests as well, one of them being his desire to teach music to the poor to offer them spiritual nourishment. This he did on Rivington Street on the lower East Side where there was a school for Jewish immigrants from Poland and Russia. This school became known as the Music School Settlement (now called The Third Street Music School Settlement), and he became committed to building this institution into something of great value. He eventually became its director and gradually devoted more and more of his time to this project. He also founded The Music School Settlement for Colored People in Harlem.

Unlike her husband, Clara did not enjoy teaching or working with the underprivileged. Also, she had always preferred performing to teaching. Therefore, it seemed that the best role for her in these projects was to take care of the management of her husband's affairs, so that he would be free to do his good works.

In 1899, Clara and David had their first child, Leopold Damrosch Mannes, and in 1904, their daughter Marya was born. Just before their daughter's birth, they started thinking of touring together as a piano-violin duo. They were both interested in chamber music, thoroughly enjoyed playing together, and made an attractive team. For Clara, this was ideal. In this way, she finally would be able to achieve her dream of having a career in chamber music. David then studied with Eugène Ysaÿe for six months, while Clara worked on her half of the repertory. When they returned from Europe, they began their concertizing. Evidently, they were the first duo in America to have an ongoing career. It lasted from 1904 to 1917. They were soon performing 40 to 50 recitals a year. It was a great contribution to music in the United States; they were instrumental in introducing to audiences fine violin-piano repertory. They played in 30 states, in England, and in Canada.

In October of 1916, Clara and David opened the Mannes College of Music (originally named the David Mannes School of Music, in spite of the fact that Clara was an equal partner). It was to differ from the Institute of Musical Art, founded by Clara's brother, Frank Damrosch: In addition to Frank's goal to train potential virtuosos and to provide them with a full education in music, Clara and David wanted Mannes College to offer an excellent music education to devoted amateurs. They felt that "a school directed solely toward education for a career runs the danger of becoming institutional, while a purely cultural school for the amateur runs the opposite risk of becoming lax in standards, bereft of the stimulus that only serious artistic qualities can give."[3] They decided not to give examinations or diplomas, so that there would be as little competition as possible. This concept was in keeping with the Mannes' pleasurable experience of playing chamber music in their home with accomplished non-professionals, as well as virtuoso professionals. They understood, too, that those who are educated musically represent the heart of audiences, make superior board members, and become enthusiastic and generous patrons and patronesses. The school opened at 154 East 70th St. in New York City. They did not have wealthy backers, but depended on small contributions. It was located in a wealthy neighborhood to make it available to those who could afford a high tuition fee. Clara managed the administrative work and taught advanced students in chamber music and ensemble work. David taught advanced violin and teaching methods, and conducted the senior orchestra. It was a success, mostly because of the Mannes's reputation, their fine faculty, and Clara's management. An important event occurred that helped them tremendously: Pablo Casals, who always came to the Mannes apartment with his cello for chamber music when he was in New York, gave a concert at the school. He and five of the city's finest string players played two Brahms sextets for strings. This attracted great attention to the new music institution.

After the war, in 1919, the school was moved to 157 East 74th St. Clara concentrated on the school. As an administrator, she was outstanding. She knew how to deal with the trustees, members of the committees, and prospective financial supporters. David was good with the students, and they both attracted outstanding teachers of the day.

The relationship between Clara and David deepened and matured. They were wonderful together. And their relationship with their children was satisfying and admirable. Their son Leopold, a young man of great charm and good looks, graduated from Harvard and pursued his two powerful interests: photography and music. He was incredibly successful in both. He and Leopold Godowsky Jr. (son of the great pianist) discovered the Kodachrome process and Kuhn, Loeb and Company subsidized their work. They received patents on which they earned royalties. In the field of music, he won a Pulitzer scholarship and the Guggenheim fellowship, both in composition, studied piano in Paris with Alfred Cortot, and became acknowledged as a professional composer and pianist. He became increasingly involved in the Mannes School and eventually became its president. During his tenure, the school leaned more toward professionalism, becoming a college accredited by the state of New York, and bestowing degrees upon students at graduation. In April 1953, it became the Mannes College of Music. However, it was still unique as a music school in that it offered a curriculum that educated students in theories of musical analysis, which helped them to emerge as well-rounded musicians. Leopold became one of the most outstanding presidents of music conservatories in the United States.

Leopold's sister Marya had always rebelled against becoming a musician and, instead, became a celebrated writer, lecturer, and television personality.

In March 1948, Clara, while walking with her husband and niece on Lexington Avenue in New York City on their way to hear their son in a piano-violin recital, had a massive heart attack and, within seconds, died. David lived another ten years. Their creation, The Mannes College of Music, is one of the outstanding conservatories in the world today.

❖ ❖ ❖

Helen Mulford Thompson (1908-1974) was born in Greenville, Ill. Her father, a druggist, was an amateur musician and supporter of Greenville's music activities. It was important to him that his children each play an instrument and participate in the town's musical events. Helen's instrument was the violin, which was given to her at the age of 6. When she was 12, she was given the job of librarian for the town's music organizations. This was the beginning of her lifelong commitment to community service, particularly in the area of music.

Helen attended DePauw University, and majored in psychology and sociology at the University of Illinois, where she received an A.B. degree and was a member of Phi Beta Kappa. Throughout her years as a college student, she continued to play the violin in her school's orchestras and ensembles. After college, she went on to take graduate courses in sociology and became a professional social worker. She worked as agency director and/or case work supervisor in Illinois, Wisconsin, and New York State from 1932-1940. Her training and experience in psychology and social work prepared her beautifully for dealing with all kinds of people. In her career as administrator, she was extremely successful in persuading those who were important to her projects to go along with her constructive and innovative ideas.

Helen married Dr. Carl D. Thompson, a research chemist. In 1940, Union Carbide and Carbon Chemicals Corporation, for whom he worked, sent him from Niagara Falls to Charleston, W.Va. Helen and Carl had just had a son, and Helen decided to retire from social work at this point. When she was settled there, she discovered that the Charleston Symphony had just been organized, and, of course, she immediately joined the orchestra, playing in the second violin section. From there, she went on to become the orchestra's manager and served in that capacity during its expansion and improvement. Composer-conductor Antonio Modarelli was the music director. Her association with him and his vision of musical development for the nation had an enormous impact on her. He believed in the growth of community orchestras and other local music activities, making use of that valuable asset: local talent.

During this time she heard of a new organization of orchestras, called the American Symphony Orchestra League (ASOL), which was founded in 1942. She joined and was soon elected to the voluntary position of secretary. In 1950, she resigned as manager of the Charleston Symphony and became the league's first full-time executive. The national headquarters of the league was set up in Charleston, W.Va. When her husband retired in 1962, the family moved and the main office was transferred to Symphony Hill, Vienna, Va. Mrs. Jouett Shouse (Catherine Filene), who had given land to the National Park System for the Wolf Trap Farm Park for the Performing Arts, had contributed 40 acres to the ASOL. The league, under Mrs. Thompson's guidance, became one of the most important and potent music organizations in the nation. Her goal has always been to help symphony orchestras of all kinds (major, metropolitan, urban or small community orchestras), and to provide them with educational programs, workshops, and source materials to help their conductors, trustees, and managers. She instilled in the league the purpose of developing an orchestra's musical quality and community service. Each year, there is a convention in one of the big cities to which each orchestra sends its representatives. In between the annual meetings, there are local workshops and conferences. It has attracted the attention and support of such wealthy institutions as the Rockefeller Foundation and the Martha Baird Rockefeller Fund for Music, which have given it large grants.

Among her many accomplishments: she obtained a repeal of the federal 20 percent excise tax on symphony tickets, an act that saved many orchestras from bankruptcy. She began the Music Critics' Workshops in 1954, resulting in the Music Critics Association. The Arts Councils of America was established because she invited arts council representatives to attend the league's meetings. In 1963, with the help of Col. Robert Benchoff, headmaster of Massanutten Military Academy, she established the Shenandoah Valley Music Festival in Orkney Springs, Va., in keeping with her philosophy that local res-

Creative Administrators

idents should have the opportunity to enjoy music of the highest quality.

In 1956, Mrs. Thompson was appointed the executive vice-chairman of the President's Music Committee of the People-to-People Program. This committee established communication between foreign and American music organizations. She was in demand everywhere, but was never too busy to answer questions, offer help, work on a new project, and be a good friend to her colleagues.

In April 1970, Helen became manager of the New York Philharmonic, the first woman manager in the history of that orchestra. She was a trustee of the Martha Baird Rockefeller Fund for Music; a member of the advisory committee of the Filene Center of the Wolf Trap Farm Park for the Performing Arts; secretary of a group of executives of national tax-exempt organizations; chairman of the steering committee of the Forum of Executives of National Arts organization; and a member of the U.S. committee on music in UNESCO, as well as other positions too numerous to mention. She received honorary doctorate degrees from Cincinnati College Conservatory of Music and Marshall University in West Virginia.

Mrs. Thompson received awards for her achievements from the American Composers Alliance, the National Association of American Composers and Conductors, the music fraternity Sigma Alpha Mu, the Community Arts Councils, Alpha Chi Omega, and the American Symphony Orchestra. She also won awards in writing and editing.

As a human being, she was remarkable. She was known for her drive, competence, fairness, honesty, and razor-sharp mind. And yet, with all the adulation showered upon her, her common sense kept her from losing her perspective. No matter how much recognition she received from the music world, she remained deeply concerned about the welfare of each orchestra (no matter how small or large) and the people associated them. Even with her enormous drive and vision, she took the time to enjoy those around her. She was a woman of great warmth, charm, and humor.

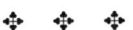

Sarah Caldwell, born March 6, 1924 in Maryville, Mo., grew up in Fayetteville, Ark. Her father was a professor at the University of Arkansas, and her mother was a pianist and taught music. She was an incredibly gifted child in both music and mathematics. Before age 10, she began giving violin recitals. She enrolled in the University of Arkansas and majored in psychology, after which she studied violin at the New England Conservatory of Music in Boston with Richard Burgin, concertmaster of the Boston Symphony Orchestra, and viola with Georges Fourel. But after studying opera production, conducting, and stage design with Boris Goldovsky, she decided to go into opera.

In 1946, Sarah went to Tanglewood to study opera. She impressed everyone. At age 18, she staged and conducted Ralph Vaughan Williams's *Riders to the Sea*. Maestro Serge Koussevitzky realized she was extremely talented and, even though she was very young, appointed her to the faculty at Tanglewood as Goldovsky's assistant. She stayed on for five years, the only female conductor there.

Goldovsky was head of the opera department at the New England Conservatory, and in 1947, hired her to be his assistant. From there, she went to Boston University, where, in 1952, she became the head of the Boston University Opera Workshop.

In 1958, she formed her own opera company, calling it the "Opera Group"; in 1965, she changed the name to "Opera Company of Boston." She wanted to reach a college audience along with professionals, intellectuals, artists, writers, musicians—everyone who was interested in opera for its own sake, rather than for social purposes. She put together amazing productions on the proverbial "shoestring" budget in the Donnelly Theater, an old vaudeville and movie theater that had been closed down. She was truly inventive, her ideas interesting and original. For one early production she created a set with $12 worth of sheets. The productions were excellent, with the finest talent. She conducts, produces, selects the cast, administrates, directs stage business, takes care of publicity, designs scenery, and makes the decisions on costumes. Among the many singers who have sung with her and been supportive of her work are Beverly Sills, Marilyn Horne, and Placido Domingo. She has a great reputation as a fine musician, a woman of tremendous energy, and almost a magician when it comes to putting on an opera. Joan Sutherland said, "Miss Caldwell is one of the great producers of the world." Laszlo Halasz agreed, saying, "One of the finest stage directors I've ever known. She's a mad genius."[4]

Because of her weight, she conducts sitting in a large armchair, which does not seem to hamper her in the least. She was able to organize support and to have important Bostonians join her board and her opera guild. She had good corporate sponsorship, as well. Nevertheless, finances continued to be a problem.

She has always been a non-conformist in the best sense. She is an individualist who knows what she wants and how to get it, and she goes after it in the simplest way possible. She has been known to wear big cloaks, carry her comb and few other articles in a paper bag, and sometimes sleep in the theater. It has been reported that "she sold her car because she got tired of trying to remember where she had parked it . . . She declared, 'I'm afraid that I do not relate well to possessions'."[5] Beverly Sills, in describing her, said Sarah kept unusual hours, and seemed to be at her best at ten o'clock at night. She said that "Sarah had a lovely house, but her real home was the theater. She slept, ate, and dressed in the theater, and usually didn't give a damn about how she looked. Sarah lives to create beauty where none has existed before."[6] One of Ms. Caldwell's statements, reported by Ms. Sills, was, "There are no boring roles. There are only boring singers."[7] She introduced the idea of audience participation. Once, when her company performed *The Daughter of the Regiment* in the gym at Tufts University, she had the people in the bleachers hold up red, white, and blue cards to form the French tricolor, as Beverly Sills entered singing an aria and banging a drum.

In the 1975-76 season, Sarah Caldwell became the first woman to conduct at the Metropolitan Opera in New York City. The performance was *La Traviata*. She has also conducted at the New York City Opera in 1973, the New York Philharmonic, and a television production of *The Barber of*

Seville. Winthrop Sargeant, a music critic, said, "Nothing in the way of eccentricity and everything in the way of bringing to light all the musical and dramatic subtleties that a score contains."[8]

Her reputation as a producer equals her reputation as a conductor. In 1978, she was the first to be presented with the Kennedy Center Award for Excellence.

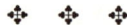

Beverly Sills (named Belle Miriam Silverman, nicknamed "Bubbles") was born on May 26, 1929, in Brooklyn, N.Y. Her brother Sidney, who became a physician, was six years older than she, and her brother Stanley, who became a publisher, was four years older. The family has always been exceptionally close. They moved about in Brooklyn, and eventually settled in Sea Gate, near Coney Island and the ocean. Her father, Morris Silverman, who was from Rumania, was an assistant manager of the Metropolitan Life Insurance Company. He was a protective father and, at the same time, authoritative. His children found him very reachable, and his daughter felt free to discuss many interesting matters with him. Yet, even though he respected her mind, he believed that, if one had to choose, it is more important for boys rather than girls to be well-educated.

Her mother, on the other hand, believed women should be equally well-educated, and was the impetus for Beverly's career. Sonia Markovna Bonchikov, Bubbles's mother, was born in Odessa. She was very musical, and from early on exposed her daughter to sophisticated cultural activities. She and Bubbles reserved every Saturday for cultural jaunts. She loved coloratura sopranos, particularly Lily Pons. She made sure that she and her daughter attended a Pons performance whenever they could. Amelita Galli-Curci was another of her favorites.

When Bubbles was 3 years old, she appeared on the radio. At age 4, after Mrs. Silverman saw an advertisement for talented children to go on "Big Brother Bob Emery's

Rainbow House" program on Saturday morning radio, she took her daughter to apply. If accepted, a training program was included. Bubbles was accepted. The host and she liked each other immediately. She sang on the program until she was 7. Then her mother took her to audition for the "Major Bowes' Original Amateur Hour." She was a hit and became a regular guest on "Capitol Family," his other program, where she stayed until she was 10. She sang on other shows, and even acted in *Our Gal Sunday* as an abused child opera singer. She not only had a lovely, sweet voice, but she was also a good little actress. She was hired to do an advertisement for Rinso White Soap and appeared on a television program entitled "Stars of the Future." She had begun to earn money at that early age. Her father did not approve, of course, and finally put a stop to it. Although he did not take her dream of becoming an opera star seriously, her mother did, and was able to persuade him, one way or another, to be supportive.

Major Bowes suggested to "Mama" that Beverly take singing lessons. Mrs. Silverman found the perfect singing teacher, Estelle Liebling (see Chapter 5). This wonderful teacher guided Beverly's career, and her student was devoted to her until her death. Miss Liebling became Beverly's guide in many areas, as well as in voice. She believed that Beverly's voice was very well-suited to French vocal music, and steered her in that direction. She insisted that she study piano (which she did, under the guidance of Paolo Gallico), and taught her to be at ease in all social situations, with famous and important people and at all kinds of elegant occasions. She introduced her to fine fashion designs and great literature. When Beverly graduated from Public School 91, she was voted "most likely to succeed." Through Miss Liebling, Beverly was introduced to J. J. Shubert who produced Broadway musicals. He hired her to go on a tour, which was a great help in gaining experience. She made her operatic debut as Frasquita in *Carmen* with the Philadelphia Civic Opera in 1947.

When her father died, her mother showed great courage, independence, and commitment to her daughter's career by moving with her to Stuyvesant Town in New York

City. She studied fashion design for a year, then started designing hats for Lily Daché and selling her designs.

Beverly Sills joined the New York City Opera in 1955, when it was at the New York City Center. At that time, Julius Rudel was assistant conductor and a good friend. She went on tour to Cleveland, where she met Peter Greenough, who was a journalist with the *Cleveland Plain Dealer* and a member of a prominent and wealthy family. They came from different worlds. Peter was a white, Anglo-Saxon Protestant, and she was a Jewish girl from Brooklyn. He was 12 years older than she, and in the process of getting a divorce from his first wife, with whom he had children. But Peter and Beverly were great together, and they were married on November 17, 1956. It is a wonderful marriage.

They moved from Cleveland to Milton, Mass., in 1960, and Peter worked for the *Boston Globe*. They have two children, and Peter has custody of his first children. Unfortunately, their son is autistic. Their daughter, who is deaf, has developed into a fine, talented, and productive young lady. Because of these problems, Beverly was able to put her career in perspective. Through bad times and good, her mother gave her strong emotional support.

When Beverly was able to pull herself together, after realizing the extent of her children's handicaps, she returned to her career. In 1962, she sang in Sarah Caldwell's production of *Manon* with Norman Treigle and John Alexander. The Boston Symphony played; Sarah Caldwell conducted and directed. They got rave reviews. Peter gave her a round-trip ticket to New York City, so that she could continue her studies with Estelle Liebling. Performing in opera had always been her love, and was an escape from her worries about the children.

She rejoined the City Opera in 1962. Tito Capobianco, director, and his wife Gigi Denda, choreographer, became part of Beverly's team at the City Opera. She admired their productions, and this association lasted through many years. In 1966, the City Opera moved to the New York State Theater in Lincoln Center. Roland Gagnon, an accompanist Beverly met when he was rehearsal accompanist for

Sarah Caldwell, also joined Beverly's team. She depended on him for his knowledge and taste in ornamentation. Their relationship, too, lasted for years. He was an excellent vocal coach.

Beverly Sills performed in *Julius Caesar* so beautifully that her name was on everybody's lips in the music world. She became an international opera star. She was known not only for her beautiful voice and her ability to perform difficult coloratura parts, but also for her intelligence and knowledge, traits not always associated with opera divas.

Beverly had sung in all the famous opera houses except the Metropolitan Opera House because Rudolph Bing, the general manager, refused to invite her—perhaps because she was the leading prima donna of the rival opera house across the plaza in Lincoln Center, or perhaps because of personality clashes. But when he left in 1972, she was asked to make her debut there, which she did on April, 7, 1975.

Peter and she decided that when she was 50 years old, she would end her singing career. He retired, having inherited a great deal of money, and became involved in philanthropic work. They moved to a nine-room cooperative on the west side of Manhattan. In December 1970, she was appointed to the Council on the National Endowment for the Arts by President Richard Nixon. She also began to be seen on television talk shows. In 1972, she became national chairman of the Mothers' March on Birth Defects.

Through the years at the New York City Opera, she had become more and more involved with the business of producing operas and the problems associated with it. Her administrative ability became apparent. At one point, the board of directors was going to shut down the company. She, Norman Treigle, Cornell MacNeil, Phyllis Curtin, and other colleagues mounted a campaign to persuade the powers that be to keep it going, and to make Julius Rudel the general director. They succeeded. In August 1977, she began serving on the board of the New York City Opera. At that time, there was a new chairman and other new board members who decided to reorganize the fund-raising and administration method. They wanted to fire the managing director, John White, who called Beverly; she then went to bat for him. She called someone she knew on the board and threatened trouble if White was fired. She was told that they would consent to keep him if she would join the board. This was agreeable. At that time, the chairman, John Samuel, suggested that, when she retired, she might consider taking over the running of the City Opera.

On October 27, 1980, she sang at the New York City Opera for the last time. She had started her career more than 30 years before, on October 28. When she retired, she became co-director with Julius Rudel. Soon after, Rudel resigned and Beverly became general director. As a board member, she had done some successful fund-raising out of town which was excellent training for her new job. As an administrator, she began to study the intricacies of her job, but she still had not seen the books, and did not realize that the City Opera was in terrible financial shape. When she became the general director, it was about $4 million in debt. Beverly Sills saved it. She went after philanthropic and financial institutions, Mayor Koch, and the city and federal governments—in fact, anybody she felt would help. Her charm and intelligence won them over. She was determined to see the New York City Opera survive.

1982 was a bad year financially, but artistically it was very good. There was one crisis after another. In 1983, the orchestra went on strike, which lasted 54 days. She made the 1983 season a mini-season, and it was a great success. After that, it was easier to raise money. Through her efforts a development department was organized. The season in 1984 opened with great optimism. She introduced many new ideas; for example, she produced not only traditional operas but also contemporary works, unknown operas, musical comedies, and operettas. This opera company is known for its excellence and innovative programming. She was instrumental in popularizing opera in America: Prices were kept low, supertitles helped to remove any mystery, and operas were produced in which the singers could act as well, and even look the part. The singers are usually young, extremely gifted American artists.

Beverly Sills retired from the management of the New York City Opera in 1988, spending some of her time producing television shows dealing with opera and singing. She received honorary degrees from Harvard University, New York University, and the California Institute of the Arts. She was given the U.S. Presidential Medal of Freedom. In 1994, she succeeded George Weisman as chair of the Lincoln Center for the Performing Arts in New York City.

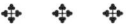

Loretta Dranoff established the Murray Dranoff International Two Piano Competition to honor the memory of her husband. She is the administrative director. When Loretta was young, she lived in New York and attended Hunter College. In 1940, she met Murray at the studio of Clarence Adler, a talented teacher who had been a student of Leopold Godowsky and whose own students included Aaron Copland and Richard Rodgers. At the time, Loretta and Murray were both rehearsing for concerts in New York. They started dating, and were married in 1941.

Clarence Adler suggested that the young couple join forces and perform as a duo-piano team. It was a brilliant suggestion. They were each sensitive to the other and performed beautifully together. Their reputation began to grow nicely, but World War II interrupted their career, and Murray was sent to Europe. While he was there, Loretta gave birth to twin girls. It was not until the children were 19 months old that he was able to return and meet his daughters.

The Dranoffs settled in Bridgeport, Conn., which was Murray's hometown. They established a music school, Studio 860, taught, and traveled regularly to New York City to study and prepare for a concert career. Just four years after Murray had returned from Europe, they received a contract for 65 concerts to be performed in that first year. (In order to travel with two pianos and all their luggage, they bought a specially designed truck.) In the 1950s and the 1960s, they were one of the busiest two-piano teams in the country. In addition to their concertizing, they both had long teaching careers. Their close family includes three children and six grandchildren.

Chapter 7

At age 49, Murray had a massive coronary, and in 1974, the Dranoffs moved to south Florida. They became involved in the music world of Miami. He taught at Barry University, and she in the Dade County school system. In 1985, Loretta's husband, close companion, and partner died. She, with the help of her children, grandchildren, friends, colleagues, and former students, founded the Murray Dranoff Foundation. The goals of the foundation were the presentation and preservation of music (especially four-hand chamber music for the piano) and the founding of a competition that would help launch two-piano teams. At one point early in their concert career, Murray had said it would have been a help in their career if there had been competitions for duo-pianists. Unfortunately, at that time, there were none. After his death, Loretta decided that the project she was about to establish in his name was one that he would have truly valued.

The foundation sponsors the International Two-Piano Competition, the International Two-Piano Symposium (for the purpose of education), the Junior Two-Piano Competition (for ages 12 to 21), and the Salon Series (with salon-sized audiences and concerts performed in the homes of patrons of the foundation). Another valuable achievement has been the commissioning of new works, many by well-known contemporary composers. The juries are composed of distinguished people in the music world, including Harold Schonberg, Joseph Horowitz, Martin Bookspan, and Charles Wadsworth.

The Murray Dranoff International Two Piano Competition, which was the first two-piano competition in America, was held in 1987. It takes place every two years in Miami. In 1995, there were 194 applications from 32 countries and 28 states. The semifinals were held in New York, Chicago, and Paris. The 10 finalists were heard in Miami. It has become an extremely prestigious competition, and is recognized by musicians all over the world.

❖ ❖ ❖

Creative Administrators

Others who deserve salutes:

Mrs. George Sheldon, a banker's wife and a capable executive in her own right, was the power behind the reorganization of the New York Philharmonic during the 1908-1909 season. She was responsible for changing the corporate structure so that the orchestra would henceforth be subsidized under the management of a committee. The season was extended from 18 to 46 concerts. In the 1908-1909 season, she wrote a letter to the *New York Times*, saying that the Philharmonic Society wanted a radical change in the organization of the orchestra. She added that there would be a board of trustees to govern the orchestra, but the conductor would control the orchestra and the concerts. The debut of the newly organized orchestra was on November 4, 1909.

Mrs. Sheldon had gathered her wealthy and influential friends to become part of the new structure. These women were not particularly knowledgeable about music but arrogant in their opinions. She decided that she would like to have Gustav Mahler as the new conductor. (He happened to be in New York at that time, and had a great reputation as a conductor of opera in Vienna.) He was hired and conducted brilliantly. Unfortunately, he had a difficult personality, and this created problems with the musicians, visiting artists, and, especially members of the board. The ladies of the board tried to tell him what to do, especially with respect to programming, and, naturally, he was furious. There were unpleasant scenes, after which he became quite ill, and the concertmaster conducted for the rest of the season. (See Chapter 4, Alma Mahler.) To avoid any public reaction, Mrs. Sheldon told the press only that she thought he was the greatest conductor in Europe and America. Since he was not well, the ladies were in a position to quietly and nicely drop him. In Paris, Alma Mahler blamed the 10 ladies of the board for the whole affair. She felt their arrogance and ignorance were inexcusable. After all, with other orchestras, particularly in Vienna, her husband made the final decisions. No one ordered him about. Word spread that these ladies were difficult to work with and, as a result, they were not able to replace Mahler with a top conductor.

Jeannette Thurber, the wife of a wealthy grocer, founded the National Conservatory of Music in New York. It was established in 1885, charged no admission until 1915, and had an excellent faculty. She was instrumental in persuading Antonin Dvořák to come over from Prague. Her goals with respect to Dvořák were to have this famous Czech composer and teacher head her conservatory in order to give it stature, to teach young American musicians, and to compose new works especially for Americans. Her goal for American music was to encourage nationalism. Serious music in the "new world" at the end of the 19th century was dominated by German composers and artists. Dvořák was known for his own nationalistic Czech compositions, and, as she had hoped, agreed with her about the need for "American" music. Dvořák believed the future of music in this country must be founded upon so-called Negro melodies, and said that the music of American Indians also was important. He explained that he meant the spirit, not an imitation of the melodies, and this spirit must be combined with modern theory. During his three years in the United States, he did indeed compose works in which he seemed to try to absorb some of the qualities he characterized as American. His compositions included the New World Symphony, the F Major String Quartet, and the E Flat String Quintet. Yet later, he denied the fact that the New World Symphony was predominantly American. Instead he insisted that it was Bohemian music. He led the conservatory from 1892 to 1895. From 1899 to 1902, it was headed by Emil Paur.

Claire Reis and Minna Lederman were primarily responsible for the founding of the League of Composers, and for making it a force for modern music. Ms. Reis became the executive director, and Minna Lederman was the editor of its publication, *Modern Music*.

Its success can be attributed to the leadership of Claire Reis. She was instrumental in the 1925-26 season in get-

Creative Administrators   233

ting Serge Koussevitzky and members of the Boston Symphony to conduct Aaron Copland's music, which the league had commissioned. She led the league to financial security by attracting wealthy patrons to the project. She had amazing organizational ability, and was truly interested in helping composers. And she fought for them. At one point, she found out that the New York Philharmonic Orchestra did not want to play a piece by Copland in a concert sponsored by the league. She marched over to Artur Rodzinski, who was the conductor at the time, and forcefully convinced him to perform it. At another time, in 1953, Copland's famous piece *Lincoln Portrait* was banned from the Eisenhower inauguration because the composer was accused of communist affiliations by the McCarthy group. Rep. Fred E. Busbey suggested the ban. Claire fired off a telegram that read, "No American composer, living or dead, has done more for American music and the growth of the reputation of American culture throughout the civilized world than Aaron Copland. To bar from the Inaugural Concert his music, and especially music about Abraham Lincoln, will be the worst kind of blunder and will hold us up as a nation to universal ridicule."[9] Unfortunately, she lost the argument.

Minna Lederman Daniel was an experienced and effective editor, as well as an illustrious writer on music. She had studied music and dance professionally, then went on to study for a degree at Barnard College. She was the editor of *Modern Music* for 22 years (1924-1946) and made the publication so prestigious that the most important people in the field of modern music wrote articles for it. (Virgil Thomson, Arnold Schoenberg, Bela Bartok, Alban Berg, Elliot Carter, Marc Blitzstein, and John Cage were just a few of the eminent contributors.) It was the first American journal for contemporary composers. In addition to her writing, in 1975, she established the Archives of Modern Music at the Library of Congress.

Marian MacDowell, a pianist and the wife of composer and pianist Edward MacDowell, was responsible for founding the MacDowell Colony in Peterborough, N.H. She had bought a summer home there in 1896 called *Hillcrest*. Edward had wanted to create a quiet center where artists could meet, work, and exchange ideas. A year before he died, in 1907, in order to realize his dream, Marian founded the colony. She was in charge of everything: the planning, maintenance, administration, and funding. There was a main house and some studios to start. She gradually added many more studios, a library, residence halls, and Colony Hall, where there was dinner and discussion. The studios were placed well apart from each other, and each one is spartan, yet has the necessary equipment. There is a cot, a chair, a bright lamp, and, for musicians, a piano. It is set in beautiful woodlands covering hundreds of acres. Many famous artists, including writers and visual artists, as well as musicians, have taken advantage of the opportunity to spend time there. Aaron Copland went on eight separate occasions and ultimately became a member of the MacDowell Association, serving as its president for a few years in the 1960s. In 1961, he received the coveted MacDowell Colony Award, which is given once a year. The MacDowell Colony is a rare, much appreciated oasis.

Marian MacDowell outlived her husband by almost 50 years. In 1910, two years after his death, she arranged an extensive and glorious pageant featuring the performance of his compositions. This was the beginning of a series of MacDowell Festivals at Peterborough.

She died in Los Angeles at age 98.

Alicia Schacter, a fine pianist, was the founder and artistic director of the Santa Fe Chamber Music Festival in Santa Fe, N.M.

Helen M. Hosmer was the founder and director of the Crane Chorus and Orchestra, which was established in 1931. She then developed the high-quality Spring Music Festival. The concert hall has 1,400 seats and is named the Helen M. Hosmer Concert Hall at the State University College in Potsdam. Ms. Hosmer has contributed greatly to the development of choral music and music education in the United States.

Creative Administrators

Helen Gunderson, who was professor emeritus of composition and theory at Louisiana State University, inspired and worked for the establishment of the Louisiana State University Festival of Contemporary Music at Baton Rouge, La. It was one of the first contemporary music festivals in the United States.

Susan Tilley has been chairman of the Van Cliburn Foundation, which is in charge of the Van Cliburn International Piano Competition.

Lina Lalandi, born in Greece, was an internationally known harpsichordist and musicologist. She was the founder and director of the prestigious English Bach Festival in Oxford and London. In 1963, Albert Schweitzer was president, as was Igor Stravinsky in later years. Leonard Bernstein became president in 1972.

Ruth, Lady Fermoy started the King's Lynn Festival of Music and the Arts in King's Lynn (96 miles north of London). It was founded in 1951 as part of the large Festival of Britain. She served as the director of this important festival for 25 years.

Chapter Eight

Remarkable Mothers and Sisters

Maria Anna Walburga Ignatia Mozart (1751-1829) was known as Marianne and called Nannerl by her brother, Wolfgang Amadeus Mozart (1756-1791), and her parents. Her family lived in Salzburg, Austria, where the two children were born. (There were seven children, but only two survived.) Her father, Leopold, was a composer, violinist, teacher of violin and keyboard, and musical theorist. Her mother was Anna Maria Pertl, whose father, in his young years, had been a singer and teacher of music, later going on to a university to receive an education in jurisprudence.

In their early years, Nannerl and her brother were inseparable, both emotionally and with respect to their interests and training. Leopold had started teaching harpsichord to his daughter when she was a small child. At the age of 3, Wolfgang listened with fascination to the musical sounds of his older sister's lessons, absorbing everything. He idolized Nannerl. She was certainly a child prodigy, but he was a musical phenomenon. Harold Schonberg, the music critic, wrote, "At the age of three, he started picking out tunes on the piano. His ear was so delicate that loud sounds would make him physically ill. And it was not only delicate, but perfect in pitch. At the age of four he was telling his elders that their violins were a quarter tone out of tune. At that age he also could learn a piece of music in about half an hour. At five, he played the clavier amazingly well. At six he started composing."[1] His father started teaching Wolfgang to play the harpsichord and the violin as soon as the child was physically able. The two children lived and worked together constantly, becoming almost as one, with their own made-up language and fantasies. They teased each other lovingly, and shared all their thoughts and feelings. He wrote to her, "I hope, my queen, that you are enjoying the highest degree of health and that now and then . . . you will sacrifice for my benefit some of your important and intimate thoughts, whichever proceed from that very fine and clear reasoning power, which, in addition to your beauty, and although from a woman, and particularly from one of such tender years, almost nothing of the kind is ever expected, you possess, O queen, so abundantly as to put men and even graybeards to shame."[2] This relationship lasted for years, but, unfortunately, when they were adults, they began to grow apart and, finally, there was a definite break.

 Nevertheless, in the early years, they thoroughly loved and enjoyed each other. Leopold gave up his own limited career and devoted himself to teaching and directing Nannerl and Wolfgang. He began arranging performances for these two young children, since he understood the theatrical value of displaying them at tender ages. He was tyrannical, manipulative, loving, and demanding. He exploited them, supposedly for their own good, but, in reality, to gain recognition, social acceptance, and financial security. He recognized his son's incredible genius, and proceeded to direct Wolfgang's every action and thought. His daughter was just as tightly controlled, and, through her life, she obeyed him almost completely in order to keep his attention and his love. Her mother, a gentle lady, did not dare to go against her husband's orders.

In 1762, Leopold took Marianne (age 10) and Wolfgang (not quite 6) to Munich, where they performed before the elector of Bavaria, and to Vienna to play for Emperor Francis I. Then, in June 1763, they started their long concert tour. Leopold arranged performances all over Europe and in London (where the boy's first symphonies were heard). They played before the most important royal families, aristocrats, and leading musicians, as well as at public concerts that anyone could attend for a fee. They became celebrated all over the continent and in England. The journey lasted three and a half years. When they started their tour, Wolfgang was 7 and Marianne was 11 (although Leopold told everyone that they were two years younger).

It was obvious to Marianne that her brother's genius overshadowed her talent. She was acclaimed as a fine pianist, and collaborated beautifully with Wolfgang in their duo recitals, but when she was 18, she decided to devote herself to giving piano lessons at home. And she was an excellent teacher. Wolfgang continued to give concerts in the capitals of Europe. While her father and brother enjoyed the excitement of mixing with nobility, the greatest musicians, and the high society of Europe, she remained in Salzburg at home with her mother. Of course, the two women resented being left at home, but said nothing (Leopold told them that the family could not afford their traveling). It probably was about this time that Marianne began to envy her brother's life and position in the family. She was still close to him, writing many supportive letters and keeping a detailed diary, which proved to be very helpful to historians.

When her father and brother left Salzburg for Wolfgang's long concert tour, she wrote in her diary, "The day of their departure I spent mostly in bed, I vomited and had an extraordinary headache."[3] Mozart neglected writing to his sister, although she had written to him of her distress, and his lack of support hurt her even more. She wrote to him, "Since you have now become so distinguished and your time is so much taken up that you cannot write to me, probably you will have no time to read a few lines from me either."[4] When her father sent her mother to travel with young Mozart to Mannheim and Paris, Marianne was left at home again. She had been close to her mother, but Anna Maria evidently was not sensitive to her daughter's feelings and made no attempt to make things easier for her.

During the time that she was abroad with her son, Marianne's mother became ill and, after a difficult time, died in Paris (with her son at her side). Now that Marianne was in charge of the household, she took on the duties of her mother, becoming more and more subservient to her father and sacrificing her own desires to his. He thoroughly enjoyed having her at home with him, and wrote about the happy hours in which they played music together. He put every obstacle he could devise in her way in order to keep her from marrying. One suitor after another was turned away. She fell in love with Captain Franz Armand d'Ippold, who loved her in return. They wanted to marry, but her father would not give his consent, and she gave him up. As had happened many times before when she was disappointed, she became ill. Her brother was supportive in his letters to her, but she could not stand up to her father. When she recovered, she accepted her position and committed herself to making Leopold's remaining life happy. In his communications with his son, he used her devotion to him as a weapon against young Mozart's desire to separate himself from his father. To the very end of his life, he played one against the other. He was successful in convincing Marianne that Mozart was to provide financial support for the family, and that she must take his side in insisting that his son owed everything to him.

Leopold wrote to Wolfgang, constantly demanding that he conform to the demands of society, behave sensibly, and have as a high priority the generation of money to support the family. But he did not recognize that Wolfgang was not the average person. His son had a greatness in him that had to evolve and to which he had to give first priority. Young Mozart had no use for bourgeois values. In addition, his personality was the direct opposite of his father's.

He was undisciplined, irresponsible about material things, and immature socially. On the positive side, he was committed to his ideals, had a deep sense of justice, was generous with his money, and had a great capacity for friendship and conviviality. Leopold succeeded in driving his son away, although their love for one another remained strong.

Their relationship deteriorated badly when Mozart married Constanze Weber, whose family had neither money nor social position. As would be expected, Leopold was totally opposed to the marriage. He continued to drive a wedge between sister and brother, and as time went on, resentment between the two mounted. He had thoroughly convinced Marianne that Mozart was in the wrong. (Perhaps she was willing to be convinced because of her brother's lack of warmth and attention, as well as her own envy.) A break was inevitable. Of course, the real culprit was their exploitive, rigid father, but this fact was never acknowledged by either one. The compensation she had for the separation from her brother and her complete emotional dependence on Leopold was that her father needed and loved her, which to her was the most important goal.

In 1784, Leopold was ready for his daughter to marry and arranged a marriage between Marianne and a wealthy, irritable, elderly man, Baron von Berchthold zu Sonnenburg. When her brother was invited to the wedding, he wrote to her ". . . It is high time I wrote to you, if I wish my letter to find you still a Vestal! Another few days and good-bye to that. My wife and I wish you all good fortune and happiness in your change of condition and are only heartily sorry that we cannot have the pleasure of being at your wedding . . . now do listen:

> The married state will teach you more
> Than you had clearly known before.
> "T'will by experience show to you
> What Mother Eve first had to do
> That ever Cain could come to life.
> But Sis, the duties of a wife

> Are heartfelt pleasure and not strife;
> Trust me, they'll not prove burdensome.
> Yet this world can't be always fun.
> Marriage brings many joys, indeed,
> But cares come too, with equal speed.
> So when your husband for an hour
> Frowns on you with a mien that's sour,
> Though faults you've not committed one,
> Tell yourself, these are mannish flights
> And murmur, Lord, thy will be done
> By day—and mine o' nights.
>   Your candid brother
>   W. A. Mozart[5]

Marianne became the stepmother to the baron's five children, and gave birth to a boy, whom she named Leopold. Her father was 65 years old by this time, and wanted that little boy for himself, to enjoy and to mold (perhaps into another musical genius). Marianne and her husband allowed him to keep the child. (There seems to be no explanation for her attitude on this, except her usual desire to please her father.) Marianne saw the boy only occasionally, but received constant accounts of him from Leopold. The child remained with his grandfather until Leopold's death, and then returned to his parents. He was raised mostly by a half-sister (and did not become a musician).

In May 1787, Leopold Mozart died. In Wolfgang's letter to his sister, he expressed his sorrow, briefly announced that he would not be returning home, and asked about the will. Then came the shock: He found out that his father had left the bulk of the estate (most of which he had earned) to Marianne, leaving only some personal effects to him. His father had said he would disinherit him if he married Constanze, but he never really believed it. Evidently, the old man had quite a large estate, which he did not reveal to his son, instead always demanding more money from Mozart. (Wolfgang, however, had suspected the truth.) Mozart found his sister to be completely unsympathetic and uncooperative, and, in fact, asked that he give up his share of the money from the sale of the personal effects. He refused. In a letter to Marianne, Mozart wrote that he probably would not be in communication with her much in the future, offering various flimsy excuses. She understood his rejection, and there was no further correspondence between them. Again, Leopold had caused dissension between his children, but their break was caused not only by the unequal legacies but by Marianne's bitterness and desire to show her brother that Leopold loved her more. In her heart, however, she probably always knew that her father lived through the achievements and talent of his son, that there was a special bond and love between the two men, and that she could never have competed with that. Mozart, although deeply wounded, had a wife and children he loved, and withdrew completely into his own world.

Marianne's husband died in 1803. She lived on comfortably until, in 1826, she went completely blind. On October 29, 1829, she died. Oddly, she was not buried near her father. Constanze, Wolfgang's wife, may have been the reason. There had been little contact between the two before 1819. (Mozart had died in 1791.) When the Baron von Berchthold died, Constanze sent a letter of condolence to Marianne, and the two sisters-in-law became somewhat friendly. Constanze had remarried. Her husband, Georg Nissen, was a legation secretary in Denmark, and when he retired, the couple moved to Salzburg, near Marianne. Georg and Constanze were both dedicated to Mozart and his music. When Nissen worked on a biography of Mozart, Marianne graciously gave him 400 family letters that the author was allowed to use for his book. Evidently, there was a friendly relationship between them. But, when Georg died, Constanze arranged to have him buried at the St. Sebastian cemetery in which Leopold was buried. (Later, Constanze and her two sisters also were buried there. Poor Leopold. Imagine his feelings if he had known that he was to be surrounded by the Weber family for eternity!) It is suspected that, when Marianne learned of Nissen's burial near her father, she changed the instructions for her own internment and chose St. Peter's cemetery.

She survived her brother by 38 years.

❖ ❖ ❖

Fanny Mendelssohn (1805-1847), born in Hamburg, Germany, was a gifted pianist and composer. Her family was extremely interesting. Her grandfather (Moses Mendelssohn) was a brilliant and internationally famous philosopher. Her father (Abraham Mendelssohn-Bartholdy) was a prominent banker. Her mother, Leah, was a talented amateur pianist who also was well-educated in literature, languages (including Greek), and visual arts. Her brother was the celebrated composer, pianist, and conductor, Felix Mendelssohn-Bartholdy (Fanny was four years older than he). Rebecca, Fanny's sister, was a singer, and Paul, her other brother, was a cellist. The family was talented, wealthy, well-educated, and cultured. Serious learning was emphasized in the lives of the children.

Originally, the family was Jewish. Moses, Fanny's grandfather, was quite observant and proud of his religion. Nevertheless, in spite of his devotion to Judaism, his intellectual curiosity led him to look into other faiths. This exposure contributed to his son's decision to join the Lutheran church when he realized that life would be difficult for his family in a society that was antisemitic. When he settled his family in Berlin, Abraham decided to convert to Protestantism. He added Bartholdy to his last name and had the children baptized. The family was accepted into Berlin society. Great men, including poets Goethe and Heinrich Heine, philosopher Georg Hegel, writer Jean Paul, and scientist Alexander von Humboldt, all frequented the Mendelssohn salon. Musicians and writers of conservative leanings regularly congregated in their home. (These associations had a great influence on the children. Felix, especially, would remain conservative in his outlook as a result, thus affecting his opinions about women performing in public and being published.) They had one of the most fashionable salons in Europe in their home at 3 Leipzigerstrasse.

Fanny started her piano studies with her mother, then went on to study piano and composition with fine professional teachers. Her interests extended to geography as well as experimental physics, but music was most important to her. In 1816, the family moved to Paris for a time so that Fanny and Felix could study piano with Marie Bigot. A few years later, they returned to Berlin, and the brother and sister studied piano with Ludwig Berger and composition with Carl Friedrich Zelter. Fanny was told by her parents that, although they recognized that she was gifted, there could be no future for her in music as a profession, because it was not appropriate for a woman. (Felix agreed with his parents, although he loved his sister and truly admired her talent.)

In 1822, the Mendelssohn family began their tradition of producing extensive musicales in their home on Sunday mornings. Her parents permitted Fanny to perform at these musicales. A small orchestra was hired to play Felix's compositions, and Fanny and Felix performed at the piano. They played and evaluated each other's music. Fanny wrote, "I have watched his progress step by step; and may say I have contributed to his development. I have always been his only musical advisor and he never writes down a thought before submitting it to my judgment. I have known his operas by heart before a note was written."[6]

By 1827, Fanny was a mature composer. Many knowledgeable musicians have judged her songs to be among the finest in the Romantic era. To protect Fanny's personal reputation and to prevent prejudiced and chauvinistic reviews about her, Felix published a few of her beautiful songs under his own name. Because of her close relationship with Felix, she spent much of her time helping him with his work, and he, in return, helped her.

Fanny had met her husband, Wilhelm Hensel, a painter, in 1821. She was 17, he 28. It was, from all accounts, love at first sight, but Fanny's parents did not want them to marry because she was so young. It was not until five years later that she finally was allowed to become engaged to Wilhelm. They were married in 1829, and moved into a small house behind her former home. Although she was happy about her marriage, she was worried that her brother Felix and she would drift apart. However, in spite of the fact that they had separate interests, their bond remained strong. They were tuned in to each other. Musically, they seemed to be on the same wave-length.

A son, Sebastian, was born to Fanny and Wilhelm a few years after they were married. Although she was a conscientious and loving mother, her work continued to be of utmost importance. They moved into the big Mendelssohn home, where she practiced and composed. As time went on, she became quite frustrated; she was not getting the recognition she felt she deserved. Leah, her mother, began to realize that her daughter's compositions merited public recognition and wrote to Felix to ask him to encourage his sister to publish. But he did not approve.

Fanny's life was thoroughly occupied with music. She arranged Sunday morning concerts at Berlin's Elternhaus from 1843, in addition to being responsible for organizing, composing, performing, and conducting the musicales at the family estate. She continued to follow Felix's life closely (he was happily married to Cecile Jeanrenaud and had four children), and performed her brother's compositions.

Fanny Hensel was not at all interested in the usual social duties of a wife. In 1838, at the age of 33, in spite of her brother's disapproval (but she had her husband's full support), she performed in her only public performance. She performed his *Piano Concerto No. 1 in G minor, Opus 25* for a charity benefit. Eventually, Fanny was able to perform her own compositions and was recognized for her talents. In 1846, some of her works were published. (Although her mother still did not want her to concertize professionally, by this time she was very much in favor of having her daughter's works published.)

When her parents died, Fanny assumed the management of the great house, and was completely in control of the Sunday morning musicales for which she continued to compose, perform, and conduct, in addition to rehearsing the chorus.

In 1846, two Berlin publishing houses asked to publish her compositions. Finally, the public was recognizing her as a composer. She wrote every type of composition except opera. During her lifetime, she composed more than four hundred works.

Unhappily, just when she was being encouraged to do more, Fanny died. On May 14, 1847, while rehearsing her chorus, she died suddenly from a stroke at the young age of 42. It was a terrible blow to her brother Felix, who collapsed upon hearing the news. He became very ill. (It is thought that he, too, had a stroke) and was not even able to attend his sister's funeral. He was unable to work much after that. Cecile, his wife, took him to Switzerland and to Baden-Baden in the hope that he would recover his health there, but that endeavor was unsuccessful. He then decided that he must visit the Mendelssohn home at 3 Leipzigerstrasse. It was such a painful experience that he had another breakdown. When he returned to Leipzig, he could not conduct, teach, or compose. On October, 28, 1847, when on a walk with Cecile, he collapsed again. On November 3, he had another physical episode, and, on November 4, he died. The Mendelssohns seem to be susceptible to strokes: Moses, Abraham, Leah, Rebecca, and quite a few of Fanny's uncles, aunts, and cousins died of strokes.

Fanny was Felix's inspiration, just as he was hers. However, it was unfortunate and disappointing to her that he discouraged her from publishing her compositions and from becoming a concert pianist. As a result, neither she nor her music are well-known.

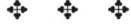

Rildia Bee O'Bryan Cliburn was born in McGregor, Texas, on October 14, 1896. Her roots in Texas were deep. Both her grandfathers had settled there. Her father, William Carey O'Bryan, was a judge and a Texas state legislator, as well as advisor to such well-known people in politics as United States Supreme Court Justice Tom Clark and United States Congressman Sam Rayburn. He married Sirilda McClain, a semi-professional actress. Rildia was the youngest of their six children.

When Rildia was a child, she studied piano with Prebble Drake, a graduate of the Cincinnati Conservatory of Music. She continued her studies at the conservatory with Shailer Evans, then at the Juilliard School of Music in New

York City in 1917 with Arthur Friedheim, who was a celebrated pianist who had studied with and was personal secretary to Franz Liszt, as well as a student of Anton Rubinstein in Russia.

Rildia Bee also studied voice with Ralph Leech Sterner, who was president of the New York School of Musical Art. She had great talent, but because of her family's opinion that a "nice" woman did not travel as a performer, her career was curtailed. She had a proper and socially prominent Texas family, and, although her parents were in favor of her developing her talent, they did not want her to be a professional performer. Because she was close to them and understood their feelings, she accepted this restriction. As a matter of fact, she was surprised to have been allowed to study and live in New York City.

Rildia Bee married Harvey Lavan Cliburn in June 1923. Their son Van was born on July 12, 1934 in Shreveport, La., where Van's father worked for the Magnolia Oil Co. as a sales representative. When Van was 6, they moved back to Kilgore, Texas, where there was an oil boom. From the boy's infant days, he would hear the piano being played for hours at a time. His mother gave lessons all day, then spent hours at the piano practicing music herself. When he was a little older, he would come from wherever he was when she was playing the piano and sit quietly and listen. When he was about 3, after a pupil left, he sat himself at the piano and played by ear the piece he had just heard. That is the point at which Rildia Bee decided it was important for Van to study formally. She recognized his gift, and was particularly impressed that, when he played a note, he did not bang, but depressed the key gently.

An unusual relationship developed between Van and Rildia Bee: that of a warm, loving mother and son, and at the same time a stern, exacting teacher and obedient pupil. She gave him a piano lesson every day, and supervised his practicing until he was 17 years old. In that way, she prevented any bad habits from developing. It was not that she forced these lessons on him; he was the one who asked for them. He really wanted to work, and at first she taught him for short periods, until he was able to work longer hours. He began to perform publicly at age 4.

As a teacher, she stressed that playing should not look difficult, that structure of the composition was important, and pedaling was to be done with great thought. She taught that inner voices should be brought out and that a singing tone is the ultimate goal. Sight-reading and memorization were important to her. Scales and arpeggios were to be practiced over and over. At times, she would accompany her students' playing on another piano, so that the young person would experience participating in a large sound. She organized music clubs for her students, and entered them in music festivals and competitions. Her preference in selecting repertoire was that of the romantic school, with a great deal of the classics added, but not much contemporary music.

Van's parents rarely treated him as if he were a child. Because they were involved in cultural activities and they all did things together, Van was exposed to the finest performances of the finest artists. They would travel for miles, putting him to sleep in the car so that he would be able to stay up late and experience all these wonders. He was a happy child, happy to be with them and happy to be with other children.

On March 12, 1948, Van made his debut at Carnegie Hall in New York City. Rildia Bee was approached by a manager, who wanted to arrange concerts for the boy. She felt strongly about not exploiting her son, and would not allow it. She wanted him to have as normal a childhood as possible, although she wanted him to perform and enter competitions. When she attended master classes at Juilliard in 1947 and 1948, she had Van accompany her, so that he would become acquainted with the school. At that time, he attended some classes in harmony, sight reading, and other subjects. Of course, she was already planning the years ahead for him, and intended to apply to Juilliard for his admission. She arranged with Van's high school principal to accelerate the boy's studies so that he could graduate early and go on to New York for his piano studies. He was accepted by the renowned piano teacher Rosina Llévinne at Juilliard (see Chapter 5). Madame Llévinne was a great inspiration to him, almost always in complete sympathy when it came to the interpretation of the music. She continued the excellent education his mother had given him, prepared him well for his professional life, and guided him in his exciting and successful career.

In the 1960s, Rildia Bee was hired by Sol Hurok, who was managing Van's career, to be in charge of her son's tours. For Van, it was wonderful having her along organizing his everyday life and giving him her sensible, expert advice. Although he has always been a very strong, self-confident person, he always listened carefully to Rildia Bee, ultimately coming to his own conclusion and making his own decisions. He relied on her, too, for reinforcing his values, for her fine musicianship and judgment in situations involving music.

When her husband died in 1974, it was a great loss to her. He had quietly but strongly supported his son's career and sacrificed time with his wife so that she could be of help to Van. She went on with her work so well that in May 1974, the Cincinnati College Conservatory of Music bestowed the Distinguished Alumnae Award on her.

Van had taken a leave of absence from his career to escape the strain of performing. In 1985, he bought a magnificent home in Fort Worth for his mother and for himself, furnishing it with beautiful antiques, several grand pianos, and a large oil painting of Rildia Bee, a gift from Imelda Marcos. But after about a decade of retirement, Van began to reactivate his piano career. Rildia Bee was delighted. In 1987, he performed at the White House for President Ronald Reagan and visiting Soviet General Secretary Mikhail Gorbachev. Then, when she was 92, her son prepared his comeback concert with the Philadelphia Orchestra, his first public concert in 11 years, and she was actively involved. She accompanied him on his Moscow tour, and the chartered jet was officially christened the Rildia Bee O'Bryan Cliburn. When she was 94 years old, Van had a spectacular party for her in Fort Worth featuring the Fort Worth Symphony Orchestra and soprano Roberta Peters. Rildia Bee Cliburn died in the summer of 1994.

❖ ❖ ❖

Jennie Resnick Bernstein, mother of Leonard Bernstein, was born in 1898 in Russia, and arrived in America in 1905. She and her family settled in Lawrence, Mass., near Boston. As a bright young girl, she did well at school and looked forward to being a teacher. Unfortunately, money was in short supply, and she had to leave school so that she could work in the wool mills.

Jennie, a pretty and intelligent young woman, met Samuel Joseph Bernstein, who also was from Russia. This was not a love match. Jennie thought Sam had a good sense of humor and would provide an escape from the mills. Sam had been in love with a gentile whom he could not marry, and probably married Jennie on the rebound. They were married in 1917 in an orthodox Jewish ceremony. At this point, she happily left her job and became a housewife. In August 1918, her son Lenny was born. (His name originally was Louis, but he was called "Leonard." He changed his name legally when he was 16 years old.)

Jennie and Sam had major differences in personality and ambition. Sam was involved with business, and enjoyed intellectual discussions about the Bible, the Talmud, business, and philosophy. Jennie was interested primarily in her family. Her husband considered her intellectually beneath him because of her lack of education and her love of "lightweight" entertainment. (She was crazy about dances, movies, and romantic novels.) Jennie resented his obsession with religion, his tight and sometimes mean budgeting, and his intense ambition in business. Several times Jennie left him and moved back with her parents, but she always returned. After Leonard was born, the couple had a mutual interest and managed to stay together, although theirs was a rocky marriage. Their anger and quarrels scarred their children. Lenny described the marriage in his operetta, *Trouble in Tahiti*. Their daughter Shirley said, "My mother and father . . . were never in love with each other, unfortunately . . . And my father was a basically melancholic man who needed a lot of love and wasn't getting it from his marriage . . . He was a manic-depressive type . . . And Lenny caught that, and so did I, in our personalities."[7] Jennie now focused on her son.

Shirley Anne was born in 1923. This was just about the time that Sam started his beauty-supply business, which ultimately became very successful. Burton, their second son, was born in 1932. Jennie's world revolved around the children, especially Lenny and his music. She had always known that he was unusual; that he was brilliant, creative, and a born leader. The fact that he was sickly probably made her even more concerned. He suffered all his life from asthma.

His father's sister Clara left her piano in Lenny's house, and the boy instantly fell in love with playing it. He went on to study with a neighborhood teacher, and from there to the New England Conservatory of Music. Sam was not happy about the direction in which his eldest son was heading; he was looking forward to Lenny's joining him in his business. But Jennie was completely supportive of her son's musical career, and actively encouraged him. She loved music, and particularly loved hearing him play. (Leonard Bernstein, when describing his mother's passion for music, said, "After a couple of weeks, I had learned to read so quickly . . . [the teacher] had to bring me harder stuff . . . After a year, she was forced to bring Chopin and Bach preludes and Chopin nocturnes . . . With the E-flat nocturne, I went mad and my mother used to stand there crying."[8] She was always on his side, encouraging him constantly. She once said, "The neighbors used to call me on the phone, 'Will you tell your son to stop banging on the piano. We can't sleep.'. . . So you know what I said to them? 'Some day you're going to pay to hear him!' and they did."[9]

At home, he spent much of his time playing the piano and composing, with his mother as his main audience. Often, she would tire and announce that she was going to bed. But Lenny, who needed and wanted her there to listen to him, would lure her back by asking for her opinions and, of course, she was not able to resist that. Most of her attention was focused on Lenny and his music. After much effort on her part, she was able to communicate her enthusiasm to her husband, who finally agreed to help pay for the music lessons. He was secretly proud of his son but was just not convinced that a career in music was practical.

Jennie grew more and more fascinated by Lenny's talent, often going to concerts with him and helping him whenever she could. In 1935, when he was conducting rehearsals of his summer amateur production of *H.M.S. Pinafore,* Jennie let the members of the cast rehearse in her living room for one month. She excused her new maid, Lilia Jiampietro, from work so that she could sing the role of Josephine in the production. To top that, she allowed them all to use her car to get to the rehearsal hall, leaving her without help with the house and without her means of transportation. She was a good sport and thoroughly caught up in her son's career.

According to her son Burton's account, his mother was unwittingly instrumental in bringing about Lenny's friendship with Dmitri Mitropoulos, the guest conductor of the Boston Symphony Orchestra. The young student was invited to attend a reception for Mitropoulos given by the Harvard Helicon Society at the Phillips Brooks House. Lenny was at home and had forgotten about the invitation. He decided that he needed a ride back to his room at the Eliot House. Jennie, who was wearing her house dress, drove him back to Cambridge. She lost her way (which she did occasionally, because of her habit of singing to the music on the radio, keeping time by tapping the accelerator, and not paying attention to the direction in which she was going). They ended up at the Phillips Brooks House. Lenny remembered the reception and convinced his mother to go in with him (even though she was not dressed for a party). Good sport that she was, Jennie agreed.[10] However, Jennie's version of the episode was that her son had asked her to drive him back to Harvard because the conductor wanted to meet him, and that the meeting had been arranged. Another version offered by a friend was that Lenny had told him that he had *not* been invited to the tea, but that he was going to "crash" it. In any case, every account agrees that they indeed went to the party. Mitropoulos was told about the talented young man, and asked him to play the piano, which Lenny did with his usual enthusiasm. The conductor was impressed with his pianistic and compositional talents (Lenny had played a Chopin nocturne and the final movement of his own sonatina) and asked him to attend his rehearsals at Symphony Hall. The young man already was in awe of Mitropoulos, and was completely overwhelmed and flattered when the older man suggested the possibility of Lenny's going into a conducting career. This was the beginning of a close association, both professional and personal.

Watching her son rise to the top was a source of great joy and fulfillment for her. When Leonard Bernstein became famous, Jennie enjoyed every moment of his success, and loved mixing with famous people. People she admired paid a great deal of attention to her, often asking for and valuing her opinions about matters in the arts. She never pretended to know more than she really did. Jennie's amusing malapropisms were a source of enjoyment to her children, and, in fact, they collected them. She had a great sense of humor, and could even join in the laughter about her own funny misstatements. Through the years, she was admired and enjoyed by all who met her. In the summer of 1940, when Lenny was studying at the Berkshire Music Center at Tanglewood with a group of prestigious teachers, he met Kiki (Jacqueline) Speyer, to whom he grew close and almost married. He invited her to his home in Sharon to meet his parents. Afterward, when describing them, she reported, "I didn't like his father. I thought he was uncouth and vulgar, throwing his weight around because he had made money. . . . His mother must have been in her early 40s when I knew her. She was a divine woman."[11] The composer David Diamond, after having met Lenny's parents, said he found Sam "aggressive and boorish. He always had his nose in the Talmud and was holier than thou, waving his finger at you self-righteously. Not what I call a man to like, but I adored Lenny's mother. She was warm and giving, and treated very badly by her husband."[12]

Jennie Bernstein became the matriarch of a close family, always believing that family is of primary importance. And her philosophy with respect to a career was, "Take any genius, I don't care who. If you don't give him the right

Remarkable Mothers and Sisters

background, he'll fall by the wayside."[13] She was completely loyal to all family members, including her husband. Actually, their relationship improved dramatically after their children insisted that Sam, who was over 60 years old at the time, go to a psychiatrist for therapy. Although he went to the sessions for only three months, they seemed to have effected a change for the better in the relationship between Sam and Jennie. They began to have the same friends and to enjoy life together. After Sam died in 1969, she moved to Newton, Mass., to be near her sisters. She carried on her life with dignity, developing new interests, traveling, and spending a great deal of time attending important cultural and social events.

On Sunday, August 19, 1990, Leonard Bernstein, who was very ill, conducted a program at Tanglewood for the Boston Symphony Orchestra's Koussevitzky Memorial Concert. This was also the 50th anniversary of the music school with which he was so closely associated. His 91-year-old mother attended, as did his family and close friends. It was a strenuous program, and Jennie witnessed her son losing his strength and coughing uncontrollably in the third movement of Beethoven's *Seventh Symphony*. Gradually, with the musicians of the orchestra giving him the musical support he needed, he recovered somewhat and was able to conduct a powerful performance of the finale. He walked off the stage, exhausted. But his mother realized that there was not much hope for her adored son. In his final days, Lenny called her to warn her that he was making a public statement that he would no longer be conducting. She wanted to be with him, but he suggested that she wait until he felt better. Then he said something that touched her deeply. He said, "Should have listened to you, Mother; I'm paying for it dearly."[14] (He was referring to the sensible advice she always gave him about taking care of himself.) He died on Sunday, October 14, 1990.

Jennie Bernstein was a strong, supportive, and remarkable mother. She died at the age of 94, surviving her son by about two years.

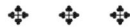

Shirley Anne Bernstein (1923-) is the daughter of Jennie and Sam Bernstein. Her brother Leonard was five years older than she. When she was born, her father had just set up his own beauty-supply company, which flourished, and eventually made him quite wealthy. She idolized Lenny; he was a combination of father, big brother, and friend to her, and most of her life she was under his influence. As a child, she was given piano lessons, but she soon realized there was no way she could compete with her talented brother. When she told her mother that she wanted to stop her lessons, much to her surprise, her mother was delighted. She did manage to play four-handed music with Lenny by "fudging" the bass parts, but definitely improved after Lenny started teaching her how to play them.

Shirley grew up on her own, to some degree. Her mother was busy with her baby brother, Burton (born in January 1932), and she kept away from her father, who frightened her because of the way he talked to her mother. He had big mood swings, which made her apprehensive when he was at home. She recalls, "Sometimes there would be scenes at the dinner table and terrible silences and he'd say, 'Tell your mother to pass the salt,' and call her ugly names under his breath. That's why to this day I have a bad stomach."[15] She decided she would never be in her mother's position. Yet she knew that her father was fundamentally a good man and that he loved his children and could be depended on to take care of her. Although his moods were unpredictable and made her uneasy, when he sank into a depression, she was compassionate, wanting only to make him feel happier.

Lenny (when she was 5 years old) included her in "Rybernia," an imaginary country. The name was an acronym of last names: Eddie Ryack, his friend, and Leonard Bernstein. Both boys were equal leaders. It was a secret society with strict rules. Shirley was the mascot. The children had a special language, private jokes, and special names for members. Burton was also included when he was old enough. The three siblings at times used this secret way of talking, even as adults. As Burton said in his book,

Family Matters, what they had achieved was "the creation of an imaginary counter-family within the real family. Our Rybernian family had a father (Lenny), a mother (Shirley), and a child (me)." They all loved to do cryptograms and other puzzles together. (Shirley testified that Burton was the champ, and Lenny said that Shirley was particularly good with musical puzzles.)

Shirley and Lenny loved to go through piano scores of operas by sharing roles. They both were crazy about opera, and Lenny used to go to the public library to take out scores and bring them home. She sang the female roles, he sang the male roles, and they both sang the choral parts. (Unfortunately, she developed nodes on her vocal chords, probably from too much strain.) At age 9, with some teeth missing, she lisped her way through a performance of his amateur operatic production, and she was good! A couple of years later, when he produced *The Mikado*, she had the female lead (Yum Yum). He had rehearsed her the winter before. They scrounged for clothes that would serve as costumes. (Shirley remembers wearing red knitting needles in her hair, a borrowed embroidered jacket, and eye makeup.) Lenny was producer, director, and pianist, and took the part of Nanki Poo.

Then, when she was 15, she acted in a fairly professional production of the opera *The Cradle Will Rock* by Marc Blitzstein, which was produced by the Harvard Dramatic Club, with Lenny organizing it and playing the piano on stage. Shirley was asked to play the important role of the prostitute and, of course, she enjoyed it. Every evening after school she would drive her mother's car to rehearsals (even though she had no license). She received fine reviews. At first, her role was a shock to her father, who was always ready to judge a woman a whore if she deviated from his rigid moral and social code. But her parents were so proud of the production and of their children that they refrained from criticizing the morality of her part.

Her big brother always tried to help and guide her. But even more important from her point of view, was that he added rich dimensions to her life, always providing love, excitement, and great fun. They were exceptionally close.

Her brother's friend (and almost his fiancée), Kiki Speyer, said, "Shirley, his sister, speaks like Leonard. She is very attractive, with slit green eyes like Leonard's, dark hair, very bright, with a sparkling intelligence." And she added, gratuitously, "I never saw her with a boyfriend."[16] Perhaps she was insinuating that the brother and sister were too close.

Shirley later concluded that the unhappy relationship of her parents was one important reason for her relying on her close relationship with her brother. Shirley explained her resistance to marriage as a reaction to her parents' constant arguments. She had broken several engagements and allowed herself to fall in love only with married men, obviously to avoid marriage (although she regretted not having children). Lenny brought Kiki home to meet his family. The young lady reported that, when she awoke in the morning in the twin-bedded room that she shared with Shirley, Lenny was in bed with his sister. She was quite shocked, but he told her that they had "cuddled" for years. Shirley later said, "There were ways we had of being together that were unique. I always looked for that kind of intimacy with others. It precluded sex, but I know why people would think so, because we were hand in hand or with our arms around each other's waists. I used to hear these incest rumors and my reaction was, 'What are they talking about? Are they insane?"[17]

Shirley attended Newton High School, even though she had passed her entrance examinations for the Boston Latin Girls School. Her father was happy to pay the fee for Lenny to attend the Boston Latin Boys School, but felt that special schools were not necessary for girls. Happily, she had done so well that she was admitted to Mount Holyoke College in South Hadley, Mass.

After graduation, she thought she might join the WAVES (Women Accepted for Volunteer Emergency Service), but Lenny asked her to be his secretary and general assistant. She moved to New York City to Lenny's apartment (until she found one of her own) and became his companion, advisor, and concert valet. Shirley loved the world of the theater, and at times worked in show business herself. In

Fancy Free, she sang a blues song for Lenny's ballet, and was in the singing chorus of *On the Town.* She also had occasional small speaking parts. Shirley finally decided to embark on her own career, and left her job as her brother's secretary and assistant. This position was taken over by Helen Coates (see Chapter 5), Lenny's former piano teacher.

Shirley was interested in many aspects of theater. In 1956 she was the producer of a television panel show called "Down You Go," on which Lenny appeared weekly for four months. No matter what she was doing, her brother remained a part of her life. A close relationship remained among all three siblings, and Lenny often invited his sister and brother to join him when he traveled on vacations or on his conducting tours, or just at home.

Lenny and Felicia Montealegre (see Chapter 4) fell in love, decided to marry, had a rocky time during their engagement, then separated. Shirley was aware that her brother was having a tremendous conflict between his homosexual and heterosexual desires. She believed that he was really bisexual. They both felt that marriage for him was the answer. She and Felicia were close friends during this separation, even during the period in which Felicia was living with the actor Richard Hart, with whom she had fallen deeply in love. When Richard collapsed with an apparent heart attack, Shirley persuaded Lenny to be with Felicia during that difficult time. Hart died within hours of his collapse, and it was not long before Felicia and Lenny, having found each other again, started dating. This time their relationship strengthened and they were married. But, the night before the wedding, they panicked. Shirley and Burton rushed over with a bag of jokes to distract them, and they calmed down. But Lenny still could not sleep, and his sister sat with him all night. She always was understanding and supportive. He, in return, cared deeply for her, and included her in as much of his life as he could.

Shirley Bernstein had formed her own theatrical agency, called the Paramuse Artists Association, representing people such as Stephen Schwartz (*Godspell, Pippin,* Disney's *Pocahontas*) and Arthur Laurents (*Gypsy, West Side*

Story), as well as movies (*The Way We Were, The Turning Point,* Joseph Stern's *Fiddler on the Roof,* and *Zorba*). But regardless of how involved she was with her own activities, she still remained very supportive of her brother. Felicia had died in 1978 of cancer and Shirley tried to help her brother and his family whenever possible. She and Burton accompanied him on a cruise to try to raise his spirits.

She became increasingly alarmed about Lenny's health and, in the spring of 1990, in order to care for him, she accompanied him to the Prague Spring Festival, where he was to conduct. On their return, she took him to his home to recuperate. Then, in August 1990, he conducted the Boston Symphony Orchestra at Tanglewood in the Koussevitzky Memorial Concert. During the performance, he was forced to leave the podium because of his terrible breathing problem, his coughing, and his general ill health (he did manage to return and conduct the final movement of Beethoven's *Seventh Symphony*). His sister and his friend Phyllis Newman accompanied him in the limousine back to New York so that he could meet with his doctors. Shirley was at his bedside the day he died on October 14.

She continues to live in New York City and is still active as president of Paramuse Artists Association.

Chapter Nine

Choreographers and Their Contributions

Many people love the performance of dance, not realizing how much the music contributes to their enjoyment. For this, we are indebted to choreographers, who appreciate and work with important compositions of the past, and who commission new works by contemporary composers.

Isadora Duncan (1878-1927) founded dance schools in Germany, Russia, and the United States that did not survive, but her style influenced dance from then on, including that of Serge Diaghilev and Michael Fokine. She was a pioneer of a style that came to be known as "modern dance," with its interpretive and expressive movement. Much of the music to which she danced was that of great classical composers, and she often introduced their music to those who ordinarily would not have heard it.

Isadora was born in San Francisco. After very little

training in ballet, she realized that she did not like it and turned to a more natural style. She always had a revolutionary and free spirit, and resented the artificial restrictions of the past. Nature was her inspiration.

Early in her life, she began touring, appearing in Chicago and New York. When she came to New York with her family, she rented a studio in Carnegie Hall and had a difficult time making ends meet. She did not achieve success in the United States at that time, and went to try her luck in Europe. In 1897, she had gone on tour in Britain with Augustin Daly's theater company. In 1899, she visited again and danced to classical music. Finally, in Paris in 1902, she had her first important successful performance. That was the beginning of the public's recognition of her style and talent. She was one of the first to interpret symphonic music in dancing. Gluck, Brahms, Wagner, and Beethoven were her favorite composers. In 1903 in Budapest, and in 1904 in Berlin, her talent was discovered and her fame became widespread in the European countries.

After she achieved recognition, she returned to Carnegie Hall in New York City. By that time, aside from her unusual style of dance, she was known for her 'sheer and abbreviated costumes and her bare feet.' The setting was simple: a bare floor with a green velvet backdrop. The music with which she worked was always of the highest caliber and, in that concert, Bach and Wagner were the composers and the orchestra was conducted by Walter Damrosch. Hers was an extremely personal interpretation of the music, and her use of an entire symphony orchestra as an accompanist to her one-woman show was daring and exciting. The house was completely packed.'

However, when she again returned to the United States after five years, she no longer was able to attract a large audience. Her shock value had lessened, because women already had begun to rebel against the prescribed dress and had started to bob their hair and wear short skirts. Yet Walter Damrosch took a gamble and asked her to perform with the New York Symphony Orchestra (of which he was the conductor) in a series of concerts in New York and on tour. These were successful, and established her art in the United States.

Her enthusiasm for Greek classic dance was soon shared by others, especially Americans, who were enraptured by its beauty. Agnes deMille said that Duncan's dancing was "not Greek at all but barefoot displays in classic tunics . . ." But, she continued, "Duncan never pretended to be Greek. 'If I [Isadora Duncan] am Greek, it is the Hellenism of Keats . . . I aim to speak the language of humanity, not the dialect of a folk.'"[1] The Grecian way of dancing gave one the feeling that the dancer moved freely. Her ideas about freedom of dress were introduced and quickly accepted. No more were women to be corseted and stiff. The new way was to be unstockinged and ungirdled, draped with flowing soft material. This kind of dancing was supposed to represent Greek culture and sculpture, the dancer striving to imitate figures on Greek vases. Members of the clergy were not in favor of this, of course. In fact, they found it scandalous.

Nevertheless, she became the center and leader of a cult. People were exhilarated by her style. There was an overwhelming demand for her performances in America, Europe, Russia, and even countries in and around the Pacific Ocean. Isadora danced for royalty, as well as for the ordinary citizen.

Although she was actually affected in demeanor and very much "on stage," her style was refreshing and a relief from the stuffy old post-Victorian presentation. She had beauty and grace, at the same time keeping the spotlight on herself by shocking the public, something she loved to do. She was never afraid of people laughing at her. She fervently valued and practiced freedom, both social and sexual.

Her belief in her causes was intense. One of them was the welfare of France, which publicly acknowledged its debt to her. (Among her many acts of generosity was her donation of her Neuilly château so that it could be used as a hospital.) During one period of her life, one of her favorite causes was communism. (During this time she happened to be on a concert tour in the United States. In her usual flamboyant way, she ended each performance by waving a red flag, causing quite a stir.)

Many of the most talented people of the time, both famous and unknown, were her friends. She influenced everyone she met. Even visual artists absorbed her style, and some used her as a model. Isadora Duncan lived fully and dramatically, entertaining lavishly in Paris after World War I, whether she was able to afford it or not. She believed that the world owed her great support, financial and otherwise. It never occurred to her to pay back any money borrowed. Her friends and admirers usually helped her when she was in trouble financially (which was often) and she, in return, was generous to them.

Her ideas on beauty and education for the young were definite and unique. Her crusades for schools of dance for children to relieve their anxieties and repression were a result of deeply felt concerns. She legally adopted and supported many children, using her original theories on raising them. Her two natural children, to whom she was completely devoted, had different fathers. She had chosen the men for their suitability as fathers. One was the stage designer Edward Gordon Craig; the other was Paris Singer, heir to the Singer sewing machine fortune and brother of the Princesse de Polignac (see Chapter 2). Isadora also had a third child who died at birth. Her two children drowned in an automobile accident in 1913, a tragedy from which she never completely recovered. Afterward, she became undisciplined, irresponsible, more outrageous than ever in her behavior, and, eventually, an alcoholic. She allowed her body to become fat and flabby. Once an inspiring human being and great dancer, she was now an object of pity. In 1921, while in the Soviet Union, she met and married Sergei Yesenin, who left her after about two years (finally committing suicide in 1925). By the time of his death, she had returned to France.

In September 1927 in Nice, at age 49, Isadora Duncan died as a result of an accident in her sports car. Her long scarf, which she was wearing at the time, caught in the wheel of her car and instantly strangled her.

❖ ❖ ❖

Martha Graham (1894-1991), dancer, teacher, and choreographer, was responsible for introducing some of the finest music of our time, as well as the great music of the past, to the dance-loving public. Martha was a creative genius in the field of modern dance, who developed a different and extremely potent technique, using powerful and unusual methods in her dance, and who had a completely different perspective from others up to that time. She changed dance forever. There was never any doubt in her mind that she was born for the purpose of expressing through dance the emotions of higher forces.

Martha was born in Allegheny, Pa. Her father, George Greenfield Graham, was a physician who specialized in mental disorders. He was a fascinating man, with a fine, original mind. Her mother, Jane Beers, was a woman of dignity and intelligence who was quite reserved (except when it came to protecting the welfare of her three daughters—Martha, the oldest, Mary, two years younger, and Geordie, the "baby," six years younger). Her parents were religious, not allowing themselves many "frivolous" pleasures, including dance. A high priority for them was to impress on their children the importance of ethics and morality. Another important influence on Martha was Elizabeth Prendergast, an Irish girl who worked for the family as a maid, nanny, cook, and general helper. Although the family belonged to the Presbyterian church, they allowed Lizzie to take the girls with her to mass at the Catholic church. Martha was impressed with the ceremony and mythology of that religion.

The family moved to Santa Barbara, in 1908. In 1911, Dr. Graham invited Martha to attend a dance concert in Los Angeles, where she saw Ruth St. Denis perform. That event awakened her profound interest in dance. Her father contributed to her evolving ideas about choreography by impressing on her the importance of watching the physical movements and facial expressions of people to determine their feelings and purpose. This was one of the bases of her philosophy of dance.

Martha always had strong, independent views, and was a very passionate woman. At one time, she told Agnes deMille, the dancer and choreographer, that she felt that virginity was an obstacle to growth. She went on to tell about an incident that had occurred when she was young: She informed her mother that she was going to a hotel with a married man, whom she loved. Her mother, who probably was stricken dumb, said nothing to stop her, and that is exactly what the headstrong girl proceeded to do. The fact that Martha was a highly sexual woman can be seen not only in her life but in her choreography. In appearance, Martha was small, although when she was dancing, she seemed larger because of her strong, intense gestures. She had an Oriental quality; her long face had white skin drawn tight across her cheeks, and her dark eyes were brilliant and deep-set. Her hair was dark and straight, her neck long, and her head seemed always to be in an attitude of alertness. Her voice was soft, except when she was angry. For most of her life, she was extremely attractive to and attracted by men.

When Martha graduated from high school, she entered the Cumnock School of Expression in Los Angeles to study drama and speech. In 1914, her father died, and in 1916, at age 22, Martha enrolled in Denishawn, a dance academy founded by her idol, Ruth St. Denis, and Miss Ruth's husband, Ted Shawn. (Ted eventually bought a place in Becket, Mass., called Jacob's Pillow for his dance group. It still exists today, and is known as the Jacob's Pillow Summer Dance Festival.) Mrs. Graham moved her family to Los Angeles to be near the school. Martha remained with the group from 1919 to 1923, becoming one of its leading dancers, even though she was quite a few years older than the other students. Her flair, vitality, acting ability, and ego were enormous. At this point in her life, the wild forces within her were hidden, although Miss Ruth and Ted could sense they were there. The fledgling dancer wanted desperately to learn whatever she could from Miss Ruth and withheld her own opinions and ideas. After two years, she became a teacher at the school.

During her years there, she met Louis Horst. He was 10 years older than Martha and a fine pianist. It was the beginning of a long relationship, both personal and professional. Louis was extremely knowledgeable about American modern dance and its music and very much involved with the musical aspects of the performances. Dancers depended upon him: he not only played the piano, directed the orchestra, and wrote music for them, but he was their advisor and confidant. He was respected throughout the world of American modern dance. In 1921, Ted took a small group to New York to dance. Martha was chief soloist. Louis was musical director. It was there that Martha and Louis became lovers. He was married, but was known for his many affairs. Always he made it quite clear that he had no intention of divorcing his wife, Betty.

When Martha left the Denishawn group, she took with her all that she had learned, repudiating many things (including Miss Ruth's employment of mysticism), but accepting others (particularly the Oriental use of ground and all that she had been taught about costuming). She went to New York in 1924, and worked in the *Greenwich Village Follies* at the Winter Garden Theater. Louis joined her in New York. At one point he brought his wife east to attempt a reconciliation. This was a difficult time for Martha. But it soon became apparent that Louis and his wife could not live together, and Betty returned to San Francisco alone, where she lived most of her long life. Martha and Louis resumed their relationship.

After two years in the *Follies*, she decided to develop her own style. In order to afford to do this, she had to teach. She took a job teaching at the school that her producer, John Murray Anderson, shared with Robert Milton for the purpose of training performers. At the same time, she taught at the Eastman School of Music in Rochester, N.Y. For a year, she commuted between the two jobs regularly. She ultimately came to the following conclusions: 1) money must not be her prime goal, 2) she must have her own company, 3) it was important to have her own school in which to train her company, 4) only those who had trained with her would be allowed to choreograph the dances, and 5) her group should not dance with any other group.

Her first independent studio was in Carnegie Hall. Then,

in April 1926, although she was in bad financial straits, Martha started her own theater. She and Louis were able to rent at cost the Forty-eighth Street Theater for one evening's performance. It was a success, and dancers rushed to study with her. Ted Shawn refused to let her use anything he had taught her, so she was completely on her own, which actually proved to be fortunate for modern dance; she was forced to depend on her own technique and creativity. She was overburdened with her responsibilities and duties. She was, after all, composing new dances, developing her own technique, training her dancers, designing and sewing all the costumes with the help of members of the company, taking care of her business affairs, and trying to find some kind of happiness in her personal life. (Louis was still adamant about not divorcing his wife.) Her creative productivity was incredible, composing piece after piece.

In 1927, she moved to a larger studio on West 10th Street. The Martha Graham Dance Company attracted talented and devoted dancers. Her students idolized her, even though she was stern and demanding. The *group* was like a family, with her students giving Martha complete devotion. (There were some, however, who could not tolerate her strict, powerful control and soon departed.) She had impressive temper tantrums, yet she could make her classes great fun, even though the instruction was very serious. The commitment and dedication of the company's members was absolute. Some have said that it was like belonging to a religious cult, based on serving the aesthetic ideal of a creative genius. At that time, the group was made up only of young women, except for Louis. He was advisor, director of music, accompanist, drillmaster, critic, and business manager. Later he taught both music and dance composition. Although he and Martha shared their professional and personal lives, they did not share an apartment, but lived very near each other.

Martha's philosophy of dance was different from that of the Denishawn school, although that is where she started to evolve her own ideas. Ruth St. Denis was one of the first to believe ardently in dance as an art in itself, instead of an addition to theatricals and operas. She instilled this belief in her students, particularly in Martha. However, while there, Martha was influenced by the ideas of Francois Delsarte about gesture and movement. Martha eliminated the exotic movements of the Denishawn method and concentrated on geometric gestures, body weight, and contraction and release of muscles. She emphasized proper breathing and percussive and sustained movements. Movement on the space of the floor as well as in the air were important to her. She was striving to express basic universal passions, never depending on grace, but on more angular, powerful, and descriptive movement. The final effect was one of starkness and control, and was quite shocking. Ballet slippers were out; innovative and earthy movements were in. Her criterion of the worth of a movement was its emotional truth. Events in the outside world such as unemployment, the Spanish Civil War, and the emergence of unions influenced her choreography. Later in her career she concentrated on American themes, creating dances like *Frontier, Appalachian Spring, Letter to the World* (concerning New England and its culture), and *El Penitente* (dealing with the Southwest culture). After that, she became interested in mythology, and the expression of psychological problems experienced by everyone.

In 1927, Martha was hired to head the dance program at the Neighborhood Playhouse, which not only attracted dancers but people such as Tony Randall, the actor, who studied with her in order to learn how to project and to move on stage. She taught that one must not follow a formula without thought. One must introduce something out of character to create interest. Although the academy stressed drama, it was unique in that it also stressed music and dance. Here Martha met some wealthy and philanthropic women interested in helping those who were poor—mostly first-generation Americans who lived on the lower east side of New York City. Two of these women were Irene and Alice Lewisohn. Their father, Leonard, had founded copper-mining companies; their uncle, Adolph, donated Lewisohn Stadium to City College of New York. (The stadium held summer concerts, with tickets inexpensive enough to allow low-income people to attend.) The sisters founded the Neighborhood Playhouse on Grand Street (later to become The School for Arts Related to the Theater), charging a small amount, if anything at all, but attracting many fine artists of all kinds to perform, lecture, and to help in many other ways. Rita Morgenthau, a sociologist and sister-in-law of Henry Morgenthau, President Roosevelt's secretary of state, was active and instrumental in strengthening the faculty. The fourth remarkable woman who helped in every way was Edith Julia Isaacs, who inherited a fortune and married a lawyer who had been a pupil of Edward MacDowell, the composer. Her salon was one of the finest in the country, having some of the most distinguished people of the time as guests. Martha was always invited, and the contacts proved invaluable.

Three other patronesses helped Martha. Miss Katherine Cornell, the actress, was one. She was not only wealthy as a result of her own success but through the inheritance of her family's fortune. (Her father, a physician, invented the windshield wiper.) Miss Cornell was a great supporter of performers, and believed that Martha was a truly great artist. Bathsabee de Rothschild of the European banking family was another (see Chapter 3). After World War II, she established a foundation in Israel for arts and sciences. She was particularly interested in science, but fell in love with the Graham dance theater when she participated in dancing classes at Martha's school in New York. From then on, she showered Martha with fine clothes, jewelry, and other luxuries. She arranged and financed the performances of the Martha Graham Company in Paris and Israel, and was supportive in whatever way she was needed. The two women became close friends. Eventually, Bathsabee increased her financial support of Israeli groups, and was not able to help the Martha Graham group as much. Lila Acheson Wallace (see Chapter 6), a great patroness of the arts, became Martha's benefactor. Mrs. Wallace, a co-publisher of the *Reader's Digest,* set up a foundation for Martha, and became the head of its board of directors. These women helped her in many important ways. Unfortunately, however, they did not provide her with a regular income on which she could depend.

Martha's career and professional standing continued to grow. In 1935, she agreed to teach at Sarah Lawrence. In 1934, she began to teach in the summers at Bennington College in Vermont, where she was the driving force at the newly founded Bennington School of Dance. (This became the forerunner of the American Dance Festival.) In 1938, she began to include men in her company. When Erick Hawkins pleaded with her to let him join, she could not resist him. Her personal relationship with Louis had always been frustrating and unsatisfying, and she was ripe for a deep, obsessive, love. Erick was 15 years younger than she and very ambitious. He tried to force his way into a major role in the company, but he was so arrogant that he antagonized everybody. Except Martha. She was madly in love with him, and he knew it. He loved and admired Martha in return, but was jealous of her recognition by the artistic world and her amazing talent. Her consuming passion for him was beneficial to her in many ways: Her technique became more human and sensual, and her inclusion of male dancers broadened her horizons. In addition to his being her male soloist, she allowed him to take over business and production matters. Because he was extremely aggressive, he was successful in effecting profitable and helpful financial arrangements. But he became more and more arrogant. Nevertheless, he and Martha were married in 1948, more than 10 years after they met. They were still very much in love. Soon after, Martha, who was in her 50s, began to have problems with arthritis that became painful. But she tried to ignore it and continued her strenuous dancing. Erick began taunting her and praising the younger girls, and their relationship deteriorated. He suddenly left her when they were performing in London. He did not want to be tied to a failing and aging woman. Actually, their marriage could never have worked. Aside from Erick's insensitivity and envy, Martha would have been destroyed if she had given in to his demand for her power and her position. They were divorced in 1954, and she was crushed. She went into a depression and began to drink. Amazingly, her creativity and productivity continued. Erick went on to try to build his own career, but it was not until 40 years later that his dancing was recognized. Martha, on the other hand, went on to increasing fame, receiving honors and awards all over the world. No matter how much her body failed her, she fought on and on until she was forced to give up dancing in 1968. She was just over 60 years old, and very ill with cirrhosis of the liver. After a long period, she recovered, and, as if reborn, she became interested and active again. She went about improving her appearance by having face lifts, dyeing her hair, and dressing to hide her bodily defects, and succeeded in creating an elegant image. Martha Graham had become a "superstar." She was as committed as ever to her artistic vision and her group.

In 1976, she received the Medal of Freedom; in 1979, the Kennedy Center Honor; and in 1985, the National Medal of Arts. She was nominated for the Nobel Peace Prize. She was an extraordinarily independent and principled woman. Two of her acts illustrating these qualities are particularly worth mentioning. In the 1930s, even though the country was segregated, her company, the Martha Graham Dance Company, was integrated. After Marian Anderson, the great black singer, was prohibited from singing at Constitution Hall, Martha refused to perform in areas of the South where the audiences were segregated. On another occasion, in 1936, Hitler extended a direct invitation to her company to perform at the 1936 Olympic Games in Berlin. This was an astounding and unexpected gesture. Nevertheless, she absolutely refused, at great expense to herself; she gave up a great deal of money and was listed as one of Hitler's enemies to be dealt with if the Nazis won the war.

This great dancer, choreographer, and teacher died at the age of 96. Martha Graham was honored in many ways on the centennial anniversary of her birth. One particularly exciting celebration was "Radical Graham" at the Brooklyn Academy of Music. This was a two-week season of performances by Martha's dance company at the Brooklyn Academy of Music. It included dances from 1929 to 1958, and a few from later years. Another excellent celebration in her memory was a year of dance in her honor at Jacob's Pillow in Massachusetts.

Martha Graham was probably one of the greatest dancers of this century, one of the great choreographers of the ages, a woman of character and integrity, an incredibly good teacher, and a woman of great originality and creativity. Not only did Martha Graham revolutionize modern dance, but her contribution to the public's acceptance of classical music in general was huge. She commissioned works at first by known composers (Debussy, Ravel, Rachmaninoff, and others), then worked with comparatively unknown composers who needed the exposure and who later became world-renowned, including Bartók and Prokofiev. She went on to American composers such as Aaron Copland and William Schuman. She was not a musician, per se, but she had an instinctive feeling for music and new styles. She opened up the world of music to those who needed its visual interpretation in order to appreciate it. Her impact cannot be overestimated.

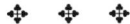

Agnes George deMille (1905-1993) was a member of an unusually interesting family. Her paternal ancestry can be traced back to 1280 in Flanders. In 1658, an ancestor of the deMille family arrived in America. Agnes's father, William deMille, and her uncle, Cecil B. DeMille, were the sons of Henry Churchill deMille and Matilda Beatrice Samuel. In spite of Henry's distinguished background, and much to his mother's dismay, he became interested in the theater, especially in writing for it.

But it was Agnes' maternal grandmother, Beatrice, who was extremely influential in the family's success in acting, directing, producing, and writing for the theater and for films. She was the daughter of an accomplished and distinguished Jewish family who arrived in New York in 1871 from Liverpool, England. They settled in a wealthy section of Brooklyn, and Beatrice was encouraged to develop her cultural interests. She soon displayed a talent for acting and, during one of her amateur performances, she and Henry, who was a student at Columbia, met. They fell in love and married. Neither family was thrilled about the other's religion; the couple was married in the deMilles' Episcopalian church. The bride's family did not attend. As time went on, Beatrice became an ardent Episcopalian, but, in spite of their religious differences and because of the birth of their grandchildren, the Samuels reconciled with their daughter and her family. (Agnes' father, William, was always proud of his Jewish roots, but his younger brother, Cecil, never acknowledged them as part of his background, dwelling instead on his paternal lineage.) Beatrice encouraged and helped her husband to succeed in the theater, and when he died, started her own business as an authors' representative, specializing in women dramatists. But most important to her were the careers of her sons. She became their manager and agent. She was indefatigable and extremely effective. William, the intellectual brother, became well-known as a playwright. Cecil, the flamboyant brother, went into acting and directing, not succeeding very well until he finally went to Hollywood to make movies. He became a legend in his own time and beyond as a director, producer, and Hollywood mogul. The whole family followed him there, and the deMille theater dynasty was on its way.

In New York in 1903, William married Anna Angela George, the daughter of Henry George, a self-educated man who was world-famous as an intellectual, social reformer, and speaker. There were two problems in the marriage from the start: First, Anna worshipped her father and his acclaim and, second, she resented her attractive husband's flirtations. However, they were very much in love in the beginning, and she truly believed her husband to be a genius as a playwright. They had two daughters. Agnes George deMille was born in 1905, and Margaret George deMille in 1908.

Agnes arrived in Hollywood from New York with her family when she was 9 years old. Her mother had a difficult time adjusting to her husband's new career in the movie industry and to the kind of people who made up Hollywood society, but she was supportive. Agnes, however, loved it. Whenever she was on vacation, she would try to spend every day on the movie set or on location. When she was 10, she had a small role in her father's film, *The Ragamuffin*, which he wrote and directed. All this exposure had the effect of making her feel very much at home in the entertainment industry and with the people involved in it. During her teens, she attended the Hollywood School for Girls, and in those years she became fascinated with dance. In 1915, she had seen Anna Pavlova dance. She also had been impressed by the dancing of Ruth St. Denis. Both of these dancers made a great impression on her, but it was not until she was 13 that she was allowed to take dance instruction. Her parents were very much against it. But her uncle, Cecil, realized how important it was for her and arranged an audition for her with Theodore Kosloff, who had danced with the Imperial Russian Ballet and now was dancing in one of Cecil's movies. Kosloff agreed to take Agnes on as a student in his school, even though she did not have the ideal ballet dancer's body (The ideal was a small torso and long legs). Her body was stocky and sturdy, but she had endurance. That, together with her energy, drive, and imagination, more than made up for the physical difference. Kosloff had a great sense of drama which interested Agnes. Her parents tried to discourage her, but she grew more and more determined to become a dancer. In 1922, to please her father, she enrolled at the University of California at Los Angeles, from which she received her degree cum laude in English. He wanted her to be a writer, but she continued her interest in dance.

Agnes and her sister were not aware just how far apart her father and mother were growing. William ("Bill") continued to have relationships with other women, and was particularly attracted to women with good minds as well as beauty. He had an affair with writer Lorna Moon, who gave birth to his son, but soon discovered that she had tuberculosis. With Bill's knowledge and consent, it was arranged that Cecil and his wife would adopt and raise him as a DeMille. (Bill's wife was not to know.) The boy,

Richard, did not learn about his natural father until he was grown, although he was always close to his "Uncle" Bill. Lorna married someone else, and died within a few years.

Bill then fell in love with Clara Beranger, who had been writing the screenplays of his films for seven years and had been in love with him even while he was having affairs with other women. They decided to marry. The day after Agnes graduated from college, her parents told her that they were divorcing. It was a great shock to her. Bill and Clara were married in 1928, and Anna and her daughters were desolate. After a miserable trip to Europe, they settled in New York City.

Agnes lost four years of her dance training when she went to college. She now had an idea of the style of dancing that interested her. It was ballet, but with drama and comedy. She joined the ballet company in Max Reinhardt's production of *A Midsummer Night's Dream* and, from then on, her life was dancing. Her mother now appreciated Agnes' talent, and concentrated on her daughter's career. She helped in every way she could, eventually acting as her manager. With the encouragement of others who were knowledgeable, the young dancer leased a rehearsal hall and hired a pianist, and began giving concerts. In December 1928, in New York, she made her choreographic debut in a program of solo dances. John Martin, the critic for *The New York Times*, said, "Here is one of the brightest stars now rising above our native horizon . . . She leaves you with the same sort of wistful laughter on your lips and the same sort of lump in your throat [referring to Charlie Chaplin]."[1] Even more important to her than the favorable reviews was the telegram she received from her father, congratulating her and welcoming her into the profession.

Agnes moved into her own apartment and was determined to become accepted as a choreographer, as well as a dancer. Her style was beginning to attract attention. In London, her concert was sold out. Marie Rambert (Mim), who had a repertory dance theater, asked Agnes to study with her and to give a series of concerts. Mim's Ballet Club met in the Mercury Theatre. Mim and her assistant, Antony Tudor, were major influences in Agnes' work. Lack of money was still a problem for Agnes, so she was happy to find that in London it was not necessary to have fashionable clothes or a car. Living there could be much less expensive. She was delighted with the arrangement.

Her first ardent love was with Ramon Reed. He was brilliant, and extremely handsome, and paralyzed from the waist down. Agnes was obsessed with him for the next two years, at one point moving in with him. Ramon believed her to be a great artist, and was as involved with her as she was with him. It was a situation that could end only in grief. His condition was the result of multiple sclerosis, which progressively worsens. While she was in rehearsal in New York, he died. It was an enormous loss for her. He had added significantly to her life. She had known love, companionship, and complete approval. But her experience with tragedy added another dimension to her art.

By this time, she was back in the States working with important people in important productions; financially, she was still having a difficult time. Finally, in 1939, Richard Pleasant formed the Ballet Theatre. Agnes was hired to create new ballets with nine of the top choreographers: Michael Fokine, Michael Mordkin, Adolph Bolm, Bronislava Nijinska, Anton Dolin, Antony Tudor, Eugene Loring, José Fernandez, and Andrée Howard. Although she did not earn much money, she had become recognized as one of the top choreographers.

A friendship developed that was important to Agnes. She was introduced to Martha Graham, and was instantly drawn to her. The two became great friends and confidantes. It was through Martha that Agnes met her future husband in 1941. Walter Prude was the manager of Graham's group. He and Agnes started dating, but a few months after their meeting he was drafted. They corresponded daily, and their relationship blossomed into a full-blown romance. They were married in California and, after a short time, Walter was sent overseas. He was in the service two and a half years. Afterwards Agnes said, "Throughout the war, as before, I had clung to Martha as to a beloved older sister. I asked her advice. I asked her reaffirmation, and she gave it steadily and wonderfully. She had introduced me to her manager and she had seen us through our courtship and pitifully brief married time together before Walter left for the war . . . Anything I could do to help Martha, I did. But what I did for her was as nothing compared with the wisdom and loving care and fortitude she gave me . . ."[2]

Martha gave her excellent advice and support throughout her career. When Agnes became a great success in her work in *Oklahoma*, she confessed to Martha that she wanted to be excellent, but was not at all sure that she could be. Martha answered, "There is a vitality, a life force, an energy, a quickening that is translated through you into action, and because there is only one of you in all of time, this expression is unique. And if you block it, it will never exist through any other medium and it will be lost. The world will not have it. It is not your business to determine how good it is nor how valuable nor how it compares with other expressions. It is your business to keep it yours clearly and directly, to keep the channel open . . . As for you, Agnes, you have a peculiar and unusual gift, and you have so far used about one-third of your talent . . ." She went on to say, "No artist is pleased [with his or her own art] . . . There is only a queer divine dissatisfaction, a blessed unrest that keeps us marching and makes us more alive than the others."[3]

In 1942, Agnes had her first outstanding success with the ballet *Rodeo*, which she had choreographed for the Ballets Russes de Monte Carlo. She had worked with Aaron Copland, the great American composer. It is one of the most beloved of American classic ballets. By that time her style was recognizable; it has action, drama, and humor. From then on, she was able to work with the best composers. Her association with Richard Rodgers started when he and Oscar Hammerstein II saw *Rodeo*. They hired her to choreograph their new Theater Guild project, *Green Grow the Lilacs* (the title was changed to *Away We Go!*, and then to *Oklahoma!*). The combination of her choreography, Rodgers' music, and Hammerstein's book and lyrics made it the most innovative, artistic production in the theater up to that time and started a completely new style of musical. The dances brilliantly emphasized character and plot. It was a smash hit. That creative team collaborated in other successful productions, including *Carousel.* Other composers with whom she worked include Kurt Weill (in *One Touch of Venus*), Harold Arlen (in *Bloomer Girl*), Frederick Loewe of the team of Alan Jay Lerner and Frederick Loewe (in *Brigadoon* and *Paint Your Wagon*), Morton Gould (in the ballet *Fall River Legend*), Benjamin Britten (in *The Rape of Lucretia,* which Agnes directed), Cole Porter (in *Out of This World,* which she directed), Virgil Thomson (in a ballet based on part of *Bloomer Girl*), and Jules Styne and Leo Robin (in *Gentlemen Prefer Blondes*).

In 1945, Walter was discharged and hired by the great impresario, Sol Hurok. He and Agnes settled down together at last. And it was a good marriage. Agnes gave birth to her son Jonathan on April 24, 1946. She continued with her unbelievably successful career, but her little family remained close and committed to each other.

Agnes has always been a woman of great character. During the dark time of Sen. Joseph McCarthy, Edward R. Murrow asked her to appear on his program. She did not attempt to hide her contempt for McCarthy and his House Un-American Activities Committee. Murrow had arranged a debate between Agnes and Hedda Hopper, the Hollywood gossip columnist who, through her column, had been instrumental in destroying many lives because of her extreme right-wing sympathies. Agnes said to Hedda, "Hedda, dear, let me tell you something . . . We have as English and American people committed every crime in the book. But this is our unique distinction, and perhaps honor. At the time of the commitment, there was always a man on his feet on the floor of the House denouncing the iniquity. This is our way of living—this way of having the freedom to stand up and say, 'This won't do.' And if ever we try to suppress our own voices to ourselves just so other people who are less informed will get a glossy picture of us—we're lost. We've given up our freedom." Hedda asked, "And our freedom is what?" Agnes answered, "The ability to protest freely among ourselves—not to subvert, not to betray—to protest and to criticize freely among ourselves in whatever medium we choose to use. Don't you agree, Hedda, dear?

I'm *sure* you agree with that." With that, Hedda conceded, saying, "Well, that shut me up completely!"[4]

When Rudolf Nureyev defected from the Soviet Union to the West, classical ballet became popular again. Those involved in ballet moved back to concert halls. So, too, did Agnes. In 1953, she established the Agnes deMille Dance Theatre. She was now considered the dean of ballet and her many lectures and books were much in demand. As she grew older, she became seriously interested in American folk music, and in 1973, she established the Heritage Dance Theater at the North Carolina School of the Arts, not only for the purpose of starting a national dance company but also of preserving forms of folk and popular dance.

On October 7, 1993, at the age of 88, Agnes deMille died from the effects of a stroke. She is survived by her son, two grandsons, and a niece. Her husband had died in 1988. She will always be revered as the choreographer responsible for the theatrical dance form, one that included ballet and modern dance, drama, well-drawn characters, and comedy, and which raised the level of dancing in musicals to an art form. Many of her ballets remain in the repertoire of the great ballet companies. Some of her honors include the National Medal of Arts, the Kennedy Center Career Achievement Award, the Dance Magazine Award, and the Handel Medallion. Kevin McKenzie, artistic director of American Ballet Theatre, stated, ". . . Agnes deMille was not simply a monumental force in American dance, but she was one of our mothers—a woman whose unwavering commitment to our company and the art form has inspired us for more than half a century. . . . She taught us that it was not good enough to dance the steps, but we had to portray a character and do so honestly, with sincerity and vitality. She possessed a choreographic genius, an awe-inspiring literacy, and a potency of character that was mesmerizing. Agnes was one of a kind . . . An American original. I will cherish my memories of her always."[5]

Notes

Chapter 1

1. Thomas Aquinas, "Summa Theologica" Supplements LXXXI, XCIII, XXXIX, in *Age of Faith* by Will Durant (New York: Simon and Schuster, 1950), p. 825.

Chapter 2

1. Arthur Rubinstein, *My Many Years*, (New York: Alfred A. Knopf, 1980), p. 104.
2. Ibid., p 107.
3. Marcel Haedrich, *Coco Chanel,* (Boston: Little Brown and Co., 1972), p. 33.
4. Ibid., p. 68.
5. Ibid., p. 90.
6. Ibid., p. 124.
7. Arthur Rubenstein, op. cit., p. 523.
8. Ibid., p. 134.

9. Leonie Rosenstiel, *Nadia Boulanger: A Life in Music*, (New York: W. W. Norton and Co., Inc. 1982), p. 80.

Chapter 3

1. Catherine Drinker Bowen and Barbara von Meck, *Beloved Friend: The Story of Tchaikovsky and Nadejda von Meck*, (New York: Random House, Inc., 1937), p. 29.
2. Ibid., p. 66.
3. Hans Gal, *The Musician's World: Letters of the Great Composers*, (London: Thames and Hudson, 1965), p. 363.
4. Catherine Dinker Bowen and Barbara von Meck, op. cit., p. 204.
5. Piotr Ilyich Tchaikovsky, *Letters to His Family: An Autobiography*, (New York: Stein and Day, 1981), p. 179.
6. Catherine Drinker Bowen and Barbara von Meck, op. cit., p. 332.
7. Ibid., p. 251.
8. Ibid., p. 343.
9. Ibid., p. 435.
10. Ibid., p. 439.
11. Albert E. Kahn, *Joys and Sorrows: Reflections by Pablo Casals*, (New York: Simon and Schuster, 1970), p. 129.
12. Agnes deMille, *Martha* (New York: Random House, Inc., 1956), p. 466.

Chapter 4

1. David Ewen, ed., *The Book of Modern Composers*, (New York: Alfred A. Knopf, 1950), p. 25.
2. Curtis Cate, *George Sand*, (Boston: Houghton Mifflin Co., Inc., 1975), p. 390.
3. Ibid., p. 479.
4. Harold C. Schonberg, *The Lives of the Great Composers*, (New York: W. W. Norton and Co., Inc., 1970), p. 170.
5. Encyclopaedia Britannica, "George Sand," (Chicago, London, Toronto: Encyclopaedia Britannica, Inc., 1960), p. 933.
6. Curtis Cate, op. cit., p. 731.
7. Hans Gal, ed., *The Musician's World: Letters of the Great Composers*, (London: Thames and Hudson, 1965), p. 304.
8. Ibid., p. 307.
9. Ibid., p. 307.
10. Ibid., p. 321.
11. Ibid., p. 322.

Notes 283

12. Thomas E. Wren, "Nietzsche," in *The New Grolier Multimedia Encyclopedia*, Grolier Electronic Publishing Inc., 1993.
13. Boris Schwarz, *Great Masters of the Violin*, (New York: Simon and Schuster, 1983), p. 231.
14. Ibid.
15. Karen Monson, *Alma Mahler: Muse to Genius*, (Boston: Houghton Mifflin Co., Inc., 1983), p. 203.
16. Kurt Blaukopf and Herta Blaukopf, *Mahler: His Life, Work and World*, (New York: Thames and Hudson, 1992), p. 161.
17. Egon Gartenberg, *Mahler: The Man and His Music*, (New York: Schirmer Books, 1978), p. 39.
18. Kurt Blaukopf and Herta Blaukopf, op. cit., p. 164.
19. Karen Monson, op. cit., p. 111.
20. Egon Gartenberg, op. cit., p. 174.
21. Karen Monson, op. cit., p. 116.
22. Ibid., p. 155.
23. Ibid., p. 310.
24. Ibid., p. 321.
25. Ellen Pfeiffer, "Koussevitzky's Widow," Boston: *Boston Herald American*, 7 Jan., 1978.
26. Ibid.
27. Arthur Rubinstein, *My Many Years*, (New York: Alfred A. Knopf, 1980), p. 247.
28. Ibid., p. 250.
29. Halina Rodzinski, *Our Two Lives*, (New York: Charles Scribner's Sons, 1976), p. 27.
30. Ibid., p. 42.
31. Arthur Rubinstein, op. cit., p. 303.
32. Harold C. Schonberg, *The Great Pianists*, (New York: Simon and Schuster, 1963), p. 413.
33. Abram Chasins, *Speaking of Pianists*, (New York: Da Capo Press, Inc. 1961), p. 108.
34. Harold C. Schonberg, *The Great Pianists*, (New York: Simon and Schuster, 1963), p. 414.
35. Halina Rodzinski, op. cit., foreword.
36. Arthur Rubinstein, op. cit., p. 601.
37. Ibid., p. 602.
38. Helena Matheopoulos, *Maestro*, (New York: Harper and Row Publishers, 1982) p. 488.
39. Galina Vishnevskaya, *Galina*, (London: Harcourt, Brace, Jovanovich Publishers, 1984), p. 208.
40. Ibid., p. 408.
41. Ibid., p. 487.
42. Ibid., p. 459.
43. Meryle Secrest, *Leonard Bernstein: A Life*, (New York: Alfred A. Knopf, 1994), p. 151.

44. Humphrey Burton, *Leonard Bernstein*, (New York: Doubleday and Co., Inc., 1994), p. 199.
45. Helena Matheopoulos, op. cit., p. 6.
46. Albert E. Kahn, *Joys and Sorrows: Reflections by Pablo Casals*, (New York: Simon and Schuster, 1970), p. 267.

Chapter 5

1. Humphrey Burton, *Leonard Bernstein*, (New York: Doubleday and Co., Inc., 1994) p. 66.
2. Abram Chasins, *Speaking of Pianists*, (New York: Da Capo Press, Inc., 1961), p. 156.
3. Josef Llevinne, *Basic Principles in Pianoforte Playing*, (Dover Publications, Inc., 1972), foreword.
4. Harold C. Schonberg, *The Great Pianists*, (New York: Simon and Schuster, 1963), p. 419.
5. Leonie Rosenstiel, *Nadia Boulanger: A Life in Music*, (New York: W. W. Norton and Co., Inc., 1982), p. 44.
6. Ibid. p. 49.
7. Aaron Copland and Vivian Perlis, *Copland: 1900 Through 1942*, (New York: St. Martin's/Marek, 1984), p. 69.
8. Harold Schonberg, *The Lives of the Great Composers*, (New York: W. W. Norton and Co., Inc., 1970), p. 548.
9. Leonie Rosenstiel, op. cit., p. 361.
10. Aaron Copland and Vivian Perlis, op. cit., p. 65.
11. Humphrey Burton, op. cit., p. 455.
12. Ibid., p. 71.
13. Ibid., p. 501.
14. Richard Dyer, "You Only Live Twice," *Opera News*, November, 1990) p. 14.
15. Ibid., p. 12.

Chapter 6

1. *Overtones*. "Mary Curtis Bok; A Tribute," Philadelphia, Curtis Institute of Music, 1974.
2. Ibid.
3. Herbert Kupferberg, *Tanglewood*, (New York: McGraw-Hill Book Co., 1976), p. 31.
4. Ibid., p. 90.
5. Ibid., p. 57.
6. Charles W. Ferguson, *Unforgettable DeWitt Wallace*, (Pleasantville, N.Y.: Reader's Digest Association, Inc., 1987), p. 14.

7. *Lila Acheson Wallace,* (New York: New York Community Trust and Community Funds, Inc., Feb. 10, 1986) p. 1.
8. Laurence Dow Lovett, *A Toast to Miss Tully,* (New York: Chamber Music Society of Lincoln Center, 1992), foreword.
9. Charles Wadsworth, *A Toast to Miss Tully,* (New York: Chamber Music Society of Lincoln Center, 1992), p. 26.
10. Martin Mayer, *The Met,* (New York: Simon and Schuster, 1983), p. 193.
11. Ibid.
12. John Dizikes, *Opera in America,* (New Haven: Yale University Press, 1993), p. 427.
13. Copyright (c) 1995 by the New York Times Company. Reprinted by permission.
14. Copyright (c) 1995 by the New York Times Company. Reprinted by permission.

Chapter 7

1. George Martin, *The Damrosch Dynasty,: America's First Family of Music,* (Boston: Houghton Mifflin Co., Inc., 1983), p. 303.
2. Ibid., p. 61.
3. Ibid., p. 238.
4. John Dizikes, *Opera in America,* (New Haven: Yale University Press, 1993), p. 538.
5. Ibid.
6. Beverly Sills and Lawrence Linderman, *Beverly,* (New York: Bantam Books, 1987), p. 132.
7. Ibid., p. 280.
8. John Dizikes, op. cit., p. 539.
9. Aaron Copland and Vivian Perlis, *Copland: 1900 Through 1942,* (New York: St. Martin's/Marek, 1984), p. 348.

Chapter 8

1. Harold C. Schonberg, *The Lives of the Great Composers,* (New York: W. W. Norton and Co., Inc., 1970).
2. Maynard Solomon, *Mozart,* (New York: Harper Collins Publishers, Inc., 1995), p. 399.
3. Ibid., p. 403.
4. Ibid.
5. Hans Gal, *The Musician's World: Letters of the Great Composers,* (London: Thames and Hudson, 1965), p. 102.

6. Janet Nichols, *Women Music Makers*, (New York: Walker and Company, 1992), p. 23.
7. Humphrey Burton, *Leonard Bernstein*, (New York: Doubleday and Co., Inc., 1994.), p. 16.
8. Ibid., p. 11.
9. Ibid., p. 27.
10. Burton Bernstein, *Family Matters*, (New York: Summit Books, 1982), p. 133.
11. Meryle Secrest, *Leonard Bernstein: A Life*, (New York: Alfred A. Knopf, 1994), p. 87.
12. Ibid., p. 84.
13. Ibid., p. 291.
14. Humphrey Burton, op. cit., p. 526.
15. Meryle Secrest, op. cit., p. 12.
16. Ibid., p. 87.
17. Ibid., p. 90.

Chapter 9

1. Anne Edwards, *The DeMilles: An American Family*, (New York: Harry N. Abrams, Inc., 1988), p. 116.
2. Agnes deMille, *Martha*, (New York: Random House, Inc., 1956), pp. 262–63.
3. Ibid., p. 264.
4. Anne Edwards, op. cit., p. 220.
5. Doris Perlman, "Obituary: Agnes deMille" in *Dance Magazine*, Dec. 1993, p. 116.

Bibliography

Bernstein, Burton. *Family Matters.* New York: Summit Books, 1982.

Blaukopf, Kurt, and Herta Blaukopf, eds. *Mahler: His Life, Work and World.* New York: Thames and Hudson, 1992.

Boretz, Benjamin and Edward T. Cone. *Perspectives on American Composers: A Symposium by Leading Musicians.* New York: W. W. Norton, 1971.

Bowen, Catherine Drinker and Barbara von Meck. *Beloved Friend: The Story of Tchaikovsky and Nadejda von Meck.* New York: Random House, 1937.

Bowers, Jane and Judith Tick, eds. *Women Making Music.* Chicago: University of Illinois Press, 1987.

Burton, Humphrey. *Leonard Bernstein.* New York: Doubleday, 1994.

Bibliography

Cate, Curtis. *George Sand*. Boston: Houghton Mifflin, 1975.

Chapin, Schuyler. *Musical Chairs*. New York: G. P. Putnam Sons, 1977.

Chasins, Abram. *Speaking of Pianists*. New York: Da Capo Press, Inc., 1961.

Copland, and Aaron, Vivian Perlis. *Copland: 1900 Through 1942*. New York: St. Martin's/Marek, 1984.

Crankshaw, Edward. *Maria Theresa*. New York: Viking, 1969.

Day, Lillian. *Ninon: A Courtesan of Quality*. New York: Doubleday, 1957.

DeMille, Agnes. *Martha*. New York: Random House, 1956.

DeWitt Wallace. New York: New York Community Trust and Community Funds, Inc., May 10, 1982.

Dizikes, John. *Opera in America*. New Haven: Yale University Press, 1993.

Durant, Will. *The Story Of Civilization*. New York: Simon and Schuster. Volume II, *The Life of Greece*, 1939. Volume III, *Caesar and Christ*, 1944. Volume IV, *The Age of Faith*, 1950. Volume V, *The Renaissance*, 1953. Volume VI, *The Reformation*, 1957.

Durant, Will and Ariel Durant. *The Story of Civilization*. New York: Simon & Schuster. Volume VII, *The Age of Reason Begins*, 1961. Volume VIII, *The Age of Louis XIV*, 1963. Volume IX, *The Age of Voltaire*, 1965.

Dyer, Richard. "You Only Live Twice." *Opera News*. p. 10, Volume 55, Number 5, November, 1990.

Edwards, Anne. *The DeMilles: An American Family*. New York: Harry N. Abrams, 1988.

Encyclopaedia Britannica. Chicago, London, Toronto: Encyclopaedia Britannica, Inc., 1960.

Ennis, Michael. *Duchess of Milan*. New York: Penguin, 1993.

Bibliography 289

Ewen, David, ed. *The Book of Modern Composers.* New York: Alfred A. Knopf, 1950.

Ferguson, Charles W. *Unforgettable DeWitt Wallace.* Pleasantville, New York: Reader's Digest Association, Inc., 1987.

Flanner, Janet. *Paris Was Yesterday.* Irving Drutman, ed. New York: Viking, 1972.

Foundation Center, compiler. *Lila Wallace-Reader's Digest Fund, Inc.* New York City: Foundation Directory, 1995.

Gal, Hans. *The Musician's World: Letters of the Great Composers.* London: Thames and Hudson, 1965.

Gartenberg, Egon. *Mahler: The Man and His Music.* New York: Schirmer Books, 1978.

Gold, Arthur and Robeert Fizdale. *The Life Of Misia Sert.* New York: Alfred A. Knopf, 1980.

Goreau, Angeline. Review of *Madame Du Deffand and Her World* by Benedetta Craveri. Boston: David R. Godine, 1994. *New York Times Book Review,* 1 January, 1995.

Graffman, Gary. *I Really Should Be Practicing.* Garden City, N.Y.: Doubleday, 1981.

Graham, Martha. *Blood Memory.* New York: Doubleday, 1991.

The New Grolier Multimedia Encyclopedia, Danbury, Ct.: Grolier Electronic Publishing, Inc., 1993.

Grout, Donald Jay. *A History of Western Music.* New York: W. W. Norton, 1960.

Grove's Dictionary of Music and Musicians, Fifth Edition, Eric Blom, Ed. New York: St. Martin's Press, 1954.

Gyles, Anna Benson (Director). *Song of the Birds.* New Jersey: Kultur International Films, Ltd., 1991.

Haedrich, Marcel. *Coco Chanel: Her Life, Her Secrets.* Boston: Little, Brown, 1972.

Hart, Philip. *Orpheus in the New World.* "The Symphony Orchestra as an American Cultural Institution: Helen M. Thompson and the American Symphony Orchestra League." New York: W. W. Norton, 1973.

Jepson, Barbara. *The Lively Arts: Dorothy DeLay Is a Violin Teacher of Genius and Geniuses.* Des Moines: Connoisseur, 1988.

Kahn, Albert E. *Joys and Sorrows: Reflections by Pablo Casals.* New York: Simon & Schuster, 1970.

Kirk, Elise K. *Music at the White House.* Chicago: University of Illinois Press, 1986.

Koopal, Grace G. *Miracle of Music: History of the Hollywood Bowl.* Los Angeles: W. Ritchie, 1972.

Kupferberg, Herbert. *Basically Bach.* New York: McGraw-Hill, 1985.

Kupferberg, Herbert. *Tanglewood.* New York: McGraw-Hill, 1976.

Landon, H. C. Robbins and Donald Mitchell. *The Mozart Companion.* New York: W. W. Norton, 1969.

Lang, Paul Henry. *The Creative World Of Mozart.* New York: W. W. Norton, 1963.

Larousse Encyclopedia of Music. Geoffrey Hindley, ed. Secaucus, N.J.: Chartwell Books, Inc., 1971.

Leinsdorf, Erich. *Cadenza: A Musical Career.* Boston: Houghton Mifflin, 1976.

Lesure, Francois. *Music and Art in Society.* State College, Pa.: Penn State University Press, 1968.

Lhevinne, Josef. *Basic Principles In Piano Playing.* New York: Dover Publications, Inc. 1972.

Libman, Lillian. *And Music at the Close: Stravinsky's Last Years.* New York: W. W. Norton, 1972.

Lila Acheson Wallace. New York Community Trust and Community Funds, Inc., Feb. 10, 1986.

Marek, George R. *Cosima Wagner.* New York: Harper & Row Publishers, 1981.

Martin, George. *The Damrosch Dynasty: America's First Family of Music.* Boston: Houghton Mifflin, 1983.

Matheopoulos, Helena. *Maestro.* New York: Harper & Row, 1982.

Mayer, Martin. *The Met.* New York: Simon & Schuster, 1983.

Mitford, Nancy. *Madame de Pompadour.* New York: Harper & Row, 1954.

Monson, Karen. *Alma Mahler: Muse to Genius.* Boston: Houghton Mifflin, 1983.

Nauhaus, Gerd, ed. *The Marriage of Robert and Clara Schumann.* Boston: Northeastern University Press, 1993.

Neuls-Bates, Carol, ed. *Women in Music.* New York: Harper & Row, 1982.

New York Times. "Margaret Ryan Tribute." April 18, 1995.

New York Times. "Anne Ratner, 90, Patron of Musicians." June 16, 1995.

New York Times. "The American Way." June 22, 1980.

Nichols, Janet. *Women Music Makers.* New York: Walker and Company, 1992.

Ogden, Christopher. *Life of the Party.* Boston, N.Y., Toronto, London: Little, Brown, 1994.

Overtones (Fiftieth Anniversary Issue). "Mary Curtis Bok." Philadelphia: Curtis Institute of Music, 1974.

Pavarotti, Luciano and William Wright. *My Own Story.* New York: Warner Books, 1981.

Pendle, Karin, Ed. *Women and Music: A History.* Indianapolis: Indiana University Press, 1991.

Perlman, Doris. *Obituary: Agnes deMille.* New York: *Dance Magazine*, December, 1993.

Pfieffer, Ellen, *Koussevitzky's Widow*, 77. Boston: *Boston Herald American*: 7 January 1978.

Pleasants, Henry. *The Great Singers*. New York: Simon & Schuster, 1966.

Rabin, Carol Price. *Music Festivals in America*. Stockbridge, Mass.: The Berkshire Traveller Press, 1979, 1981, 1983.

Rabin, Carol Price. *Music Festivals in Europe and Britain*. Stockbridge, Mass.: Berkshire Traveller Press, 1980.

Reich, Howard. *Van Cliburn*. Nashville: Thomas Nelson, Inc., 1993.

Rodzinski, Halina. *Our Two Lives*. New York: Charles Scribner's Sons, 1976.

Rosenstiel, Leonie. *Nadia Boulanger: A Life In Music*. New York: W. W. Norton, 1982.

Rubinstein, Arthur. *My Many Years*. New York: Alfred A. Knopf, 1980.

Sand, Barbara. *A Toast to Miss Tully*. New York: Chamber Music Society of Lincoln Center. 1992.

Schickel, Richard. *World of Carnegie Hall*. New York: Julian Messner, Inc. 1960.

Schnabel, Artur. *My Life and Music*. New York: Simon & Schuster, 1963.

Schonberg, Harold C. *The Lives of the Great Composers*. New York: W. W. Norton, 1970.

Schonberg, Harold C. *The Great Conductors*. New York: Simon & Schuster, 1967.

Schonberg, Harold C. *The Great Pianists*. New York: Simon & Schuster, 1963.

Schwarz, Boris. *Great Masters of the Violin*. New York: Simon & Schuster, 1983.

Secrest, Meryle. *Leonard Bernstein: A Life*. New York: Alfred A. Knopf, 1994.

Bibliography 293

Shead, Richard. *Music in the 1920's*. New York: St. Martin's Press, 1976.

Sills, Beverly and Lawrence Linderman. *Beverly*. New York: Bantam Books, 1987.

Slonimsky, Nicholas, ed. *The Concise Baker's Biographical Dictionary of Musicians*, 8th Edition. New York: Schirmer Books, 1994.

Solman, Joseph. *Mozartiana: Two Centuries of Notes, Quotes and Anecdotes about Wolfgang Amadeus Mozart*. New York: Vintage Books, 1990.

Solomon, Maynard. *Mozart*. New York: HarperCollins, 1995.

Symphony Newsletter: The Newsletter of the American Symphony Orchestra League. Vol. 25, Number 5. "Helen Thompson Remembered." Washington, D.C.: American Symphony Orchestra League, October–November 1974.

Tchaikovsky, Piotr Ilyich. *Letters to His Family: An Autobiography*. New York: Stein and Day, 1981.

Thomas, Jurgen A. "*Olga Koussevitzky.*" Pittsfield, Mass.: Berkshire Eagle, 6 January 1978 and 12 January 1978.

Thompson, Virgil. *American Music Since 1910*. New York, San Francisco: Holt, Rinehart and Winston, 1970.

Vishnevskaia, Galina. *Galina*. London: Harcourt, Brace, Jovanovich, 1984.

Wechsler-Vered, Artur. *Jascha Heifetz*. New York: Schirmer Books, 1986.

Women's Studies/Women's Status. Boulder, Colo.: The College Music Society, Inc., 1988.

Zweig, Stefan. *Marie Antoinette: The Portrait of an Average Woman*. New York: Viking, 1933.

Index

Acheson, Barclay, 192
Acheson, Mary Huston, 191
Acheson, Reverand T. Davis, 191
Adler, Clarence, 229
Adler, Felix, 183
Aeschylus, 2
Agoult, Countess d' (Marie Catherine Sophie de Flavigny), 100–101
Albert of Belgium, 81
Alençon, duc d', 60
Alenn, Emilienne d', 46
Alembert, Jean Le Rond d', 33, 36, 38
Alexander II, Czar, 48
Alexander VI. Pope (Rodrigo Borgia), 24
Alexander VII, Pope, 31
Alexander the Great, 3
Alexander, John, 226
Alphonso II of Naples, 25
Amati, Andrea, 32
Amati family, 11, 32
Amati, Nicòlo, 32
Anderson, John Murray, 267
Anderson, Marian, 272
Anderson, Sherwood, 53
Aquinas, St. Thomas, 5
Aristophanes, 2
Arlen, Harold, 279
Armsby, Leonore W., 207
Arrau, Claudio, 141
Aspasia, 19–21
Auer, Leopold, 123, 169, 185
Auersperg, Countess Wilhelmina, 63
Auger, Arleen, 206

Auric, Georges, 43, 51
Austen, Jane, 41
Averino, Olga, 175
Bach, Johann Sebastian, 12, 32, 65, 71, 158, 206, 235, 262
Ballets Russes, 48, 167, 278
Balsan, Étienne, 45
Balzac, Guez de, 28
Balzac, Honoré de, 86, 131
Bampton, Rose, 186
Barber, Samuel, 155, 166, 185
Barrett, Mrs. William Fulton, 189
Barry, Comtesse du (Jeanne Becu), 64, 69
Bartók, Bela, 233
Bartoli, Cecilia, 207
Bauer, Clara, 207
Beaujoyeux, Balthazar de, 59
Beethoven, Ludvig van, 16, 262
Behm, Ada and William, 200
Belmont, August, 115, 201, 202
Belmont, Eleanor Robson, 201–2
Bembo, Pietro, 25
Benchoff, Colonel Robert, 220
Benedict XIV, Pope, 37
Bennett, Maria Zimbalist, 186
Berchthold zu Sonnenburg, Baron von, 241–43
Berchthold zu Sonnenburg, Leopold, 242
Berg, Alban, 233
Berger, Ludwig, 245
Berlioz, Hector, 40
Bernhardt, Sarah, 188
Bernstein, Alexander Serge, 145
Bernstein, Burton, 145, 252, 253, 256, 257

Bernstein, Clara, 252
Bernstein, Felicia Montealegre Cohn, 139, 140–48, 173, 174, 259
Bernstein, Jamie, 144
Bernstein, Jennie Resnick, 251–55
Bernstein, Leonard, 139, 141–48, 154, 169, 172–74, 185, 235, 251–60
Bernstein, Nina, 145
Bernstein, Samuel Joseph, 251–58
Bernstein, Shirley Anne, 142, 143, 145, 147, 173, 251–52, 256–60
Bigot, Marie, 245
Bing, Rudolph, 202, 204, 227
Bisceglie, Duke of (Don Alphonso), 25
Bismarck, Otto von, 14
Bliss, Anthony A., 201
Bliss, Cornelius, 201
Blitzstein, Marc, 166, 233, 257
Block, Ernest, 180
Bloomingdale, Donald, 83
"Blue stockings," 16
Boijen, William Bouwens van der, 161
Bok, A. Margaret, 187
Bok, Cary, 183, 186
Bok, Curtis, 183
Bok, Edward W., 182–84
Bok, Mary Louise Curtis. See Zimbalist
Bolet, Jorge, 185
Boleyn, Anne, 60
Bolm, Adolph, 277
Bonnard, Pierre, 41, 52
Bookspan, Martin, 230
Borgia, Cesare, 22, 24–25
Borgia, Lucrezia, 24–26
Bori, Lucrezia, 202
Borie, Victor, 95

Index 297

Boulanger, Henri Alexandre Ernest, 159–61
Boulanger, Lili, 161–65
Boulanger, Nadia Juliette, 51, 52, 158–69, 188, 213
Boulanger, Raïssa Ivanovna Myschetsky, 159–68
Bourges, Michel de, 91
Bowes, Major, 225
Brahms, Johannes, 16, 98–99, 106, 262
Bramante, Donato d'Angelo, 22
Brandenburg, Marie-Eleanore of, 29
Brèze, Louis de, 26
Brezhnev, Leonid, 139–40
Britten, Benjamin, 279
Bronstein, Raphael, 169–70
Brooks, Rosamund Dixey, 189, 190
Browning, John, 156
Bruckner, Anton, 16
Bulganin, Nikolai, 134–35
Bull, John, 61
Bull, Ole, 109–10
Bull, Sara Olea, 109–10
Bull, Sara Thorpe, 109–10
Bülow, Hans von, 40, 101–5
Burckhard, Max, 111
Burgin, Richard, 222
Busbey, Fred E., 233
Busch, Adolf, 205
Busoni, Ferruccio, 215
Byrd, William, 60–61

Cage, John, 233
Caldwell, Sarah, 222–24, 226, 227
Callistus III, Pope (Alphonso de Borgia), 24
Capdevila, Madame, 150
Capel, Boy, 47–48
Capobianco, Tito, 226
Cara, Marchetto, 23
Carnegie, Andrew, 115, 212
Carter, Artie Mason, 199
Carter, Elliot, 166, 233
Caruso, Enrico, 42
Casals, Enrique, 151
Casals, Marta Montañez, 148–52
Casals, Pablo, 81–82, 148–52, 205, 213, 217
Catherine of Aragon, 10
Cattani, Vannozza, 24
Chabrier, Emmanuel, 50, 51
Chaliapin, Feodor, 163
Chandler, Dorothy Buffam ("Buff"), 201
Chandler, Harry, 201
Chandler, Norman, 201
Chanel, Adrienne, 45–47
Chanel, Antoinette, 45–47
Chanel, ("Coco") Gabrielle, 44–50
Chapin, Schuyler, 168
Chaplin, Charlie, 276
Charles V of France, 22, 23
Charles VI of Austria, 61–63
Charles VIII of France, 22
Charles IX of France, 58
Charles X of Sweden, 30
Charpentier, Marc Antoine, 34
Chasins, Abram, 127, 156
Châteauroux, Duchesse de, 37
Chausson, Ernest, 51
Chekhov, Anton, 41
Chevigné, Comtesse Adhéaume de, 52
Chopin, Frederic, 15, 85, 91–95
Christina of Sweden, 29–32
Chung, Kyung Wha, 205
Churchill, Winston, 49
Cicero, Marcus Tullius, 4
Clark, Tom, 247
Clarke, Mrs. Chauncey D., 200

Index

Clement VII, Pope, 23, 58
Clésinger, Auguste, 94
Cliburn, Harvey Lavan, 248, 249, 250
Cliburn, Rildia Bee O'Bryan, 247–50
Cliburn, Van, 156, 158, 205, 235, 248–50
Clinton, President Bill, 171, 206
Coates, Helen, 142, 144, 172–74, 259
Cocteau, Jean, 43, 53
Cohn, Clemencia Montealegre, 140
Cohn, Roy Elwood, 140
Coll, Luis and Rosa Cueto, 152
Conti, Princess of, 28
Coolidge, Elizabeth Sprague, 179–81
Coolidge, Dr. Frederic Shurtleff, 179
Copland, Aaron, 166–67, 233, 234, 273, 278
Corbett, Patricia, 209
Correggio, Nicòlo da, 22
Corelli, Arcangelo, 32
Corelli, Pierre, 28
Cornell, Katherine, 270
Cortot, Alfred, 218
Cothran, Tom, 147
Couperin, François, 34, 71
Craig, Edward Gordon, 264
Cramp, Theodore H., 183
Curtin, Claudia Madeleine, 175–76
Curtin, Phillip, 175–76
Curtin, Phyllis Smith, 175–77, 227
Curtis, Charlotte, 146
Curtis, Cyrus H. K., 182
Curtis, Louisa, 182–83

Daché, Lily, 226

Dachs, Joseph, 153
Daladier, Edouard, 148
Daly, Augustin, 262
Damrosch, Clara. *See* Mannes
Damrosch, Frank, 212, 213, 215, 217
Damrosch, Helene, 211, 213, 214
Damrosch, Hetty Mosenthal, 214
Damrosch, Leopold, 211, 214, 215
Damrosch, Margaret Blaine, 214
Damrosch, Walter, 165, 167, 212, 213, 262
D'Annunzio, Gabriele, 162
Davenport, Marcia, 186
Debussy, Claude, 41, 43, 51, 73, 273
Deffand, Marie de Vichy-Champrond du, 37–39
Defilló family, 149
Delacroix, Eugène, 93
DeLay, Dorothy, 169–71
Delormé, Philibert, 26
Delsarte, Francois, 269
deMille, Agnes, 273–80
deMille, Anna Angela George, 274–76
DeMille, Cecil B., 273, 274, 275
deMille, Clara Beranger, 276
DeMille, Henry Churchill, 273–74
deMille, Margaret George, 274–76
DeMille, Matilda Beatrice Samuel, 273–74
DeMille, Richard, 275–76
deMille, William, 273–76
Denda, Gigi, 226
Descartes, René, 29
Diaghilev, Serge, 42–44, 48, 50, 51, 52, 163, 261

Index 299

Diamond, David, 166, 254
Dichter, Mischa, 156
Diderot, Denis, 14, 33, 38
Disney, 259
Dmitri, Grand Duke, 48
Dohna, Count, 30
Dolin, Anton, 277
Domingo, Placido, 223
Douglas, Mrs. Lewis, 204
Downes, Olin, 189
Drake, Prebble, 247
Dranoff, Loretta, 229–30
Dranoff, Murray, 229–30
Dreyfus, Jean Tennyson, 209
Drexel, George W. Childs, 183
Dudevant, Amantine Aurore Lucile Dupin. *See* Sand, George
Dudevant, Baron Casimir, 88–90
Dudevant, Maurice, 88–89, 93
Dudevant, Solange, 88–89, 93–95
Dudley, Robert, Earl of Leicester, 60
Dumas, Alexandre *fils*, 86
Duncan, Isadora, 261–64
Dupin, Caroline, 87
Dupin, Hippolyte, 87
Dupin, Maurice, 86
Dupin, Madame Sophie-Victoire Delaborde, 86–88
Durey, Louis, 43

Edward VI of England, 10, 60
Edwards, Alfred, 42
Einstein, Albert, 148
Eisenhower, President Dwight D., 233
Eleanor of Aquitaine, 55–57
Eleanora of Aragon, 21
Elgar, Sir Edward, 180
Elisabeth of Belgium, 80–82
Elizabeth I of England, 10, 59–61

Elizabeth Christine of the Hapsburg family, 62
Emery, Bob, 224
Emmanuel II of Italy, 14
Ercole I of Ferrara, 21
Ericsson, Leif, 110
Essipov, Annette, 153
Este family, 8, 21
Este, Isabella d', 21–23
Esterhazy, Prince Anton, 66
Esterhazy, Prince Nikolaus, 67
Etioles, Alexandrine d', 68, 72
Etioles, Charles Guillaume Le Normant d', 68–70
Euripides, 2
Evans, May Garrettson, 208
Evans, Shailer, 247

Fabiola of Belgium, 82
Falla, Manuel de, 51, 180
Faurè, Gabriel, 40, 41, 42, 51, 160, 161
Federigo of Mantua, Marquis, 21
Fels, Mrs. Samuel, 183
Ferdinand of Aragon, 7
Ferdinand, Archduke of Austria, governor of Milan, 66
Fermoy, Ruth Lady, 235
Fernandez, Josè, 277
Ferrante I of Naples, 21
Ferrara, Duke of (Alphonso), 25
Flagler, Harry Harkness, 165
Flaubert, Gustave, 95
Fleisher, Leon, 185
Flesch, Carl, 185
Fokine, Michael, 261, 277
Foss, Lukas, 155, 185
Fossombroni, Madame Patersi de, 101
Fraenkel, Dr. Joseph, 117

Index

Francis I of Austria (Francis Steven of Lorraine), 63–64, 239
Francis I of France, 22, 58
Francis II of Austria, 67
Francis II of France, 58
Franco, Francisco, 148–49
Francueil, Madame Dupin de, 86–88
Frank, Pamela, 186
Franklin, Benjamin, 39
Franz Joseph I of Austria, 114
Frederick the Great of Prussia, 71
French, Daniel Chester, 188
Freud, Dr. Sigmund, 116
Friedheim, Arthur, 248
Frolowsky, Philaret Vasillievitch, 72

Gabor, Eva, 142
Gagnon, Roland, 226–27
Galamian, Ivan, 170–71
Gallico, Paolo, 225
Galli-Curci, Amelita, 157, 224
Garden, Mary, 209
Garina, Vera Nikolayevna, 133
Gaulle, Charles de, 83
Gebhard, Heinrich, 172
Geoffrin, Marie Thérèse Rodet, 38
George, Henry, 274
Gian Francesco of Mantua, 21–22
Gibbons, Orlando, 61
Gide, André, 41, 52
Gillespie, Mrs. E, D., 207
Gluck, Christoph Willibald, 65, 71, 262
Godebski, Cipa, 52
Godebski, Cyprien, 39–41
Godebski, Ida, 52
Godowsky, Leopold, 155, 229

Godowsky, Leopold, Jr., 218
Goethe, Johann Wofgang von, 244
Goldovsky, Boris, 175, 185, 222
Gonzaga, Elisabetta, 22
Goode, Richard, 186, 207
Gorbachev, Mikhail, 140, 250
Gould, Morton, 279
Gounod, Charles, 160
Graffman, Gary, 155, 185, 186, 187, 205
Graham, Geordie, 265
Graham, George Greenfield, 265
Graham, Jane Beers, 265–66
Graham, Martha, 3, 83–84, 265–73
Graham, Mary, 265
Grandsagne, Stephane Ajasson de, 88
Greenough, Peter, 226–27
Greffulhe, Comtesse Henri, 43, 52
Grolle, Johann, 183
Gropius, Alma. See Werfel, Alma Schindler Mahler Gropius
Gropius, Manon, 119–20
Gropius, Walter, 115, 119–20
Groves, Paul, 204
Guarneri, Andrea, 32
Guarneri family, 11, 32
Guggenheimer, Minnie, 189
Gunderson, Helen, 235
Gustavus II of Sweden, 29

Hadley, Dr. Henry Kimball, 188
Halasz, Laszlo, 223
Hale, Mary, 209
Halir, Carl, 215
Hammerstein, Oscar II, 278–79

Index

Handel and Haydn Society of Boston, 17
Handel, George Frideric, 15, 32, 65, 71
Hapsburg Dynasty, 16, 62, 110
Harris, Roy, 166, 180
Hart, Richard, 142–43, 174, 259
Hawkins, Erick, 271
Haydn, Joseph, 16, 65, 66–67, 71
Hegel, Georg, 244
Heifetz, Jascha,169
Heimburg, Marie von, 211, 213
Heine, Heinrich, 86, 244
Hemingway, Ernest, 53, 167
Hènault, Charles, 38
Henry II of England, 56–57
Henry II of France, 26
Henry III of France, 58, 60
Henry IV of France (Henry of Navarre), 11, 27, 58
Henry VIII of England, 10, 60
Hensel, Sebastian, 246
Hensel, Wilhelm, 245–46
Hepburn, Mrs. Andrew H. *See* Brooks, Rosamund Dixey
Herford, Julius, 209
Hershey, Myra, 201
Hindemith, Paul, 180
Hitler, Adolph, 108, 272
Hofmann, Josef, 155, 183, 184, 185
Hogg, Ima, 208
Holmes, Bettie Fleischmann, 208
Holy Roman Empire, 10
Honegger, Arthur, 43
Hong, Hei-Kyung, 204
Hoover, J. Edgar, 146
Hopper, Hedda, 279–80
Horace, Quitus Flaccus, 4
Horne, Marilyn, 204, 223
Horowitz, Joseph, 230
Horowitz, Vladimir, 155
Horst, Betty, 267
Horst, Louis, 266–68, 271
Horszowski, Mieczyslaw, 149, 185
Hosmer, Helen M, 234
Houghton, Amory, 195
Houghton, Arthur, 195
Howard, Andrée, 277
Howe, Mary, 208
Hughs, Adella Prentiss, 208
Hugo, Victor, 86
Humboldt, Alexander von, 244
Hurok, Sol, 128, 250, 279
Hutcheson, Ernest, 158
Hutchins, Robert, 199
Hutchinson family, 16

Indy, Vincent d', 51
Ippold, Captain Franz Armand d', 240
Irish, Florence Behm, 200
Irish, Leiland Atherton, 200
Isaacs, Edith Julia, 270
Isabelle I of Castile, 7
Istomin, Eugene, 149, 152, 185, 205

Jedliczka, Ernst, 158
Jefferson, Thomas, 14
Jiampietro, Lilia, 253
Joachim, Joseph, 98–99, 109
John, king of England, 57
Johnson, Mrs. Owen, 188
Johnstone, Winifred Hope, 168
Joseph II of Austria, 63–67

Kahane, Jeffrey, 207
Kahn, Otto Herman, 202–3
Kammerer, Paul, 118

Index

Kapell, William, 158
Keats, John, 263
Kennedy, Edward, 139
Kennedy, President John, 149, 151
Kennedy, Nigel, 171
Kennedy, Robert, 145
Khrushchev, Nikita, 134–35
Klimt, Gustav, 111
Koch, Edward, 228
Kokoschka, Oskar, 118–19
Kosloff, Theodore, 275
Koussevitzky, Natalie, 121–22
Koussevitzky, Olga Naoumoff, 121–23
Koussevitzky, Serge, 121–23, 143, 148, 189, 190, 222, 233
Kreisler, Fritz, 158
Kurth, Mrs. J. Edward, 209

La Fayette, Comtesse de, 28, 33
Lalandi, Lina, 235
Lambert, Marquise de, 38
Lancie, John de, 186
Landowska, Wanda, 51, 185
Lantelmle, Geneviève, 42
Lanvin, Jeanne, 53, 168
Laredo, Jaime,186
Lasker, Mrs. Albert, 204
Laurents, Arthur, 259
Leczinska, Marie, queen of France, 69
Leczinski, Stanislas of Poland, 69
Lederman, Minna, 233
Lenclos, Ninon de, 35–36
Lenin, Vladimir Ilich, 138
Leopold II of Austria, 63
Lermontov, Mikhail, 131
Lerner, Alan Jay, 279
Leschetizky, Theodor, 154, 199

Les Six, 43, 53, 167
Letz, Hans, 169
Leventritt, Edgar M., 205
Leventritt, Rosalie J., 205
Levi, Hermann, 108
Levine, James, 204
Lewisohn, Adolph, 269
Lewisohn, Alice and Irene, 269–70
Lewisohn, Leonard, 269
Lhévinne, Josef, 155
Lhévinne, Rosina, 155–57, 249
Liadov, Anatoli, 124
Liebling, Estelle, 157, 225, 226
Lin, Cho–Liang, 171
Lincoln, President Abraham, 233
Lipkin, Seymour, 185
List, Eugene, 158
Liszt, Blandine, 100
Liszt, Daniel, 100
Liszt, Franz, 15, 40, 86, 91, 99, 100–102, 106–7, 212, 248
Livy (Titus Livius), 4
Locke, John, 14
Loewe, Frederick, 279
Loring, Eugene, 277
Louis II, Duc de Bourbon (The Great "Condé"), 35
Louis VII of France, 55–56
Louis XII, 22–25
Louis XIII, 27
Louis XIV, 13, 34, 36
Louis XV, 34, 36, 37, 39, 67–72
Louis XVI, 69
Lovett, Laurence Dow, 197
Ludwig II of Bavaria, 104–7
Lully, Jean Baptiste, 34, 35
Luther, Martin, 9

Index

MacDowell, Edward, 233–34, 270
MacDowell, Marian, 233–34
MacNeil, Cornell, 227
Maggio Musicale, 17
Mahler, Alma Schindler. *See* Werfel, Alma Schindler Mahler Gropius
Mahler, Anna Justine, 114, 117, 120
Mahler, Gustav, 16, 112–18, 119, 231
Mahler, Maria Anna, 114
Maine, Duchesse du, 38
Manceau, Alexandre, 95
Mannes, Clara Damrosch, 211–18
Mannes, David, 214–18
Mannes, Leopold Damrosch, 216, 218
Mannes, Marya, 216, 218
Marchesi, Mathilde, 157
Marcos, Imelda, 250
Marguerite of Valois, 58
Maria Theresa, empress of Austria, 62–67, 71
Marianne of the Hapsburg family, 62
Marie Antoinette of France, 63, 64
Marín, Gov. Muñoz, 151
Marshall, Harriet Gibbs, 208
Martin, John, 276
Mary I of England, 10
Massenet, Jules, 160
Massine, Leonide, 43
Mather, Cotton, 188
Mather, Richard, 188
Matisse, Henri, 53
Mave, Rolf, 51
McCarthy, Eugene, 145
McCarthy, Joseph, 233, 279
McClain, Sirilda, 247
McKenzie, Kevin, 280

Mdivani, Roussadana, 44
Meck, Julia von, 73
Meck, Karl George Otto von, 72–73
Meck, Nadezhda Philaretovna von, 72–80
Meck, Vladimir von, 73, 80
Medici, Catherine de, 26, 58–59
Medici family, 8, 58
Mendelssohn, Moses, 244–45, 247
Mendelssohn–Bartholdy, Abraham, 244–45, 247
Mendelssohn–Bartholdy, Cecile Jeanrenaud, 246–47
Mendelssohn–Bartholdy, Fanny, 244–47
Mendelssohn–Bartholdy, Felix, 244–47
Mendelssohn–Bartholdy, Leah, 244, 246, 247
Mendelssohn–Bartholdy, Paul, 244
Mendelssohn–Bartholdy, Rebecca, 244, 247
Menotti, Gian-Carlo, 185
Menuhin, Yehudi, 170, 205
Merimée, Prosper, 86
Mestastasio, Pietro, 66
Metcalfe, Susan, 150
Meyer, Marcelle, 51
Midori, 171
Mikoyan, Anastas, 134
Milan, duchess of (Beatrice), 21, 22
Milhaud, Darius, 43, 52
Milton, Robert, 267
Minnesingers, 7
Mintz, Schlomo, 171
Mitropoulos, Dmitri, 253, 254
Mlynarski, Alina, 124
Mlynarski, Emil, 123, 124, 184

Modarelli, Antonio, 219–20
Moffo, Anna, 186
Moliere (Jean Baptiste Poquelin), 28
Moll, Carl, 118
Monaco, the reigning family, 51, 168
Montañez, Rafael, 149
Montenuovo, Prince, 114
Montesquieu, Baron de, 14, 33, 38
Moon, Lorna, 275
Mordkin, Michael, 277
Morgan, Anne, 188
Morgan, J. P., 115, 188
Morgenthau, Henry, 270
Morgenthau, Rita, 270
Mosler, Archie, 157
Mottl, Felix, 108
Mozart, Anna Maria Pertl, 237, 239, 240
Mozart, Constanze Weber, 241, 242, 243
Mozart, Leopold, 237–43
Mozart, Maria Anna ("Nannerl" or "Marianne"), 65, 237–43
Mozart, Wolfgang Amadeus, 12, 16, 65, 66, 71, 77, 237–43
Munch, Charles, 191
Munz, Mieczyslaw, 125–26
Murat, Joachim, 86
Murat, Princesse Lucien, 52
Murrow, Edward R., 279
Musset, Alfred de, 86, 91

Napoleon, 14, 15
Napoleon III, 15, 91
Natanson, Matylda, 40, 41
Natanson, Thadée, 41–42
Naumburg, Elkan, 212
Naumburg Family, 208
Naoumoff, Alexander, 121

Naoumoff, Anna, 121
Newhouse, Edward, 170
Newman, Phyllis, 260
Nicklass-Kempner, S., 157
Nietzsche, Friedrich Wilhelm, 106, 107, 111
Nijinska, Bronislava, 277
Nijinsky, Vaslav, 43, 51
Nippert, Louise, 209
Nissen, Georg, 243
Nitze, Paul, 199
Nitze, William A., 198
Nixon, President Richard, 227
Noailles, Duchesse Anna de, 51
Nureyev, Rudolf, 280

O'Bryan, William Carey, 247
Odoevsky, Count, 109
Ohlsson, Garrick, 156
Oistrakh, David, 82
Oliver, Miriam, 188
Orléans, Henri, Duc d', 58
Orléans, Philippe, Duc d', 36, 37
Orsini family, 27
Ovid (Publius Ovidius Naso), 4
Oxenstjerna, Count Axel, 29
Ozawa, Seiji, 139

Paepcke, Elizabeth Nitze, 198–99
Paepcke, Walter, 198–99
Pagello, Pietro, 91
Parr, Catherine, 60
Paul, Jean, 244
Paur, Emil, 232
Pavlova, Anna, 275
Pavlovna, Grand Duchess Helena, 74
Pergolesi, Giovanni Batista, 34
Pericles, 19–21

Périer, Jean, 196
Perlman, Itzak, 170, 171
Persinger, Louis, 169–70
Peter the Great of Russia, 12
Pfeifer, Ellen, 123
Philip II of Spain, 58, 60
Phipps, Mrs. Ogden, 204
Piatigorsky, Gregor, 83
Picasso, Pablo, 43, 53, 167
Piston, Walter, 166
Plato, 2
Pleasant, Richard, 277
Plessis, du (family), 88
Pleyel, Camille (of the firm of Ignace Pleyel et Fils Aîné), 92, 93
Poisson, Abel, 68
Poisson, François, 68
Poisson, Madame, 68, 69, 70
Poitiers, Diane de, 26–27, 58
Polignac, Prince Edmond de, 50–51
Polignac, Princesse Edmond de (Winaretta Singer), 50–51, 53, 163, 167, 264
Polignac, Comtesse Jean de (Marie-Blanche), 52, 168
Pompadour, Marquise de (Jeanne Antoinette Poisson), 34, 36, 39, 67–72
Pons, Lily, 224
Porter, Cole, 51, 279
Post, Marjorie Merriweather, 208
Potemkin, Anastasia, 72
Poulenc, Francis, 43, 51, 52
Prendergast, Elizabeth, 265
Press, Michael, 169
Prokofiev, Sergei, 133, 167, 273
Proust, Marcel, 41, 43
Prude, Jonathan, 279
Prude, Walter, 277–78
Pugno, Raoul, 162–63

Pulitzer, Joseph, 115, 218
Pushkin, Aleksandr, 131

Rachmaninoff, Serge, 163
Ralli, Hélène, 51
Rambert, Marie (Mim), 276
Rambouillet, Marquise de (Catherine de Vivonne), 27–28
Rambouillet, Marquis de (Charles d' Angennes), 27
Rameau, Jean Philippe, 34, 71
Randall, Tony, 268
Raphael (Raffaello Sanzio, or Santi), 23
Rasputin, Grigory Yefimovich, 48
Ratner, Anne, 206–7
Ravel, Maurice, 41, 42, 43, 51, 52, 167, 273
Rayburn, Sam, 247
Reagan, President Ronald, 250
Reed, Ramon, 277
Regneas, Joseph, 175
Reiner, Fritz, 185
Reinhardt, Max, 184, 276
Reis, Claire, 232–33
Renoir, Auguste, 41
Respighi, Ottorino, 180
Ribbentrop, Joachim von, 49
Richard the Lion-hearted (Richard I, king of England), 57
Richelieu, Cardinal, 28
Richter, Hans, 40, 106
Ritter, Fanny Raymond, 207
Robin, Leo, 279
Rochefoucauld, François de la, 28
Rockefeller Foundation, 220
Rockefeller, John D., 115
Rockefeller, John D. III, 204

Rockefeller, Martha Baird, 204, 220
Rodgers, Richard, 229, 278–79
Rodzinski, Artur, 124, 185, 233
Rodzinski, Helena Lilpop, 124, 125, 126, 128
Rohan, Duchesse de, 28
Rorem, Ned, 185
Rosanoff, Professor Lief, 149
Rostropovich, Elena, 135
Rostropovich, Galina Pavlovna Vishnevskaya, 130–40, 185
Rostropovich, Mstislav ("Slava"), 134–40, 185
Rostropovich, Olga, 135
Rothschild, Baron Edmond de, 82
Rothschild, Bathsabee de, 82–84, 270
Rothschild, Guy de, 83
Rothschild, Jacqueline de, 83
Rousseau, Jean Jacques, 14, 33, 34, 71
Rousseau, Madame (glazier's wife), 36
Rubin, Mark Illich, 133–35
Rubinstein, Alina, 128
Rubinstein, Aniela (Nela) Mlynarski, 123–39
Rubinstein, Anton, 40, 74, 123, 155, 156, 213, 248
Rubinstein, Artur, 43, 49, 50, 51, 124–30
Rubinstein, Eva, 128
Rubinstein, John, 128
Rubinstein, Nikolai, 74
Rubinstein, Paul, 128
Rudel, Julius, 226, 227, 228
Ryack, Eddie, 256
Ryan, Margaret Kahn, 202–4
"Rybernia," 256

Saarinen, Eliel, 190
St. Bernard of Clairvaux, 56
St. Denis, Ruth, 265–69
Saint-Saens, Camille, 163
Saint-Simon, Count Henri, 89
Salerno-Sonnenberg, Nadja, 171
Salieri, Antonio, 65
Salmond, Felix, 169
Salzedo, Carlos, 184
Samaroff, Olga Hickenlooper, 158
Samuel, John, 228
Sand, George (Amantine Aurore Lucile Dupin Dudevant), 85–95
Sandeau, Jules, 89–91
Sanger, Eleanor N., 208
Sarasate, Pablo, 109
Sargeant, Winthrop, 43, 51, 52, 53, 224
Satie, Erik, 167
Savelli, Giulia, 27
Saxe, Maréchal de, 86
Sayn-Wittgenstein, Princess Carolyne, 101
Scarlatti, Alessandro, 32
Schacter, Alicia, 234
Schenck, Janet, 208
Schiff, Andras, 207
Schiff, Jacob, 203
Schindler, Alma. See Werfel, Alma Schindler Mahler Gropius
Schindler, Anna von Bergen, 110–11
Schindler, J. Emil, 110–11
Schirmer, Gustave, 212
Schneider, Alexander ("Sasha"), 149–51
Schoenberg, Arnold, 16, 111, 120, 164, 180, 233
Schonberg, Harold, 166, 230, 238

Index

Schubert, Franz, 16
Schuman, William, 197
Schumann, Clara Wieck, 96–99
Schumann, Robert, 96–98
Schwartz, Daniel, 146
Schwartz, Stephen, 259
Schweitzer, Albert, 199, 235
Scriabin, Alexander, 155
Sembrich, Marcella, 183, 185
Semyonov, Vladimir, 138
Seneca, Lucius, Annaeus, 4
Serkin, Peter, 186
Serkin, Rudolph, 149, 185, 186, 205
Sert, José Maria, 42–44, 48
Sert, Misia, 39–44, 48, 49, 50, 52,
Servais, Adrien-François, 40
Servais, Eugènie, 40
Sessions, Roger, 166
Sevigné, Madame de, 28, 33
Seymour, Elizabeth Damrosch, 213, 214, 215
Sèze, Aurelien de, 88–89
Sforza family, 8
Sforza, Giovanni, 24
Shaham, Gil, 171
Shakespeare, William, 61
Shaw, George Bernard, 202
Shaw, Robert, 209
Shawn, Ted, 266–68
Sheldon, George R., 115
Sheldon, Mrs. George R. Sheldon, 115, 117, 231–232
Shostakovich, Dmitri, 133, 136–37
Shouse, Catherine Filene, 205–6, 220
Shubert, J. J., 225
Sibelius, Ainö, 85
Sibelius, Jean, 85
Sibley, Edward A., 183

Sills, Beverly, 157, 209, 224–29
Silverman, Morris, 224–25
Silverman, Sidney, 224
Silverman, Sonia, 224–25
Silverman Stanley, 224
Singer, Paris, 264
Smith, Betty R., 175
Smith, Charles Robinson, 187
Smith, Ella May, 208
Smith, E. Vernon, 175
Smith, Gertrude Robinson, 187–91
Smith, Hilda, 188
Smyth, Ethel, 51
Society of Jesus (Jesuits), 10, 62
Socrates, 2, 20
Solzhenitsyn, Alexander, 137–39
Sondheim, Stephen, 141
Sophocles, 2
"Spatz" (Baron von D.), 49
Speilter, Mrs. Heidy, 209
Speyer, Jacqueline ("Kiki"), 254, 258
Sprague-Smith, Mrs. Charles, 206
Staal-Delauney, Madame de, 38
Stade, Frederica von, 204
Stalin, Joseph, 131, 133, 134
Stein, Gertrude, 53–54, 167, 188
Stein, Leo, 53
Steinberg, William, 205
Steinway, Theodore, 212
Stern, Isaac, 149, 170
Stern, Joseph, 260
Stern, Mrs. Sigmund, 206
Sterner, Ralph Leech, 248
Stevenson, Christine Wetherill, 200
Stoeckel, Ellen Battell, 207

Stokowski, Leopold, 158, 183, 184, 185
Storer, Maria Longworth Nichols, 207
Stowe, Harriet Beecher, 188
Stradivari, Antonio, 32
Stradivari family, 11, 32
Strauss family, 16
Stravinsky, Igor, 43, 51, 52, 164, 167, 235
Styne, Jule, 279
Suggia, Guilhermina, 150
Suh, Ju Hee, 186
Sutherland, Joan, 223
Sylvan, Sanford, 176
Szell, George, 205
Szigeti, Joseph, 149
Szymanowski, Karol, 44

Tacitus, Cornelius, 4
Taft, Annie Sinton, 208
Taft, Helen H., 208
Tailleferre, Germaine, 43
Tappan, Mary Aspinwall, 190
Tappan, William Aspinwall, 189
Tchaikovsky, Alexandra, 76
Tchaikovsky, Anatol, 75, 78
Tchaikovsky, Antonina Ivanova Miliukova, 75–76
Tchaikovsky, Modeste, 75
Tchaikovsky, Peter (Piotr) Ilyich, 74–80
Tencin, Claudine Alexandrine Guerin de, 36–37
Theodor, Duke of Bavaria, 80
Thomas, Theodore, 179
Thompson, Dr. Carl D., 219
Thompson, Dorothy, 184
Thompson, Helen Mulford, 219–21
Thompson, Dr. Randall, 184
Thomson, Virgil, 53, 148, 166, 233, 279
Thurber, Jeannette, 232

Tilley, Susan, 235
Titian (Vecellio Tiziano), 25
Toch, Ernest, 180
Toklas, Alice B., 53
Tolstoy, Count Leo, 41, 131
Tonton, 39
Toulouse-Lautrec, Henri de, 41
Tournehem, M. Le Normant de, 68
Treigle, Norman, 226–27
Tromboncino, Bartolommeo, 23
Troubadours, 6–7, 56, 57
Trouvères, 57
Tudor, Antony, 277
Tully, Alice, 195–98
Tully, Clara Houghton, 195
Tully, William J., 195
Tureck, Rosalyn, 158
Turgenev, Ivan, 95

Urban II, Pope, 4
Urch, Ernest, 183

Valente, Benita, 186
Vengerova, Isabelle, 153–55, 173, 185
Vergil (Publius Vergilius Maro), 4
Vieuxtemps, Henri, 40, 109
Vigny, Alfred de, 86
Vinci, Leonardo da, 22
Vintimille, Marquise de, 69
Vishnevsky, George, 133
Vivaldi, Antonio, 32
Voltaire (François Marie Arouet), 14, 33, 38, 71
Vuillard, Edouard, 41, 52

Wadsworth, Charles, 197–98, 230
Wagner, Cosima Liszt von Bülow, 100–9, 112
Wagner, Eva, 105, 108

Index

Wagner, Isolde (given family name: von Bülow), 104
Wagner, Minna Planer, 102-3, 105
Wagner, Richard Wilhelm, 100-8, 212, 262
Wagner, Siegfried, 105, 108
Wagner, Wieland, 109
Wagner, Winifred, 108
Wagner, Wolfgang, 109
Wales, Prince of, 43
Wallace, Dr. James, 192
Wallace, Lila Bell Acheson, 199-95, 270
Wallace, William Roy DeWitt, 191-95
Walpole, Horace, 38
Walter, Bruno, 113, 117, 120
Walter, William E., 183
Webern, Anton, 180
Weill, Kurt, 279
Weisman, George, 229
Weissenberg, Alexis, 158, 205
Werfel, Alma Schindler Mahler Gropius, 110-21
Werfel, Franz, 119-21
Werfel, Martin, 120
Wesondonck, Mathilde, 102
Westminster, Duke of, 48-49
Weyerhaeuser, Mrs. Frederick K., 205
Wharton, Edith, 188
Whitestone, Annabelle, 130
Widor, Charles Marie, 161
Wiechman, Marie Damrosch, 213, 214
Wieck, Friedrich, 96-97
Wieck, Marianne Tromlitz, 96
Wilde, Oscar, 41
Wilder, Thornton, 199
Willeke, Sally, 180
Willeke, William, 180
William I of Prussia, 15
William X, Duke of Aquitaine, 55
Wister, Frances A., 207
Wolfe, Tom, 146
Woolf, Virginia, 50
Wren, Sir Christopher, 182

Yesenin, Sergei, 264
Ysaÿe, Eugène, 81, 216
Yusupoff, Prince Felix, 48

Zelter, Carl Friedrich, 245
Zemlinsky, Alexander von, 111-12
Ziegler, Edward A., 183
Zimbalist, Alma Gluck, 186
Zimbalist, Efrem, 158, 184-86
Zimbalist, Efrem, Jr., 186
Zimbalist, Mary Louise Curtis Bok, 181-87
Zola, Emile, 41
Zuckerman, Pincus, 205

About the Author

Mona S. Mender is a teacher of piano and music theory and the author of *Music Manuscript Preparation: A Concise Guide* (Scarecrow Press, 1991). After studying piano and composition in New York City, she received her bachelor's degree from Mount Holyoke College and continued with postgraduate courses in music therapy at Montclair State College, New Jersey, and in music manuscripts at the Julliard School. She has been the state chair of education and the docent program, New Jersey Symphony Orchestra League; chair of the board of regents, and member of the board of directors, New Jersey Symphony Orchestra; and a member of the governing committees of Young Artists Auditions and Education. Currently, her main occupation is writing books about music and musicians.